JAN -   2006

Karen Rupp-Serrano
Editor

Licensing in Libraries: Practical and Ethical Aspects

Licensing in Libraries: Practical and Ethical Aspects has been co-published simultaneously as *Journal of Library Administration*, Volume 42, Numbers 3/4 2005.

Pre-publication
REVIEWS,
COMMENTARIES,
EVALUATIONS . . .

"ALL INFORMATION PROFES-SIONALS–FROM SEASONED WORKERS IN THE TRENCHES TO WIDE-EYED NOVICES–CAN BENEFIT FROM THIS TIMELY RESOURCE. This book is a welcome state-of-the-art look at a rapidly evolving concept in libraries. It provides a balanced examination of issues and trends in licensing electronic resources for libraries, offering hope that the give-and-take of negotiations can be equitable to all parties involved. As we all know, the devil is in the details, and in this collection of papers, information professionals share their experiences, suggest best practices, and offer some examples of workable licenses."

The Haworth Information Press®
An Imprint of The Haworth Press, Inc.

Licensing in Libraries: Practical and Ethical Aspects

Licensing in Libraries: Practical and Ethical Aspects has been co-published simultaneously as *Journal of Library Administration*, Volume 42, Numbers 3/4 2005.

Monographic Separates from the *Journal of Library Administration*™

For additional information on these and other Haworth Press titles, including descriptions, tables of contents, reviews, and prices, use the QuickSearch catalog at http://www.HaworthPress.com.

Licensing in Libraries: Practical and Ethical Aspects, edited by Karen Rupp-Serrano, MLS, MPA (Vol. 42, No. 3/4, 2005). *Presents state-of-the-art information on licensing issues, including contract management, end-user education, copyright, e-books, consortial licensing software, legalities, and much more.*

Collection Management and Strategic Access to Digital Resources: The New Challenges for Research Libraries, edited by Sul H. Lee (Vol. 42, No. 2, 2005). *Examines how libraries can make the best use of digital materials, maintain a balance between print and electronic resources, and respond to electronic information.*

The Eleventh Off-Campus Library Services Conference, edited by Patrick B. Mahoney, MBA, MLS (Vol. 41, No. 1/2/3/4, 2004). *Examines–and offers solutions to–the problems faced by librarians servicing faculty and students who do not have access to a traditional library.*

Libraries Act on Their LibQUAL+™ Findings: From Data to Action, edited by Fred M. Heath, EdD, Martha Kyrillidou, MEd, MLS, and Consuella A. Askew, MLS (Vol. 40, No. 3/4, 2004). *Focuses on the value of LibQUAL+™ data to help librarians provide better services for users.*

The Changing Landscape for Electronic Resources: Content, Access, Delivery, and Legal Issues, edited by Yem S. Fong, MLS, and Suzanne M. Ward, MA (Vol. 40, No. 1/2, 2004). *Focuses on various aspects of electronic resources for libraries, including statewide resource-sharing initiatives, licensing issues, open source software, standards, and scholarly publishing.*

Improved Access to Information: Portals, Content Selection, and Digital Information, edited by Sul H. Lee (Vol. 39, No. 4, 2003). *Examines how improved electronic resources can allow libraries to provide an increasing amount of digital information to an ever-expanding patron base.*

Digital Images and Art Libraries in the Twenty-First Century, edited by Susan Wyngaard, MLS (Vol. 39, No. 2/3, 2003). *Provides an in-depth look at the technology that art librarians must understand in order to work effectively in today's digital environment.*

The Twenty-First Century Art Librarian, edited by Terrie L. Wilson, MLS (Vol. 39, No. 1, 2003). *"A MUST-READ addition to every art, architecture, museum, and visual resources library bookshelf." (Betty Jo Irvine, PhD, Fine Arts Librarian, Indiana University)*

The Strategic Stewardship of Cultural Resources: To Preserve and Protect, edited by Andrea T. Merrill, BA (Vol. 38, No. 1/2/3/4, 2003). *Leading library, museum, and archival professionals share their expertise on a wide variety of preservation and security issues.*

Distance Learning Library Services: The Tenth Off-Campus Library Services Conference, edited by Patrick B. Mahoney (Vol. 37, No. 1/2/3/4, 2002). *Explores the pitfalls of providing information services to distance students and suggests ways to avoid them.*

Electronic Resources and Collection Development, edited by Sul H. Lee (Vol. 36, No. 3, 2002). *Shows how electronic resources have impacted traditional collection development policies and practices.*

Information Literacy Programs: Successes and Challenges, edited by Patricia Durisin, MLIS (Vol. 36, No. 1/2, 2002). *Examines Web-based collaboration, teamwork with academic and administrative colleagues, evidence-based librarianship, and active learning strategies in library instruction programs.*

Evaluating the Twenty-First Century Library: The Association of Research Libraries New Measures Initiative, 1997-2001, edited by Donald L. DeWitt, PhD (Vol. 35, No. 4, 2001). *This collection of articles (thirteen of which previously appeared in ARL's bimonthly newsletter/ report on research issues and actions) examines the Association of Research Libraries' "new measures" initiative.*

Impact of Digital Technology on Library Collections and Resource Sharing, edited by Sul H. Lee (Vol. 35, No. 3, 2001). *Shows how digital resources have changed the traditional academic library.*

Libraries and Electronic Resources: New Partnerships, New Practices, New Perspectives, edited by Pamela L. Higgins (Vol. 35, No. 1/2, 2001). *An essential guide to the Internet's impact on electronic resources management past, present, and future.*

Diversity Now: People, Collections, and Services in Academic Libraries, edited by Teresa Y. Neely, PhD, and Kuang-Hwei (Janet) Lee-Smeltzer, MS, MSLIS (Vol. 33, No. 1/2/3/4, 2001). *Examines multicultural trends in academic libraries' staff and users, types of collections, and services offered.*

Leadership in the Library and Information Science Professions: Theory and Practice, edited by Mark D. Winston, MLS, PhD (Vol. 32, No. 3/4, 2001). *Offers fresh ideas for developing and using leadership skills, including recruiting potential leaders, staff training and development, issues of gender and ethnic diversity, and budget strategies for success.*

Off-Campus Library Services, edited by Ann Marie Casey (Vol. 31, No. 3/4, 2001 and Vol. 32, No. 1/2, 2001). *This informative volume examines various aspects of off-campus, or distance learning. It explores training issues for library staff, Web site development, changing roles for librarians, the uses of conferencing software, library support for Web-based courses, library agreements and how to successfully negotiate them, and much more!*

Research Collections and Digital Information, edited by Sul H. Lee (Vol. 31, No. 2, 2000). *Offers new strategies for collecting, organizing, and accessing library materials in the digital age.*

Academic Research on the Internet: Options for Scholars & Libraries, edited by Helen Laurence, MLS, EdD, and William Miller, MLS, PhD (Vol. 30, No. 1/2/3/4, 2000). *"Emphasizes quality over quantity. . . . Presents the reader with the best research-oriented Web sites in the field. A state-of-the-art review of academic use of the Internet as well as a guide to the best Internet sites and services. . . . A useful addition for any academic library." (David A. Tyckoson, MLS, Head of Reference, California State University, Fresno)*

Management for Research Libraries Cooperation, edited by Sul H. Lee (Vol. 29. No. 3/4, 2000). *Delivers sound advice, models, and strategies for increasing sharing between institutions to maximize the amount of printed and electronic research material you can make available in your library while keeping costs under control.*

Integration in the Library Organization, edited by Christine E. Thompson, PhD (Vol. 29, No. 2, 1999). *Provides librarians with the necessary tools to help libraries balance and integrate public and technical services and to improve the capability of libraries to offer patrons quality services and large amounts of information.*

Library Training for Staff and Customers, edited by Sara Ramser Beck, MLS, MBA (Vol. 29, No. 1, 1999). *This comprehensive book is designed to assist library professionals involved in presenting or planning training for library staff members and customers. You will explore ideas for effective general reference training, training on automated systems, training in specialized subjects such as African American history and biography, and training for areas such as patents and trademarks, and business subjects.* Library Training for Staff and Customers *answers numerous training questions and is an excellent guide for planning staff development.*

Collection Development in the Electronic Environment: Shifting Priorities, edited by Sul H. Lee (Vol. 28, No. 4, 1999). *Through case studies and firsthand experiences, this volume discusses meeting the needs of scholars at universities, budgeting issues, user education, staffing in the electronic age, collaborating libraries and resources, and how vendors meet the needs of different customers.*

Licensing in Libraries: Practical and Ethical Aspects

Karen Rupp-Serrano
Editor

Licensing in Libraries: Practical and Ethical Aspects has been co-published simultaneously as *Journal of Library Administration*, Volume 42, Numbers 3/4 2005.

The Haworth Information Press®
An Imprint of The Haworth Press, Inc.

New York • London • Victoria (AU)
www.HaworthPress.com

Published by

The Haworth Information Press®, 10 Alice Street, Binghamton, NY 13904-1580 USA

The Haworth Information Press® is an imprint of The Haworth Press, Inc., 10 Alice Street, Binghamton, NY 13904-1580 USA.

Licensing in Libraries: Practical and Ethical Aspects has been co-published simultaneously as *Journal of Library Administration*™, Volume 42, Numbers 3/4 2005.

The development, preparation, and publication of this work has been undertaken with great care. However, the publisher, employees, editors, and agents of The Haworth Press and all imprints of The Haworth Press, Inc., including The Haworth Medical Press® and Pharmaceutical Products Press®, are not responsible for any errors contained herein or for consequences that may ensue from use of materials or information contained in this work. Opinions expressed by the author(s) are not necessarily those of The Haworth Press, Inc. With regard to case studies, identities and circumstances of individuals discussed herein have been changed to protect confidentiality. Any resemblance to actual persons, living or dead, is entirely coincidental.

Cover design by Lora Wiggins.

Library of Congress Cataloging-in-Publication Data

Licensing in libraries : practical and ethical aspects / Karen Rupp-Serrano, editor.
    p. cm.
    "Co-published simultaneously as Journal of library administration, volume 42, numbers 3/4."
    Includes bibliographical references and index.
    ISBN-13: 978-0-7890-2878-5 (hc. : alk. paper)
    ISBN-10: 0-7890-2878-6 (hc. : alk. paper)
    ISBN-13: 978-0-7890-7879-2 (pbk. : alk. paper)
    ISBN-10: 0-7890-2879-4 (pbk. : alk. paper)
    1. Copyright licenses–United States. 2. Computer software industry–Licenses–United States.
3. Libraries–United States. I. Rupp-Serrano, Karen. II. Journal of library administration.

KF3002 .L53 2005
346.7304'82–dc22
                                                                                      2004030491

Indexing, Abstracting & Website/Internet Coverage

This section provides you with a list of major indexing & abstracting services and other tools for bibliographic access. That is to say, each service began covering this periodical during the year noted in the right column. Most Websites which are listed below have indicated that they will either post, disseminate, compile, archive, cite or alert their own Website users with research-based content from this work. (This list is as current as the copyright date of this publication.)

Abstracting, Website/Indexing Coverage . . . . Year When Coverage Began

- *AATA Online: Abstracts of International Conservation Literature (formerly Art & Archeology Technical Abstracts) <http://aata.getty.edu>* 2004

- *Academic Abstracts/CD-ROM* 1993

- *Academic Search: database of 2,000 selected academic serials, updated monthly: EBSCO Publishing* 1995

- *Academic Search Elite (EBSCO)* 1993

- *AGRICOLA Database (AGRICultural OnLine Access) A Bibliographic database of citations to the agricultural literature created by the National Agricultural Library and its cooperators <http://www.natl.usda.gov/ag98>* 1991

- *AGRIS <http://www.fao.org/agris/>* 1991

- *Business & Company ProFiles ASAP on CD-ROM <http://www.galegroup.com>* 1996

- *Business ASAP* 1994

- *Business ASAP–International <http://www.galegroup.com>* 1984

- *Business International and Company ProFile ASAP <http://www.galegroup.com>* 1996

- *Business Source Corporate: coverage of nearly 3,350 quality magazines and journals; designed to meet the diverse information needs of corporations; EBSCO Publishing <http://www.epnet.com/corporate/bsourcecorp.asp>* 1993

(continued)

(continued)

(continued)

*Special Bibliographic Notes related to special journal issues
(separates) and indexing/abstracting:*

- indexing/abstracting services in this list will also cover material in any "separate" that is co-published simultaneously with Haworth's special thematic journal issue or DocuSerial. Indexing/abstracting usually covers material at the article/chapter level.
- monographic co-editions are intended for either non-subscribers or libraries which intend to purchase a second copy for their circulating collections.
- monographic co-editions are reported to all jobbers/wholesalers/approval plans. The source journal is listed as the "series" to assist the prevention of duplicate purchasing in the same manner utilized for books-in-series.
- to facilitate user/access services all indexing/abstracting services are encouraged to utilize the co-indexing entry note indicated at the bottom of the first page of each article/chapter/contribution.
- this is intended to assist a library user of any reference tool (whether print, electronic, online, or CD-ROM) to locate the monographic version if the library has purchased this version but not a subscription to the source journal.
- individual articles/chapters in any Haworth publication are also available through the Haworth Document Delivery Service (HDDS).

Licensing in Libraries:
Practical and Ethical Aspects

CONTENTS

ABOUT THE EDITOR

Karen Rupp-Serrano, MLS, MPA, has held her position as Head of Collection Development at the University of Oklahoma Libraries since 2000 and directs license reviews and negotiations. Additionally, she collaborates with colleagues in the Greater Western Library Alliance to negotiate consortial licenses and determine collection development policies. She is the author of many articles on collection development and librarianship and the editor of *Collection Management: Preparing Today's Bibliographer for Tomorrow's Library.*

Preface

While libraries have been immersed in licensing for a number of years, permutations on the subject continue. Various building blocks, such as LibLicense, ICOLC guidelines, COUNTER-compliant statistics, and similar efforts have been laid as a foundation, but there is still a great deal of latitude in the final product. The variation in finished licenses depends greatly upon local and consortial needs and the abilities of the negotiator.

The need to share information about licensing experiences, learn from the parties involved, and understand the impact of licensing throughout libraries remains. Thus, these articles address a variety of issues and viewpoints in the licensing process as it currently stands.

Stephen Bosch shares a step-by-step analysis of the use of model licenses. Kristin Gerhard explores producer pricing models, discussing their positive and negative aspects. Anna Wyatt summarizes current legal aspects of licensing for libraries. David Fowler offers a history of licensing to ground the discussion.

Stepping back from the library community, several authors provide a different perspective on licensing. Tracey Armstrong explains the expanding role of the Copyright Clearance Center in providing materials for the electronic environment. Andrea Ramsden-Cooke and Priscilla McIntosh describe "how the other half lives," giving a glimpse of the factors that must be balanced by a vendor in the provision of licensed products. Anne McKee serves up a view of the complexity of consortial licensing, offering practical tips for fair and equitable license negotiation.

Several contributors shed light on the impact of licensing for various library services. Janet Croft discusses the influence of licensing on interlibrary loan processes, arguing for a proactive approach. Jill Emery

[Haworth co-indexing entry note]: "Preface." Rupp-Serrano, Karen. Co-published simultaneously in *Journal of Library Administration* (The Haworth Information Press, an imprint of The Haworth Press, Inc.) Vol. 42, No. 3/4, 2005, pp. xxi-xxii; and: *Licensing in Libraries: Practical and Ethical Aspects* (ed: Karen Rupp-Serrano) The Haworth Information Press, an imprint of The Haworth Press, Inc., 2005, pp. xv-xvi. Single or multiple copies of this article are available for a fee from The Haworth Document Delivery Service [1-800-HAWORTH, 9:00 a.m. - 5:00 p.m. (EST). E-mail address: docdelivery@haworthpress.com].

reminds us of the obligation to educate our users about the licensing terms of products we provide for their use. Richard Fyffe and Beth Forrest Warner urge us to consider carefully how we undertake the provision of unique materials to the public. Yem Fong and Heather Wicht review the numerous products available to libraries for managing licenses and compliance, speaking to the needs of libraries in that regard. Emilie Algenio and Alexia Thompson-Young address permutations on e-book licensing.

I wish to express my thanks to these contributors for their hard work and willingness to share their licensing insights. It is no small effort to do so and I trust you will find what they have to offer of value.

Karen Rupp-Serrano

Pricing Models for Electronic Journals and Other Electronic Academic Materials: The State of the Art

Kristin H. Gerhard

SUMMARY. This article presents a state-of-the-art description of pricing models for electronic academic materials. Relevant, interwoven topics are discussed: the complex context of electronic pricing, range of models available and variables involved, and usefulness of economic analyses of electronic scholarly publishing in evaluating fair price or pricing structure for a particular product. The goals of publishers, library users, and librarians in evaluating pricing are discussed, as well as the importance of understanding the findings of economic studies in order to negotiate a fair deal. Finally, some future directions for pricing models are posited. *[Article copies available for a fee from The Haworth Document Delivery Service: 1-800-HAWORTH. E-mail address: <docdelivery@haworthpress.com> Website: <http://www.HaworthPress.com> © 2005 by The Haworth Press, Inc. All rights reserved.]*

KEYWORDS. Electronic journals, pricing, economic analysis, scholarly publishing, collection development, acquisitions

---

Kristin H. Gerhard is Professor and Associate Dean for Collections and Technical Services, Iowa State University Library, 203 Parks Library, Iowa State University, Ames, IA 50011 (E-mail: kgerhard@iastate.edu).

[Haworth co-indexing entry note]: "Pricing Models for Electronic Journals and Other Electronic Academic Materials: The State of the Art." Gerhard, Kristin H. Co-published simultaneously in *Journal of Library Administration* (The Haworth Information Press, an imprint of The Haworth Press, Inc.) Vol. 42, No. 3/4, 2005, pp. 1-25; and: *Licensing in Libraries: Practical and Ethical Aspects* (ed: Karen Rupp-Serrano) The Haworth Information Press, an imprint of The Haworth Press, Inc., 2005, pp. 1-25. Single or multiple copies of this article are available for a fee from The Haworth Document Delivery Service [1-800-HAWORTH, 9:00 a.m. - 5:00 p.m. (EST). E-mail address: docdelivery@haworthpress.com].

1

INTRODUCTION

There is a large body of literature on electronic journals and pricing models to synthesize in order to present the reader with a state-of-the-art description of pricing models for electronic academic materials. As a result, this article must address several interwoven topics somewhat sequentially. First, it discusses the complex context in which electronic product pricing currently exists. Second, it describes the range of pricing models currently available, and the variety of variables that may go into the pricing of any one product or group of products. Some of the issues raised by various pricing models for libraries are discussed briefly in this section.

Thirdly, there have been a number of studies providing economic analyses of pricing models, both current and potential, and some key findings from those works are presented here. This introduces an approach to analysis that may be unfamiliar to many librarians. The fourth section presents publisher goals in setting pricing models, a discussion of the goals of the academic library user relative to access and publishing opportunities, and goals of librarians in evaluating specific pricing for specific products. The fifth section picks up on a frequently neglected resource in negotiating a fair deal, giving an overview of the findings of some of the economic studies that have been done relevant to electronic journals. The final section of this paper posits some directions for the future of pricing models, taking all of the above into account.

THE CONTEXT FOR ELECTRONIC JOURNAL PRICING

To discuss pricing models with any sense of reality, one must begin with the quite complex context in which the pricing of electronic journals takes place. The question of pricing models for academic electronic materials is one that can only be considered in the context of the larger venues of library budgets, evolution within the scholarly communication market, technological advances, patron expectations, and the political realities of the library as part of a large institution.

For the purpose of this article, *any electronic product for which a library must pay an annual or other periodic fee is considered an electronic serial.* This is a practical definition rather than a theoretical one, because where pricing is concerned, any product that requires an annual fee must be treated in budgeting as part of the serials budget. Pricing does not care whether there are distinguishable, sequential parts, numbered or unnumbered; only that there is an ongoing cost to provide the library's users with access.

The Library Budget as Context

There is no question that library budgets are struggling to manage. Caught between the Scylla of limited dollars in a tough economy and the Charybdis of rapidly increasing costs even of print journals, librarians are struggling to make the best purchasing decisions for their institutions. We are asked routinely to do more and more with less and less. Articles from the early nineties proclaim, "Librarians Must Have the Authority to Cancel Subscriptions to Seldom-Used Journals"[1] and "Can Research Libraries Keep Pace?"[2] Ford points out that "most academic libraries have, since 1972, had several rounds of serial subscription cancellations, with varying degrees of trauma."[3] Serials cancellation projects are occurring at increased frequency and the dollars cut in these projects are growing larger as libraries try to make room for newer materials in their acquisitions budgets. Among the new materials added, of course, are electronic resources.

In addition to newly available electronic resources, acquisitions budgets are now frequently expected to contribute funds towards a variety of library services. Taken together with traditional acquisition of physical materials for the permanent collection, these services provide as full an access to the information universe as the library can afford. To give a sense of the variety of expenses now paid in part or in full by acquisitions budgets, Ford enumerates a representative list: "the budgeting process for the acquisition of information now has to take account of the prices of alternative document delivery systems, copyright fees, license agreements, the (often) premium prices for electronic products which have added value by comparison with their print near-equivalents, and then cost of software and hardware upgrades necessary to accommodate each new product."[4] Acquisitions budget managers have a great deal to juggle on a shrinking plate of resources.

This balancing act is not helped by common misconceptions about the impact of electronic journals on the library's financial health. Of the "seven common myths about acquiring and accessing e-journals" identified by Tonkery,[5] three are related to imputed cost savings in subscription costs alone:

Myth no. 1: Publishers are rushing to convert their print journals to e-journal form to reduce costs

Myth no. 2: E-journals will solve the serials pricing crisis in libraries

Myth no. 5: The costs of e-journals will be passed to the end users, thus saving acquisitions funds

Two additional myths discussed by Tonkery relate to expectations in cost savings due to saved staff time.

It is not surprising that these beliefs would be present in the library community, at least in the early days of the conversion to more electronic information provision: these beliefs represent the dearest hopes of many an acquisitions budget administrator and many a director and provost. The reality, however, is that electronic journals are turning out to be at least as costly as their print counterparts. Frequently, they are considerably more expensive.

Electronic titles also add to the complexity and number of tasks that must be performed by library staff. A recent task force at Iowa State University identified 49 issues that we are currently facing, all related to providing cohesive management of our electronic subscriptions. The subgroups of issues fell under headings such as access, payments and reports, acquisitions/cataloging communication, Web page management, and proxy server issues. The final report from this group clearly indicates that a great deal of communication and coordination is required to do a responsible job of managing electronic resources. Lee summarizes the situation well when he suggests, "On the whole the deals are seen to be overly complicated, administratively a burden, restrictive, and of course, too expensive."[6]

The Scholarly Communication Crisis as Context

The impending crisis in the scholarly communication system is another important piece of the pricing context. The crisis follows to a large extent from the budget dilemma described above. Acquisitions budgets are pinched as state budgets and endowments alike face a poor economic situation, yet more and more is published, and inflation rates continue to run considerably higher than average inflation of goods and services.

There is plenty of responsibility to assign in analyzing the crisis in scholarly communication. A good bit can be laid at the feet of for-profit publishers. Academic publishers tend to have monopolies or near-monopolies on academic journal articles reporting research results. The economic competition that tends to bring prices down in other product arenas does not appear to hold for information products.

Journals have been created for every conceivable specialty and subspecialty, seemingly no matter how small the interested population would be. Journals have become longer, with more pages per issue, and have an increased number of issues per volume as well. Costs go up due to increased content, in order to make a profit from a relatively small number of subscriptions, and to increase profit for shareholders. For-profit publishers' first concerns are for these shareholders. They have fewer vested interests for the short run in achieving the most effective exchange of scholarly information, at the least cost to information users. As Tenopir and King conclude, "Some high journal prices are inevitable when circulation is low because publishers must recover the high cost of processing scholarly articles. However, this does not necessarily mean that all journal prices need to be as high as they currently are. Publishers need to be concerned about costs and librarians and readers should be vigilant about the reasonableness of journal prices."[7]

Responsibility for the current situation must also be assigned to the academy. Faculty members are required, explicitly or implicitly, to publish their research in peer-reviewed, preferably prestigious, journals. They are forced to rely on publication in specific journals, the standard-bearers in their field of expertise, in order to attain tenure or promotion. The amount of profit attained by the publisher as libraries are forced to purchase access to this research is not part of the equation for the majority of university faculty or administrators.

Tenure and promotion requirements, and the newer post-tenure review requirements at many institutions, provide direct support to a system that is financially unsustainable. Faculty members need more journals, and more specialized journals; they need enough places to publish enough articles to pass muster within their institution. Publishers have so far been more than willing to accommodate this university-created need. Libraries are left struggling in the middle.

Improved Information Technologies as Context

Technological advances are bringing a constantly growing number of increasingly sophisticated electronic information products to the academic market. Cross-platform and cross-vendor standards have led to deeper linking within the web of electronic information. Linking provides the connective tissue between citations and full text, as well as between related articles. The growing sophistication of software platforms for electronic information allows more browsing and serendipity to occur, without requiring faculty members to leave their offices. Digitization efforts have picked up a great deal of speed. E-journals increasingly offer (at a separate price) backfiles in electronic form, decreasing still further the need for students or faculty to visit the physical library. Portals are the current hot topic, providing search engines that can cross a wide variety of academic e-journals and indexes. This development will bring university library patrons closer to a model where one search may turn up everything they need to see–and that is a large universe for libraries to finance.

Patron Expectations and University Politics as Context

This leads to the question of patron expectations and of the university as a political arena. For university libraries, patron expectations are frequently indicative of broader political realities on campuses. Library users expect to find everything electronically. Unreasonable licenses and costs do not douse their fervor for the latest product or a product that was available at their previous institution. They express this fervor freely and sometimes loudly to their department head, library liaison, faculty senate representative, and any university administrator willing to listen.

Simultaneously, the majority of faculty and graduate students do not want to see any further journal cancellations. In a recent discussion about the possibility of substituting article-on-demand at no cost for articles in journals that are rarely used in our library, one faculty member proclaimed that not having an article that was wanted at the moment that it is wanted is not an acceptable solution to the budget problem. This resistance is best summarized as "you can cancel journals as long as you don't cancel journals." Any delay whatsoever is judged unacceptable for at least some subset of library users.

The need to publish for tenure and promotion is a critical part of our campus cultures, and access to the research record is an essential ingredient for this process. Active support for the library from students, faculty, and university administrators is essential for the library to gain and retain adequate resources to serve its community. Willingness to fund, without funding to give, or with specific guidelines about what is to be purchased, may not provide the best possible access for library users. In the end, managing the serials budget becomes a campus-wide endeavor, driven at least as much by what is politically possible as by strict rationality.

PRICING MODELS FOR ELECTRONIC INFORMATION PRODUCTS

In the first days of electronic access, there were virtually the same numbers of pricing models as there were products. The last five or six years have brought about some movement toward standardization of approaches to pricing. Nonetheless, there is still a broad range of models to document and describe, for there are many variables that function more on a sliding scale than a binary basis in determining price and pricing options for any given electronic product. Sharon McKay summarizes the situation well: "There are no industry standards about charging for electronic information, and providers use many different pricing mechanisms. Different pricing formulas have pros and cons from the consumer perspective–in this case, the library–and there does not seem to be a universally accepted model. No consensus exists among libraries regarding pricing, other than the universal desire for a model that produces the lowest initial as well as ongoing cost."[8]

Existing Pricing Models

A number of sources describe current models in depth, from particular perspectives, or for specific purposes.[9] One particularly concise report lists 16 pricing models.[10] Rather than duplicating the previous work by enumerating each model and describing it at length, this section will give an overview of the pricing models (or perhaps more accurately, the pricing structure variables) currently in play. It then proceeds to examine how these models relate to the concerns of publishers, scholars, and librarians: what do these models accomplish? What difficulties do they pose? Are there observable directions in the movement of current pricing models?

Analysis shows that the following variables appear in one way or another in most currently available models:

1. General price-for-value class: inexpensive, reasonable, expensive
2. Clarity or firmness: fixed ticket price, discounts on fixed price, negotiable price

3. Number of simultaneous users: single user only, incremental numbers of users, site-wide license, consortial license, state-wide license, multi-consortial license
4. Type of users: based on all library users at all libraries in consortium, based on all individual campus library users, based on undergraduate FTE, based on number of faculty and graduate students in a specific group or department
5. Location of seats: number of workstations on single network, in a specific building, in a specific IP range
6. Amount of use: pay per view, pay per time used, unlimited usage
7. Unit priced: article, issue, journal, bundle
8. Timing of payments: one-time payment, one-time cost spread over several payments, annual subscription payment, maintenance fees
9. Division of pricing (where consortium exists): proportional to usage, proportional to FTE, equally divided

Given the number of variables, let alone the number of potential combinations of variables, it is no surprise that Machovec identifies "understanding how publishers, aggregators, and other information providers charge for electronic access"[11] as one of the greatest challenges facing librarians working with electronic purchases. By the time each variable is set and the resultant cost announced to the library, it can be difficult to detect rationality in the price offered–even when rationality is present.

Assessing the Appropriateness of a Pricing Model

Different pricing models may be more appropriate for different types of products. The unit of purchase also plays a role in the pricing models of electronic materials. What makes sense for one database may be nonsensical for another. The distinctions between annually paid databases, aggregated journal databases, and e-journals can become relevant for some products in some pricing models. For example, aggregated general undergraduate databases rationally relate more to undergraduate FTE than a more specialized database, say, a highly specialized physics database. A one-time purchase of a journal backfile, with a small annual maintenance fee, appears more rational than charging (and paying) a large annual subscription price.

Large packages of e-journals may be available under group or individual title models, and the most desirable model in this situation will depend on how much use those journals will receive as a whole. If the level of use of a journal is high enough that the cost of obtaining individual articles across a year exceeds the journal's annual cost, a title-level description is more reasonable.[12] If the level of use of a significant enough portion of a publisher's title is high, the so-called "Big Deal" begins to appear more attractive.

The "Big Deal"

The purchase of bundled journals presents its own issues. The attraction of such an arrangement is that libraries may be able to provide a much wider range of journals electronically than they had previously subscribed to in print. A great quantity is supplied to the campus community, and librarians are loath to reduce the number of titles supplied. But as political realities in the university make it difficult to cancel a large bundle of titles from a single publisher, publishers (generally for-profit) are moved into the driver's seat. Large packages inflate, and their pricing becomes more complex and less negotiable. Libraries purchase, and then maintain, what Kern Simirenko calls maximized, rather than optimized, collections.[13]

Ken Frazier, Director of Libraries at University of Wisconsin-Madison, stated his stance on these packages baldly: "Academic library directors should not sign on to the Big Deal or any comprehensive licensing agreements with commercial publishers."[14] He uses game theory to demonstrate the long-term effects of purchasing such commercial packages and the extent to which the scholarly communication system is likely to emerge the loser. He describes subscribing to the Big Deal as removing librarians' ability to select stronger journals and leave weaker journals aside, and as increasing libraries' dependence on commercial journals.

Usage Statistics as Evaluation Resource

While not strictly a pricing model variable, the importance of meaningful, manipulable usage statistics, which can be compared across titles and across vendors, cannot be overestimated. The availability of reliable, standard statistics, particularly those that are COUNTER compliant, allows librarians to make fair comparisons of usage, and to share objective usage data in the event of a cancellation project. Lacking this data, it is difficult to cancel low-use titles believed by faculty to be important. The data allows the serials budget the opportunity to be run on a realistic, rather than an idealistic, basis. Realism is critical to a positive outcome that supports genuine user needs (represented here by use).

GOALS AND CONCERNS RELATED TO PRICING: PUBLISHERS, SCHOLARS, AND LIBRARIANS

Publishers' Goals and Concerns: Impact in Pricing and Sales

Pricing models are generally constructed by, and offered by, publishers. Publishers' first questions regarding pricing are likely to be the effect of pricing on sales, and how to create or sustain the level of profit sought by their parent organization.[15] How are these models constructed? What considerations go into their creation? Publishers have to be concerned that they do not end up making a bad deal, one that loses money. They must determine what distinguishes a poor pricing model for their product from one that gives whatever they consider a reasonable rate of return. Publishers who participate as fair-dealing partners in the scholarly communication system add a third question: what makes a reasonable deal, based on value for cost and usage, within the context of current library budgets?

Publishers need and deserve a fair return on their investment. In general, librarians and publishers have not agreed as to how to define what is a fair return. For-profit publishers generally seek to maximize their profit; society publishers aim to maintain either a steady income to support other society activities, or to break even while maintaining low membership costs. It is interesting to note that in a very good publication published by the Association of Learned and Professional Society Publishers, providing guidelines for good practice to would-be journal publishers, the question of setting a cost is barely mentioned and no specific approach is proposed.[16] Small publishers are generally on their own in determining what a reasonable or good price would be for their publication.

Inflation of e-journals, as inflation of print journals, is an important adjunct to the initial pricing model. Increasing materials costs are the result of a combination of factors. Some inflation is to be expected, based on increases in the costs of paper (print versions only), production (editorial work, printing to paper or publishing to the Web), and distribution (mail, user interface). Some inflation is due to the straightforward increase in volume: new journals founded, journals splitting into multiple specialized journals, more articles being accepted and published (increasing the size of individual journals, or the number of issues published per volume). Some inflation is due to publisher profit-taking. Jean-Mark Sense suggests "electronic publication does not really revolutionize scholarly publication but accentuates some of the existing tensions in terms of fluctuating prices, durability, duplication of information, innovation and obsolescence related to the transient life of serials."[17]

As stated above, it can be difficult to know whether an offer is rational and fair, simply because of the many variables involved. When the value of a product is perceived as very high (by the campus community–politics will play here–and/or by the library), libraries are vulnerable to paying unreasonable and irresponsibly high inflation rates. Librarians as a whole are handicapped by a lack of knowledge of economic theory, and its applications to pricing models, long or short-term, for academic e-journals.

Scholars' Goals and Concerns: Impacts on Accessibility and Publishing Opportunities

It is important to remember also that publishing scholarly research does not require that a researcher involve a for-profit or scholarly society publisher. Publishing models under current discussion in the library community include models where self-publishing, posting to an institutional repository, or posting to a subject-based open access e-journal play a larger role, and costs of access are shared between funding agencies and the academic institutions from which the scholarship emerges. These publishing pricing models are more user-centered, in that they rely on financing from the individuals or institutions producing the works to be published. While grant funding is also involved, grants are generally awarded to individuals or institutions, which brings us back to the producers of the knowledge to be disseminated.

As noted above, faculty members need access to information in order to create their own research program. The increasing demands for quality and quantity of articles in the promotion and tenure process places scholars in an unfortunate role. They are the participants in the scholarly communication process who are both most in need of both wide access (causing pressure on libraries to purchase journals not necessarily in the best interest of the campus as a whole) and a wide range of possible publication venues (causing publishers to increase publication and legitimize a certain amount of the inflation charged). As users and creators of information, as well as editors and reviewers for academic journals, the role of faculty members in the long term will be pivotal to the success of scholarly communication system.

Academic Library Goals and Concerns: Impact of Pricing on Purchasing Decisions

Publishers want to make a fair return, or better, on their investments. They cannot afford to make a bad–money losing–deal. Librarians' first priority is getting the best possible terms for their users, for the products that best meet university strategic priorities. They cannot afford to make a bad–overpricing–deal. The better the terms for any product, the further librarians can stretch existing acquisitions dollars to cover more needed materials. The questions from the library point of view are, how does one assess what makes a reasonable pricing offer? And, what distinguishes a bad deal, a fair deal, and a great deal?

This section of the paper outlines the issues collections managers and budget planners must take into consideration in evaluating a specific pricing structure for a specific product. These include content, archival rights, a clear understanding of internal budgeting, predictability of pricing (knowable pricing), local demand, the ability to evaluate pricing offers, and the ability to negotiate terms with confidence.

Content Purchased. The first issue must be content. What exactly would the library be buying? Can the publisher or vendor give a complete and accurate accounting of what is contained? For some large e-journal bundles, verifying the titles included and excluded may be the most time-consuming part of the purchasing process. Is the content guaranteed, and to what degree? Will the content grow over time, or is it static? Under what circumstances will a title (or an article) be withdrawn? What happens if the publisher acquires an additional set of e-journals? Will the library be required to pay an additional fee for these, or will the library have the option to not subscribe to the new titles? Aggregated databases present specific issues of content consistency. It is a good thing to ask, in regard to these products, for the record of consistency. Over the previous year or two, how many titles been dropped from coverage, and how many titles picked up? Is there a clause in the license that allows discontinuation of the subscription mid-license if content changes significantly? It is essential that the library understand what it is and is not buying, and what it is legally committed to buying during the term of the license. This understanding is then considered in the library's evaluation of the pricing offered.

Archival Access. Closely related to evaluation of content covered are the terms of long-term, archival access. Are archival rights to the material purchased included in the purchase price, or is the purchase for access only for the duration of the license? If ongoing archival access, following cancellation of a current subscription, has an ongoing maintenance fee, what order of magnitude is that fee? Where there is no archival access, the library must essentially repurchase the same material year after year. For some content, in some situations, this is acceptable. But for research journals of record, archival rights are an important item to consider in the price. A lack of archival rights justifies a significantly lower price for the annual subscription when it comes time to negotiate.

Clarity of Budget Priorities. Another issue of importance in evaluating a specific price for a specific product is the librarian's depth of understanding of the budget and budgeting process. Sometimes budgets are carried on from year to year, with whatever additions or removals of dollars, but without significant reevaluation. Few academic librarians have the luxury of time to create a zero-based acquisitions budget. However, a budget established long ago and carried forward on this mainly historical basis, risks budget divisions and allocations that are far removed from the current university strategic plan.

Librarians must have a firm grasp on the main purposes of the budget, and those purposes must relate tightly to institutional priorities. Fortunate is the librarian with a well-written library strategic plan! This can be invaluable in making hard allocation decisions, and determining the appropriate levels of funding both by formats (the serial/monograph split, proportion to electronic and to print products) and by subject. This also allows budget assessment–the process of documenting both how well the library is able to meet institutional needs, and what reasonable funding requests might be made to the central university administration.

Local Demand. The next issue can be seen as related to institutional priorities, though this is not always the case. Wiemers reminds us that "demand drives content" and sometimes forces us into purchases we would on ideological grounds prefer not to make.[18] It is frustrating to find that an evaluation of pricing for a product argues against its purchase, while a significant constituency of the campus community is calling for it. Still more frustrating is the situation where the campus community's demand coincides with the university's priorities. These situations can be reduced to an extent by educating provosts, university presidents, the faculty governance organization, and department heads about the current struggles of the scholarly communication system. However, despite best efforts to educate, there will inevitably be situations where political reality requires the purchase of materials with inappropriate pricing or licensing.

Comprehensible Pricing That Can Be Evaluated. Known, or at least comprehensible, pricing is another issue librarians face as they set out to negotiate an agreement. It is an amazing thing to be negotiating with a publisher without any idea of where their price comes from; or worse, to negotiate without even knowing what pricing they typically offer. At least one publisher Iowa State has dealt with has insisted on a fully negotiated license before giving an actual dollar figure. Some publishers bait and switch–offering a price, negotiating the license, and then announcing that the changes in the license make a difference (in their favor) in price; or stretching out the negotiations over such a long period of time that they can say the publisher's pricing or terms have changed since the beginning of the process.

Further, a number of commercial publishers maintain that their pricing offers are confidential information, which may not be shared with other institutions; some have contract clauses prohibiting discussion of license terms with other institutions. It is a reasonable thing for librarians to want clear, public sticker prices. Without a solid sense of the money involved, or what comparable institutions have paid, librarians will be at a distinct disadvantage in the negotiation process.

Another way to get up-to-date pricing information for general comparison is the use of periodicals price indexes and pricing predictions from serials vendors. As McKay puts so plainly, "Librarians need up-to-date information on prices. It is a key factor in planning–and all budgets must be planned. The librarian is both aided and hindered by the existence of a variety of published price indexes for books and periodicals. The most directly useful are the periodicals price indexes published annually by Blackwells . . . and by Faxon. . . . These two international subscription agents, handling subscriptions to thousands of serials, are well placed to calculate average prices and to predict trends. . . ."[19]

A recent paper by Bluh et al. suggests that the model of using pricing indexes alone to predict publication prices may not be as helpful to budget planners now as it has been in the past. They point out that libraries "use the price indexes in different ways. . . . Exclusive reliance on the price indexes is a thing of the past. Libraries now use these indexes in conjunction with a variety of other tools and other sources of information."[20] Price indexes are particularly problematic in that they do not yet explicitly include electronic serials. Neal points out, for instance, the need to track and predict costs of bulk purchases, and the need for measures of not only quality, but functionality as well. Nonetheless, he identifies both internal and external uses librarians currently make of these indexes in their budget planning. He concludes, "Publication price indexes present an important continuum of usability as a tool for collection development and fiscal decisions. Are indexes primarily political, communication, planning, budgeting, or allocation tools? In most academic library settings, all of these uses apply, but with varying levels of relevance and confidence."[21] In the absence of fully disclosed, comprehendible pricing from a publisher or vendor, price indexes may be the only source for this particular kind of data for librarians. However, the Bluh et al. discussion makes clear the importance of the other kinds of information, outlined in this article, in evaluating a pricing model or offer. An understanding of each of these issues is critical in order to begin a negotiation from a position of strength.

Ability to Negotiate. The ability to negotiate a fair price is not an ability most humans are born with. It requires both a knowledge set about the specific deal, and a skill set specific to the negotiation process. These can include things as simple as projecting confidence and willingness to treat the partner in negotiation with respect. However, for most current library administrators, these were not skills taught during their M.L.S. program.

Kern-Simirenko discusses the importance of librarians developing active negotiating strategies. "Publishers are likely to be surprised when confronted with librarians who refuse 'standard' terms, that is, terms set by the publishers in the same 'take-it-or-leave-it' mode as the traditional print market. However, negotiating mutually beneficial contracts is the norm in the business world, and it behooves librarians to sharpen their negotiation skills."[22] One thing that would aid many librarians in their role as negotiators is a better understanding of the economics involved.

ECONOMIC STUDIES ON ELECTRONIC JOURNAL PRICING

This paper does not attempt to provide an exhaustive summary of the available economic analyses of the scholarly communication system, or even of the more specific literature analyzing the present and probable future courses of e-journal economics. Rather, this section will provide some basic findings and references to a handful of papers that librarians can consult as they seek a better understanding of the economic workings of the e-journal market.

Jean-Mark Sense provides an analysis of the actions of commercial scientific publishers, and compares them to the role of non-profit scientific publishers. He concludes that, in our current system, commercial publishers are mainly responsible for the current inflation rates. He also concludes that libraries must find better ways to measure their collections and services than sheer numbers of journals, if they are to reduce the role of the commercial publishers as inflationary middlemen in the scholarly communication system.[23]

Do electronic site licenses for individual academic journals benefit the scientific community? This is the question addressed in an analysis by Bergstrom and Bergstrom.[24] They investigate whether there is a fiscal function performed by site licenses, and if so, what it is. They conclude that there are straightforward ways to determine when site licenses actually benefit a university and when they do not. According to their analysis, libraries "should agree to purchase a journal site license only if the subscription price is close to the publisher's average cost."[25] In the case of non-profit journals, both the university and the scientific community benefit from libraries' purchase of site licenses. They conclude, "the scientific community would benefit if overpriced journals were displaced by journals committed to price approximately at average cost. This suggests that non-profit professional societies and university presses would benefit the academic community by expanding their existing journals or starting new ones. Individual scholars could advance this process by refusing to do unpaid referee work for overpriced journals and by favoring reasonably priced journals with their submissions."[26]

Brendan Wyly compiled economic data in 1997 and conducted an analysis of the profits achieved by a set of publicly held commercial publishers, focusing on profits from sales of subscriptions for academic research journals. Published through the Association of Research Libraries, Wyly's information demonstrates profits that are significantly beyond those of average periodicals publishers in a number of commercial publishers' account sheets. "If the net margins of Wolters Kluwer, Reed Elsevier, Wiley, and Plenum had been 5.0% (the median in the overall periodical publishing industry as measured by Dun & Bradstreet's Industry Norms & Key Business Ratios 1997-98) the customers of the three companies would have saved approximately $884,653,000 in 1997."[27]

Wyly continues his analysis with the goal of determining whether a competitive market exists for research journals. "Wolters Kluwer provided a higher return on equity in 1997 than 482 of the S&P 500 companies, Reed Elsevier higher than 448, Plenum higher than 361, and Wiley higher than 302. . . . A detailed analysis of the origins of these returns on equity is beyond the scope of this article, but a high return on equity is at least a potential indicator that equity holders are benefiting from investing in activities not subject to competitive forces."[28] A non-competitive market means that there is no motivation for commercial publishers to price more reasonably, and accept lower return. Wyly's proposed solution is for the academy to contribute to the development of genuine alternatives to commercial journals, creating, through innovation, the possibility of a more competitive marketplace. He mentions the SPARC initiatives as a specific example of this kind of innovation.

Fishwick et al.'s study of scholarly electronic journals and their economic implications was carried out and published in 1998. It examines and analyzes from an economic standpoint the various strategies libraries were then using to deal with the problem of journal inflation so rapidly outpacing library budget growth. They conclude that mixed pricing models–multiple ways to price and pay for a given journal–would best serve the scholarly community.[29]

The Wellcome Trust commissioned a report entitled Economic Analysis of Scientific Research Publishing, available at the time of this writing in a revised (October 2003) edition.[30] At 33 pages in length, this is a concise, yet very comprehensive report on the current state of scientific, technological, and medical publishing, and is well worth librarians' time to read. It provides analysis on scholarly journals in STM, their function, journal bundling, new technologies, archiving, search engines, pressure groups, the publishing market, supply and demand for STM journals, and so on. It presents a cogent picture of the roles currently played by commercial and society publishers, and by academics themselves.

The first conclusion in the executive summary is a clear announcement of our present situation: "The current market structure does not operate in the long-term interests of the research community."[31] The report is also interesting in its statement that, while Elsevier is leading the way in overly inflated pricing, and being cast in the role of Evil Empire within the library community, other commercial publishers are providing the same type of bloated pricing, hiding behind the long shadow cast by Elsevier. An excellent analysis of the position of academic society publishers is also provided in this report.

For a longer and more detailed analysis of the economics and politics of electronic journals, a near-exhaustive study by Tenopir and King[32] covers the cost, value, and roles of scientific journals in virtually every section of the book. One chapter is devoted entirely to the use and economies of library-provision of scientific articles; another is on the cost of scientific scholarly e-journal publishing. It is not a fast read, but it presents its data and arguments in a straightforward manner, readily accessible to those lacking background in economics.

THE FUTURE
OF ELECTRONIC JOURNAL PRICING MODELS

Ultimately, the degree of fit between publisher pricing models; libraries' budgets, services, and policies; and the needs of the scholars who create and consume academic information, will determine the direction of scholarly publishing and pricing models for electronic academic materials. In looking to the future, we must consider the role of library budget management, the "Big Deal," the units of information routinely purchased, the role of consortia, and the potential of the open access movement.

Library Budget Management

As we move into the future, librarians' ability to tie their budget planning tightly to institutional priorities is critical. Additionally, librarians must educate their campuses–in particular faculty and administrators–on the contribution local decisions have on the international pricing practices for e-journals. When local political demand for a product conflicts with what is for the long term good of the entire scholarly communication system, the only way out of a forced purchase will be to have this education solidly in place ahead of time.

Additionally, as Ford states, "in these circumstances the relationships between performance and budgeting, and the choices between alternative ways of meeting users' needs will of necessity become more explicit."[33] Libraries will have to make decisions about the place of bundled packages of e-journals, and of desktop delivery of single articles, in their overall collection program.

With those decisions must come serious movement in what statistics are collected and reported by academic libraries. A full and accurate measure of access cannot be based solely on the number of subscriptions purchased or donated. This goes to Kern-Simirenko's argument about the value of an optimized rather than a maximized collection.[34] Libraries will also have to develop routine mechanisms to collect, analyze, and report usage statistics on the e-journals subscribed to, and to make these available to the campus community.

The Future of the "Big Deal"

Library Journal's annual periodicals price survey for April 2003 was titled, "Big Chill on the Big Deal?" and issues surrounding the purchase of pre-packaged e-journal bundles permeate the text. Van Orsdel and Born report that "the big scientific and medical publishers are being criticized openly and often by customers. . . ."[35] The big deals offered by these publishers are being reexamined. "Some of these Big Deals don't look so good two and three years into the contracts. It remains to be seen whether librarians will find a way to uncouple from the Big Deals and force publishers to give them more discretion over the purchase of their content."[36] Given the number of states in serious budget crisis, the survey suggests that how libraries respond to the bundles coming up for renewal this year will be telling.

These questions and Ken Frazier's predictions in his article on "The Big Deal" have proven to be prophetic. In November 1993, Cornell University Library announced that it would be ending its subscription to Elsevier's ScienceDirect journal package and interface at the end of its 2003 contract. Cornell closed renewal negotiations for 2004. The Library said that its decision was business, rather than ideologically, based, and that purchasing access to these materials as a single large package was not cost-effective. This followed public statements from Harvard and the University of California indicating that their renewal negotiations were not going satisfactorily.[37] It remains to be seen what other libraries follow this trend; the numbers of those backing away from the Big Deal will be significant information in assessing the future of commercial e-journal publishing.

Size of Standard Unit Purchased

Just as purchasers of large bundles are buying journal literature at a macro level, libraries have the option of purchasing journal literature at a micro level. The two levels relate well to just-in-case and just-in-time scenarios for library collections. Purchasing individual articles at the time they are needed by a researcher allows the most tailored approach to collection development possible.

Initiating such an approach requires a great deal of preplanning and follow-up. Birch and Young describe the start-up of unmediated document delivery at Leeds University.[38] The Leeds project presents a good example of implementing one step at a time, over time. By taking this approach, librarians were able to both target specific populations, and to collect both quantitative and qualitative information about their experimental trial. Librarians moved this forward over the course of a year, until they established it as a formal trial service for science and engineering schools at the university. Response has been positive on both the library and user sides.

Establishing unmediated document delivery requires that the library determine what journals should be covered and which exempted, what amount per article the library is willing to pay, and whether some portion of the cost should be borne by the department or faculty member. There must be reliable mechanisms in place to track and process payments for these articles. Statistical information about journals sources, user department, numbers of articles requested, etc., must be collectable.

Robertson investigated the impact of electronic journals on academic libraries, looking specifically at the roles and functions of serials, acquisitions, and interlibrary loan. She suggests that if ILL transactions continue to drop, staff and functions may be absorbed into the serials or acquisitions departments.[39] Managing an unmediated document delivery service is a logical role for interlibrary loan staff, and the tasks involved might provide a complement to the work level generated by actual ILL tasks.

There are three routes to article-level access: access through individual publishers, access through an aggregator, or access through a document delivery service. First, more publishers are positioning themselves to provide this type of access. This is becoming a significant enough move that lack of progress in this direction is being viewed as a negative in the business community. According to an October 14, 2003 posting to LibLicense-L, "financial analysts at BNP Paribas issued the following report on Reed Elsevier stock this afternoon: 'BNP Paribas expresses its concern regarding the company's current subscription based access, as compared to the newer and more successful article-fee based open access system.'" This mechanism of access seems better suited to individual users than to a large group of users, as billing for a large group of users would come from a wide range of publishers and many payments would have to be made.

Vendors whose mission it is to provide an aggregated document delivery service provide materials from a wide range of publishers. The advantage to this approach for libraries lies in unified billing and authentification, reducing the need to work with multiple accounts and multiple individual payments to individual publishers. This is a way to pick up parts of specific journals, or materials at a specific level (often undergraduate) without having to enter individual subscriptions for each title in full. The downside, according to Kern-Simirenko, is that these databases "add and drop titles over time, without any concomitant price adjustment. If the database contains unique material that users become dependent on, librarians may quickly find themselves in an untenable position."[40]

Document delivery services may be the least expensive way to provide patron-directed document delivery, with the advantages of unified billing and authentification, and a relatively small initial fee. Most document delivery services cover quite a wide range of journal materials. If a document delivery service is combined with an appropriate aggregated database, this may provide the maximum benefit to users for the least total cost.

The Future Role of Consortia

Consortia have risen up in droves over the past seven to ten years, and will continue to be important for a substantial proportion of academic libraries. For very expensive purchases, consortial purchasing may in many cases be the only viable option for many academic libraries. While acknowledging that libraries are not going to save money because of the move to e-journals, Ford suggests, "The tendency for electronic publications to be priced higher than their print equivalents is counterbalanced to a certain extent by the trend towards consortium purchase agreements. . . ."[41]

The Solinet Lexis-Nexis pricing offered a number of years ago was the first identified case where a large number of consortia joined together to buy a product as a super-consortium. This approach to buying has become formalized enough that it has developed the outward signs of any visible movement: an international organization, and a journal. "The International Coalition of Library Consortia (ICOLC), founded in 1997, represents over one hundred major consortia around the world. . . . Another indicator of the growth and importance of the consortial movement was the establishment, in 1999, of a new journal called Library Consortium Management: An International Journal."[42]

The Open Access Movement

The International Association of Scientific, Technical and Medical Publishers (STM) released a statement November 5, 2003, which said, "Broadening and ensuring continuity of information access for researchers, scholars, and practitioners is a critical mission for all publishers." It continues on to state that research in STM areas is more accessible than ever before, that its publisher members have invested a great deal of money to create this accessibility. The Association presents a case that it is these dollars that have led to technologies such as cross-linking protocols and the digital object identifier that have made navigation and discovery more transparent for scientists. It points out differences in journal content, services, and publishing models among its members. Finally, it concludes with the following statement: "Abandoning the diversity of proven publishing models in favour of a single, untested model could have disastrous consequences for the scientific research community. It could seriously jeopardize the flow of information today, as well as continuity of the archival records of scientific progress that is so important to our society tomorrow. It is the competitive and well-functioning market, and not governments, that must choose which business models and which publishers are best equipped to stay apace of the ever-increasing demand for information exchange."[43]

The statement is presumed to be, more than anything, a response to the growing open access movement. One could describe the current STM publishing system as one controlled by the publisher community, in that it accepts or rejects material for publication, and sets pricing and access policies. Scientists at research institutions produce research, funded either by their home institution or outside granting agencies. They may or may not pay page charges for publication of accepted articles, depending on standard practices in the field involved. Access to these articles, frequently owned in full by the publisher through the signing over of copyright by the authors, is then on a fee basis only.

The open access movement has a number of threads running through it. The basic model assumes that scientists produce research, self-archive either on their own university computer account, or institutionally archive if their research center or university provides institutional archiving services. Articles may be posted to a subject-based preprint archive, where they may be reviewed and commented on by others in the field. These subject preprint archives may be operated on grant funds, or by a research institution. One model has authors paying to have their work posted on a preprint server.

There is a great deal of conversation and excitement around open access and repository approaches to recording the research record. In December 2003, LJ Academic Newswire interviewed Georgia Tech economist Mark McCabe. He identifies the strength of an open access model as the reintroduction of competition to a market that lacks it. The payment of authors for the consideration of their work, while making the reviewed and accepted material available to users for free, "offers more efficiency . . . because it reintroduces faculty to the costs of disseminating research in their academic field. The current practice–libraries purchasing site licenses–in contrast divorces faculty members from the costs of publishing."[44]

CONCLUSIONS

It is clear that the state-of-the-art for e-journal pricing models is in extreme flux. The system appears poised to make serious changes, but it is not possible to know whether a significant enough group of libraries (and their universities) will step actively into that change process. Universities are traditionally slow to move, though modern models of higher education offer ways to make necessary responses (or to take proactive steps) at a faster pace. Library budgets cannot continue in their current approach indefinitely. Wise budget managers are educating their campuses and helping faculty and administrators recognize that, without making changes in their behavior, they are contributing to the scholarly communication crisis on an ongoing basis. Walking the line between individual and collective interest in providing journal access through appropriate pricing mechanisms will continue to be a careful balancing act for all librarians for some time to come. Sharper negotiating skills, more communal approaches, and stronger campus support are going to be necessary to manage our way through this period of change.

REFERENCES

1. Dougherty, Richard M. "Librarians Must Have the Authority to Cancel Subscriptions to Seldom-Used Journals." *Chronicle of Higher Education*, January 9, 1991, p. A56.

2. Jones, Dawn L. "Can Research Libraries Keep Pace?" *Touchstone*, August 1990, p. 2-7.

3. Ford, Geoffrey. "Financing and Budgeting." In Jenkins, Clare, and Morely, Mary. *Collection Management in Academic Libraries*, 2nd ed, p. 45-46.

4. Ford, op. cit., p. 45-46.

5. Tonkery, Dan. "Seven Common Myths About Acquiring and Accessing E-Journals." In Bluh, Pamela, ed. *Managing Electronic Serials: Essays Based on the ALCTS Electronic Serials Institutes, 1997-1999*. Chicago: ALA, 2001, p. 86-94.

6. Lee, Stuart D. *Electronic Collection Development: A Practical Guide*. New York: Neal-Schuman; London: Library Association Publishing, 2002, p. 58.

7. Tenopir, Carol and King, Donald W. *Towards Electronic Journals: Realities for Scientists, Librarians, and Publishers.* Washington, DC: SLA, 2000, p. 36.

8. McKay, Sharon Cline. "Managing Electronic Serials: An Overview." In Bluh, op. cit. (2001), p. 63.

9. See, for instance, McKay, op. cit.; Hanson, Kathlene, "Electronic Serials Costs: Sales and Acquisitions Practices in Transition." In Wayne Jones, ed., *E-Serials: Publishers, Libraries, Users, and Standards,* 2nd ed. New York: The Haworth Press, Inc., 2003; Knight, Nancy H. and Hillson, Susan B. "Electronic Pubs Pricing in the Web Era: NASIG Conference workshop identifies pros and cons of 16 models." *Information Today* 15(8), pp. 39-40; Cox, John. "Pricing Electronic Information: A Snapshot of New Serials Pricing Models." *Serials Review* 28(3), Autumn 2002, pp. 171-175.

10. Knight and Hillson, op. cit.

11. Machovec, George. "Management and Technical Considerations for Acquiring and Accessing Electronic Serials." In Bluh, op. cit. (2001), p. 70.

12. For a worked example, see Snyder, Herbert and Davenport, Elisabeth, *Costing and Pricing in the Digital Age: A Practical Guide for Information Services.* New York: Neal-Schuman, 1997, p. 133-134.

13. Kern-Simirenko, Cheryl. "Perspectives on the Library as E-Journal Customer, Intermediary, and Negotiator in a Time of Crisis." In Jones 2003, op. cit., p. 82.

14. Frazier, Kenneth. "The Librarians' Dilemma: Contemplating the Costs of the 'Big Deal.'" D-Lib Magazine 7(3), March 2001, p. 2.

15. We are clearly living in the age of constant publisher mergers, sales and acquisitions, but it is easy to forget that these changes can have an impact on specific publisher financial goals.

16. Brown, Diane; Stott, Elaine; and Watkinson, Anthony. *Serial Publications: Guidelines for Good Practice in Publishing Printed and Electronic Journals,* 2nd ed. Clapham, Worthing, West Sussex: Association of Learned and Professional Society Publishers.

17. Sense, Jean-Mark. "Moving Digits in Serial Life." *Library Philosophy and Practice* 6(1), Fall 2003. Viewed September 22, 2003 at <http://www.webpages.uidaho.edu/~mbolin/sens.html>.

18. Wiemers, Eugene L. "Seamless Information Environments and Seamless Management Structures: Where are our Aspirations Leading Us?" In Johnson, Peggy; and MacEwan, Bonnie, eds. *Virtually Yours: Models for Managing Electronic Resources and Services.* Chicago: American Library Association, 1999, pp. 25.

19. McKay, op. cit., p. 65.

20. Bluh, Pamela; Neal, James G.; and Call, J. Randolph. "Predicting Publication Prices: Are the Old Models Still Relevant?" *Library Resources & Technical Services* 47(4), October 2003, p. 189.

21. Ibid., p. 190.

22. Kern-Simirenko, Cheryl, op. cit., p. 81.

23. Sense, op. cit.

24. Bergstrom, Carl T.; and Bergstrom, Theodore C. "Do Electronic Site Licenses for Academic Journals Benefit the Scientific Community?" December 7, 2002. Viewed at <http://www.econ.ucsb.edu/~tedb/Journals/sitelicense.html>, December 2003.

25. Ibid., p. 11.

26. Ibid., p. 12.

27. Wyly, Brendan J. "Competition in Scholarly Publishing? What Publisher Profits Reveal." *ARL: A Bimonthly Newsletter of Research Library Issues and Actions*

#200, October 1998. Viewed at <http://www.arl.org/newsltr/200/wyly.html>, November 2003.

28. Ibid.

29. Fishwick, Francis; Edwards, Louise; and Blagden, John. *Scholarly Electronic Journals: Economic Implications, a Supporting Study in the JISC Electronic Libraries (eLib) Programme.* London: Library Information Technology Centre, 1998.

30. Economic Analysis of Scientific Research Publishing: A report commissioned by the Wellcome Trust. Histon, Cambridgeshire: SQW, January 2003. Rev. ed. October 2003.

31. Ibid., p. iv.

32. Tenopir, Carol; and King, Donald W. *Towards Electronic Journals: Realities for Scientists, Librarians, and Publishers.* Washington, DC: SLA Publishing, 2000.

33. Ford, Geoffrey, op. cit., p. 45.

34. Kern-Simirenko, op. cit., p. 84.

35. Van Orsdel, Lee; and Born, Kathleen. "Big Chill on the Big Deal? Periodicals Price Survey 2003, 43rd Annual Report." *Library Journal*, April 15, 2003.

36. Ibid.

37. *Library Journal Academic Newswire*, November 13, 2003.

38. Birch, Katie; and Young, Ian A. "Unmediated Document Delivery at Leeds University: From Project to Operational System." *Interlending & Document Supply* 29(1), pp. 4-10.

39. Robertson, Victoria. "The Impact of Electronic Journals on Academic Libraries: The Changing Relationship between Journals, Acquisitions and Inter-Library Loans Department Roles and Functions." *Interlending & Document Supply* 31(3), 2003, pp. 174-179.

40. Kern-Simirenko, op. cit., p. 86.

41. Ford, op. cit., p. 67.

42. Machovec, op. cit., pp. 74-75.

43. Viewed at <http://www.stm-assoc.org>, November 2003.

44. *Library Journal Academic Newswire*, December 2, 2003.

Is Our Best Good Enough?
Educating End-Users
About Licensing Terms

Jill Emery

SUMMARY. Educating end-users about licensing terms is an on-going systematic activity at most academic research institutions and there have been many methods employed by various institutions to address this concern. Through the use of rudimentary surveys and the responses to these surveys from librarians, content providers, and management providers, this paper outlines some of the ways libraries have been addressing these educational issues, how content providers feel libraries are attempting to meet these needs, and introduces resources from the library marketplace that can help facilitate this educational goal. Finally, best practices for educating users about the contractual agreements are suggested. *[Article copies available for a fee from The Haworth Document Delivery Service: 1-800-HAWORTH. E-mail address: <docdelivery@haworthpress.com> Website: <http://www.HaworthPress.com> © 2005 by The Haworth Press, Inc. All rights reserved.]*

Jill Emery is Director, Electronic Resources Program, University of Houston Libraries, 114 University Library, Houston, TX 77204-2000 (E-mail: JEmery@uh.edu). She is a member of ALA-ALCTS Serials Section, the North American Serials Interest Group, and the Texas Library Association.

[Haworth co-indexing entry note]: "Is Our Best Good Enough? Educating End-Users About Licensing Terms." Emery, Jill. Co-published simultaneously in *Journal of Library Administration* (The Haworth Information Press, an imprint of The Haworth Press, Inc.) Vol. 42, No. 3/4, 2005, pp. 27-39; and: *Licensing in Libraries: Practical and Ethical Aspects* (ed: Karen Rupp-Serrano) The Haworth Information Press, an imprint of The Haworth Press, Inc., 2005, pp. 27-39. Single or multiple copies of this article are available for a fee from The Haworth Document Delivery Service [1-800-HAWORTH, 9:00 a.m. - 5:00 p.m. (EST). E-mail address: docdelivery@haworthpress.com].

http://www.haworthpress.com/web/JLA
© 2005 by The Haworth Press, Inc. All rights reserved.
Digital Object Identifier: 10.1300/J111v42n03_02

KEYWORDS. Acceptable use, content providers, contracts, electronic resources, electronic resource management, license, licensing terms, end-user education

Last spring, when asked to respond to a column on how to best inform end-users of the licensing terms for a library's electronic users, the response given by this author was a statement which was somewhat flip, sardonic, and by and large evasive (Bazirjian 2003, 86). The basic tenet was and still is to a certain degree that a library has to determine what its best practices are and adhere to its own self-imposed standards and procedures when it comes to this matter. Because of the participation in that column, the author has now been asked to write this article to further the proposition of determining best practices when it comes to educating end-users of licensing terms. This time around, more research has been performed, members of the academic library community have been surveyed about this topic, members of the academic publishing community have been surveyed, and follow-up has been performed on the development of various products that can and should help libraries do a better job when it comes to informing users about what they can and cannot do with regard to electronic resources.

Therefore, this article will look at the current practices used by many academic institutions to inform users about licensing terms, it will provide a synopsis of what the publishing community thinks in relation to libraries informing users of licensing terms, it will provide a rudimentary investigation into tools on the market that can help improve our best practices in this arena, and lastly will show how educating users about these matters is a practice that needs to be adopted by the whole library throughout all the mechanisms used in instruction of end-users. Many libraries have embarked on what is referred to as best practices when it comes to informing users of licensing terms, but given that breaches do occasionally occur, and continue to occur, our best may not be quite good enough. Many of the librarians responding to the surveys conducted for this article have indicated that more can be done to educate end-users about terms of use and that this is a concern all libraries are attempting to address from every point of service offered in relation to electronic resources.

CURRENT BEST PRACTICES EMPLOYED

In the Winter 2000 issue of *Colorado Libraries*, Donnice Cochenour outlined many ways that libraries have been informing users of the licensing terms of their electronic resources (Cochenour 2000, 45). A synopsis of these findings indicates that some libraries were scanning licenses and providing links to license files from cataloging records, some had developed a general statement that was being linked from Web pages, some had created pass-through pages that spelled out licensing terms, and some were in the process of creating management systems that outlined licensing terms (Cochenour 2000, 46). The findings in Cochenour's article were followed up by electronic mail messages to selected librarians who work at institutions involved in the Digital Library Federation's Metadata for Electronic Resource Management Initiative or who were known to have developed some type of local electronic resource management tool (Chandler 2003). The questions asked of these librarians were:

1. Does your library currently have a mechanism in place to inform library users of the licensing terms of electronic resources and if so, can you describe briefly how the mechanism works?
2. Do you feel this mechanism effectively communicates licensing terms to the end-user?
3. What do you consider to be the most effective way(s) to educate library users of licensing terms?
4. In general, do you think libraries try to communicate too much or too little information about licensing terms to their library users?
5. Do you think publishers/vendors are constructing their resources to better inform end-users about permitted and allowable use in a way that removes the library from having to share or carry this responsibility solely?

It can be concluded that not much has changed in three years. If a library has created some sort of homegrown electronic resource management tool or subject guide tool to its electronic resources, there are usually only basic terms listed or indicated, with either text or specific icons next to each resource to indicate who may use what and how this use is limited (Medeiros, Bills, Blatchley 2003, 33). In some cases, libraries have scanned licenses and provide a link to the scanned contract for the end-user from their OPAC. The most common practice is to have some type of terms of use statement written in plain language that an end-user can comprehend, made available on all Web pages that link to electronic resources. This statement spells out what users can and cannot do with electronic resources in general. In some cases, the library has developed this statement as a splash page that a user needs to ac-knowledge before moving on to the resource.

Many universities do have computer-use agreements to which students and faculty have to agree; within these are usually one or two statements about the proper use of electronic, copyrighted material. Many times though, these statements are drafted by a campus computing department or informational technology department without the consultation of the library and do not exactly address all the issues a library may want to cover. Another practice is to have licensing terms listed on the user authentication page. In this instance, as the user is typing in her/his name and authentication code, the person has the opportunity to read through a statement concerning how the resource can be used for the research process. Lastly, a few libraries put licensing statements in different note fields of their OPAC records to inform users about the specific licensing terms for those resources.

All in all, what these practices tend to show is that libraries are attempting to comply with license agreements that request the signer or designated institution to inform third-party users of the basic tenets of electronic resource use. One way to view these attempts is to consider the signs posted at your local fishing hole: they tell you what the daily catch limit is, that you should have a current fishing license on your person, which specific lures or fishing techniques are not allowed, and which areas of the pond are currently open for fishing. Generally, these postings are provided at the main entry into your fishing spot.

What happens when you access the pond from an unmarked entrance or come across the pond while trekking through the underbrush and decide you want to try a hand at fishing? More than likely, if a park ranger happens by, you can claim a certain amount of ignorance in relation to knowing what your catch limit is, or any fishing techniques banned by this particular park or fishing venue. If you're lucky, you may end up with a stern warning or a small fine, or at most be forbidden from fishing there in the future. The same occurs with end-users and licensed library materials. When faculty and students bookmark sites directly, or more likely type a journal name or database name into Google™ and then access licensed resources from this point, the users are most likely bypassing the local portal that explains the use terms governing their research or information gathering. When signing licensing agreements, both the University's designated signatory and the information resource provider agree to a false conceit that the resources are only available in one manner, through the library's Web pages or portal. So when members of a University community breach the terms of use, the person can oftentimes plead the same ignorance as the errant fisherman, that the terms of using the resources were not directly provided to them.

Let's also talk for a minute about what terms are usually provided to the end-user. By and large, the terms most often spelled out are an explanation of the authorized users and the reiteration of a copyright statement. Both of these have been deemed by the academic library community to be the biggest concerns that need to be conveyed to an end-user when attempting to access a resource. We recognize that there are often many other terms that are just as important to communicate to the end-user (Reference and User Services Association/Machine-Assisted Reference Section/Management Committee 1998, 277). These terms can include that the activity is being recorded in some mechanized way and not always anonymously; that the number of pages or issues which they download or print are being noted and there is a point at which most information providers consider the downloads and printing to be *excessive*; that they shouldn't be e-mailing articles or other bits of information to people beyond the university community; and lastly, and in many cases most importantly, that the resources are provided on an *as is* basis and there is no guarantee that the information will continue to be available in an hour's time, tomorrow, a year from now, or even that the information provided is correctly presented in any way.

Academic libraries and information providers alike have so far accepted that a library posting the general terms of use statement is a *best efforts* or a *reasonable* attempt by the library to notify the end-user of terms. Some licenses specifically call for this type of notice to be implemented; for the most extreme cases of proprietary databases, you must authenticate end-users to a page that provides the use terms spelled out along with a specific gateway to the resource. Despite these reasonable efforts, breaches of contractual agreements occur. There is probably not an academic library in the United States that has not received a dreaded e-mail or call from the information provider, stating that misuse of a resource has been detected. At this point, libraries and information providers work together to try to identify where the breach occurred. The end-user or department receives a stern warning, a cease-and-desist mandate, or in some extreme cases, access is denied to an individual or set of individuals.

Librarians like to see themselves as helpful stewards of information. Ushering end-users to the resources that are needed to further their scholarly endeavors is one of our most important responsibilities. We do not like to see ourselves as security control when it comes to providing access to these resources to end-users. We expect the public to act in accordance with the laws of the public good and assess between right and wrong. This can be a naïve and simplistic view. The beauty of the World Wide Web, from many people's viewpoint, is the ability to provide resources in an unfettered and readily accessible manner. Many of our users cannot tell the difference between a licensed resource and one freely available. We are no longer in an era when simply posting a sign by a photocopier suffices and indemnifies us in relation to the use or misuse of intellectual property. A more active role in informing users of the proper and improper uses of electronic material should become as much of a characteristic of our profession as is our assistance in resource discovery.

THE VIEW FROM THE INFORMATION PROVIDER

Publishers and information providers tend to see the attempts that libraries have taken to educate end-users as *good faith efforts*, and state that breaches are relatively rare given the large numbers of authorized users utilizing their content. Some publishers feel that end-users understand the general gist of proper user behavior but may not be aware of specific terms that relate to specific electronic collections of content. Every information provider surveyed responded that libraries appear to be doing a good job of trying to inform end-users of the terms of use.

Societies, institutional publishers, and publishers that provide individual subscriber access to their electronic content, feel they do inform the end-user about licensing terms by having end-users who register for access to content from the parent institution pass-through or click an *I agree* button. No one publisher/content provider surveyed indicated that there is further education beyond this initial introduction to content on their Web sites. Every electronic information provider tends to provide copyright statements directly or re-enforce awareness of their ownership of content or the fact that the information is provided on behalf of a specific content owner. These statements appear on just about every page on which proprietary content is hosted. All content providers have drafted a basic terms of use statement in plain language for their Web sites.

The survey sent to selected content providers asked these questions:

1. In general, do you think libraries have made a good faith effort to inform users about the licensing terms of their electronic resources?

2. What in your opinion would be a good faith effort by a library to inform users of licensing terms?
3. Do you think this responsibility lies with the library or with the content provider?
4. Does your content platform make terms of use readily known to the end-users of your content?
5. Do you think societies and publishers are now trying to educate users directly about the terms of use?

All of the content providers responding felt that informing users of the terms of use fell solely to the subscribing institution since the subscribing institution signed the licensing agreement. A further consideration that came up from talking to a few librarians after surveying the content providers was how to reconcile inherently contradictory confidentiality clauses as part of the contract; a confidentiality clause generally states that a library should not make any part of the signed contract readily available to people outside of university's acquisitions or business office. Given the increasing number of confidentiality clauses in licenses, this does put a library at a disadvantage as far as informing users of terms of use? It quite possibly gives libraries a legal loophole, since providing users with the terms of the agreement would run counter to the confidentiality clause. At the very least, informing end-users of the terms of a contract should be a way to negotiate out of some confidentiality clauses.

A couple of the content providers surveyed think that there are standard introductions-to-the-library classes being offered at most academic institutions in the United States, and that general information concerning licensing terms and the proper use of electronic resources is a component of these classes. While this does occur during instruction sessions, we will later see that information literacy professionals are still grappling with how to best include this type of information as a regular part of their sessions. Another belief presented by many content providers was that terms of use statements are provided as printed material near or at public workstations in libraries much like copyright statements are posted near photocopiers. However, given ergonomic workstation design, the advent of flat monitor screens, the introduction of wireless connectivity, laptop check-outs, and the general need to squeeze many workstations into controlled areas in a library, this type of signage is not always readily available to an end-user.

One member from the publishing community felt that the content provider should have a pop-up screen at the start of every session but eventually, we will reach a point when the proper use of electronic material is commonly known and accepted and these types of alerts will no longer be necessary. Generally, these types of splash screens or pop-up windows are considered to be bad Web design and the majority of content providers do not use them. An interesting proposal that was presented by one of the members from the publishing community was that publishers/content providers should be talking to their authors/contributors/editors about the proper use of electronic material. It was felt that information kits could be devised and distributed with their review copies and flyers presented at major society/member conferences. It was even suggested that content providers could cooperate with institutions of higher learning to set up group learning sessions, demos at conferences, and training in order to create an exchange for better end-user awareness, as well as promotion of their content.

Let's go back to our fishing metaphor for a moment. Who buys the fishing license? Wal-Mart™ may be a place where one can get a fishing license, but we certainly do not expect the salesperson there to be held responsible for the catch limit of an individual who has purchased the fishing license. The content providers have a valid point, they have sold libraries their goods with specific terms outlined in a signed agreement and it is up to the libraries to make sure the resources are used in accordance with the rules and regulations of the agreement. Overall, the publishing community feels that libraries are making reasonable efforts to inform end-users of terms of use and it is primarily librarians who tend to feel like there is more that could be done.

NEW TOOLS TO TACKLE THE PROBLEM

In the spring of 2003, Innovative Interfaces, Inc. released a new module marketed as ERM™ (Electronic Resource Management). This module allows libraries to create a separate tracking mechanism for their electronic resources and more fully utilize the integrated library system for the management of electronic products. The product is available as a stand-alone module or as part of the Innovative Interfaces platform as a whole. Endeavor Information Systems, Inc. is working to have a product in release in 2004. EBSCO Subscription Services has EJS (Electronic Journals Service) which has a sophisticated authentication device built into the system and is looking at how to better aid in the registration of electronic material. Electronic journal management systems have been developed by several players in the industry and many of these providers are beginning to understand the need of enhancing their products to make electronic content licensing information easier to manage and disseminate. In particular, GoldRush™ from the Colorado Alliance has a robust licensing management mechanism for libraries and librarians.

How helpful are these tools? It depends on the information the library wishes to provide to end-users. At this point, you still need someone with a good enough grasp of licensing terms and legalese to determine what a license allows. A library still needs to determine for itself which terms of use should be conveyed to the end-user. In the mechanics of these systems, the entering of most standard terms can be as easy as clicking a check-box which indicates what uses are and are not allowed, or as complex as entering a free-text message. By and large, the technology is maturing and helping us better disseminate this information. Then there is the question of whether the licensing terms appear solely in a Web A to Z list, as part of a federated search mechanism, as part of the open URL device, or in the OPAC; presently, there are no systems that allow libraries to make licensing terms ubiquitously available to the end-user at the point of entry.

On the Electronic Resources in Libraries electronic discussion list, this question was posed to the audience: Is anyone using their purchased/ licensed electronic journal management system to notify end-users of licensing terms? For example, if your library is using Serials Solutions A to Z title list, TDNet, EBSCO's A-Z, UNCG's Journal Finder, etc., do you use any type of note field to explain who can access the electronic title, if there are printing restrictions for that title, or any other restrictions of the content? The responses indicated that most libraries using these products are not utilizing the available note fields to provide this information. A small group of libraries are beginning to discuss using these note fields more creatively and a subset of these libraries is beginning to actually enter this information into the appropriate fields.

So why aren't more libraries beginning to take advantage of these tools? Because, if faced with the choice of purchasing and processing more full-text content or a management system to aid in the distribution of the full-text content, the management system is still considered secondary. It's much harder to prove the worth of a management system and the processing time to the user community than it is to state that hundreds of new titles are electronically available to a library community. Generally, libraries choose cheaper products that do not always provide the easiest way to enter and display licensing information. It is much easier to click through a number of boxes than it is to agree upon a standardized statement to be entered into free-text fields. Also the management of these notes can be difficult. In the print world, serials librarians didn't have to worry too much if journal X came from publisher A or publisher B as long as the subscription agent could provide it. In the online world though, when a title switches from publisher A to publisher B suddenly we have to sign an addendum agreement with publisher B, change the URL, and quite possibly also change the terms of use that display with journal X. Providing terms of use on such a granular level is seen by most librarians as something of a Sisyphean act.

IS USER INSTRUCTION THE ANSWER?

As stated previously, there is a common belief in the publishing community that we are spending a reasonable amount of time educating users on the proper usage of electronic resources in classroom settings and through hands-on workshops. While this type of training occurs quite often and educating end-users of licensing terms is included in the ACRL Information Literacy Competency Standards, many instructors find it hard to include this information in their sessions due to time limitations. The primary focus of instruction sessions is still resource selection to use for subject-specific research. Secondary instruction centers on the basic interface of these products. Even when federated search mechanisms are available, the majority of information sessions tend to focus on the specific database interface navigation. In many of the cases that were described, end-users were given rudimentary overviews of licensing terms concentrated on defining authorized users.

Here are the questions that were asked of instruction librarians:

1. In the ACRL Best Practices Guidelines for Information Literacy or in the ACRL Guidelines for Instruction Programs, are there any specific statements that in your opinion support or speak directly to educating end-users of licensing terms for electronic resources?
2. How do you incorporate Terms of Use statements into your instruction sessions?
3. Where do you think the responsibility for educating end-users about licensing terms lies?
4. Do you think trying to educate end-users of licensing terms is a lost cause for librarians and feel that this is better accomplished through publisher devices on their Web sites or via scripted, click-through licensing pages?

5. In your opinion, what is the best way or best practice to educate users about licensing terms?

The instruction librarians identified Standard Five of the ACRL Information Literacy Standards as best covering this topic: "Standard 5: The information literate student understands many of the economic, legal, and social issues surrounding the use of information and accesses and uses information ethically and legally" (Association of College and Research Libraries 2000). There are other areas in the standards where educating end-users about licensing terms can be inferred but this is the most obvious statement available. Most instruction librarians assert that conveying the cost of their university's electronic resources has more of an impact than reciting the restrictions that might accompany a product's use. If there are specific restrictions that an end-user will encounter when using a product, these restrictions will be covered in the overview of the interface. However, the general consensus was that the most important aspect to cover is who is authorized to use what material and how this material can be retrieved or accessed.

Instruction librarians are quick to point out that teachers should take advantage of any opportunity to educate end-users about the terms of use issues and concerns. The time constraints of most teaching sessions leave few suitable circumstances in which to cover licensing terms and many of today's reference interviews result in a patron receiving an answer to her/his query. No one has found a way to make this type of user information fun and catchy, and librarians often rely on the end-users having a basic understanding of what is right and wrong, hoping the students will do the right thing rather than pointing out the rules. Click-through or splash pages are seen as an annoyance by the instruction librarians. According to members of the instruction field, these types of alerts and/or notices are never read and are a waste of programming time. One way to grab end-users attention is to mention the cost of resources and many instruction librarians agree that this act does have an impact on the end-user during instruction sessions. By playing up the high cost spent on electronic resources and the penalties for abuse, these librarians feel that they can instill a respect for the material in that way.

For public services librarians, the best way to educate end-users about licensing terms is by reviewing the information in a subject-oriented session or by introducing the terms of use in an instruction session when showing end-users how to access the information. Generally, it is felt that instructors show end-users how to navigate a database or a content platform, but rarely point out the rules and regulations of access. To return again to our fishing metaphor, we're teaching them how to fish but neglecting to tell them about their responsibilities and obligations before they head out on their own.

CONCLUSION

So are our best practices good enough? As with just about everything, there is always room for improvement. We need to tell end-users more than just who can access what–we need to explain specific limitations that may be associated with each resource. While it is helpful to have terms of use spelled out more specifically through electronic resource management tools and through the OPAC, the tools available right now do not provide the ubiquity needed to make this effort completely worthwhile. Many librarians feel that their OPACs are no longer the main entry point to resources. It is obvious that electronic resource librarians need to provide more in-house training to their public services staff to insure the terms of use are being taught in instruction sessions and pointed out during extended reference interviews. Of all the practices currently in use by libraries, the best of the best practices appears to be having the terms of use statements incorporated into the user authentication page. This way, it does not matter how or when the user has come across a resource, the person is presented with the terms of use as they authenticate themselves as a valid user. In the end, we need to make sure that as we're teaching the art of fishing for resources, we remind the end-user that you still need to understand the fishing license before setting out on a research expedition.

BIBLIOGRAPHY

Association of College and Research Libraries. "Information Literacy Competency Standards for Higher Education." ACRL Web Site (document posted: January 2000): http://www.ala.org/Content/NavigationMenu/ACRL/Standards_and_Guidelines/Information_Literacy_Competency_Standards_for_Higher_Education.htm, accessed last 11/3/2003.

Bazirjian, Rosann [column editor]. "Group Therapy Column." *Against the Grain*. V. 15, no. 2 (April 2003): 86-7.

Chandler, Adam and Jewell, Tim. "A Web Hub for Developing Administrative Metadata for Electronic Resource Management." Web Site. (Updated 2/26/2003): http://www.library.cornell.edu/cts/elicensestudy/home.html, accessed last 11/3/2003.

Cochenour, Donnice. "How Will They Know? Libraries' Responsibility to Inform Users of License Restrictions for Electronic Resources." *Colorado Libraries*, V. 26, no. 4 (Winter 2000): 45-6.

Medeiros, Norm; Bills, Linda; Blatchley, Jeremy. "Managing Administrative Metadata: The Tri-College Consortium's Electronic Resources Tracking System (ERTS)." *Library Resources & Technical Services*, V. 47, no. 1 (January 2003): 28-35.

Reference and User Services Association/Machine-Assisted Reference Section/Management Committee. "Guidelines for the Introduction of Electronic Information Resources to Users." *Reference & User Services Quarterly*, V. 37, no. 3 (Spring 1998): 277-8.

SUGGESTED READING

Buttler, Dwayne K. "Little or New Choice: Copyright, Licensing, and Electronic Resources." *Serials Review*, V. 29, no. 2 (Summer 2003): 69-71.

Drake, Miriam, A. "Technological Innovation and Organizational Change Revisited." *Journal of Academic Librarianship*, V. 26, no. 1 (January 2000): 53-9.

Ebbinghouse, Carol. "Legal Aspects of Information Technology." *Searcher*, V. 8, no. 1 (January 2000): 18+.

Ebbinghouse, Carol. "Ferreting Out Terms and Conditions." *Searcher*, V. 7 no. 2 (February 1999): 14-17.

Miller, Ruth H. "Electronic Resources and Academic Libraries, 1980-2000: A Historical Perspective." *Library Trends*, V. 48, no. 4 (Spring 2000) 645-70.

Von Elm, Catherine and Trump, Judith F. "Maintaining the Mission in the Hybrid Library." *Journal of Academic Librarianship*, V. 27, no. 1 (January 2001): 33-5.

Interlibrary Loan and Licensing:
Tools for Proactive Contract Management

Janet Brennan Croft

SUMMARY. Licensing agreements can profoundly affect the operation of interlibrary loan departments. How do academic libraries cope with the variety of ILL clauses included in database licenses? This article examines the avoidance approach (lend nothing from electronic sources) and the reactive approach (maintain files on which databases permit which types of loans), but recommends a proactive approach in which licensing negations include local interlibrary loan requirements from the start. Included are recommended resources for developing negotiating skills. *[Article copies available for a fee from The Haworth Document Delivery Service: 1-800-HAWORTH. E-mail address: <docdelivery@haworthpress.com> Website: <http://www.HaworthPress.com> © 2005 by The Haworth Press, Inc. All rights reserved.]*

Janet Brennan Croft is Head of Access Services, University of Oklahoma Libraries, 401 West Brooks, Norman, OK 73019 (E-mail: jbcroft@ou.edu). She has written on library issues for *Archival Products News*, *College & Undergraduate Libraries*, *Interlending and Document Supply*, *Journal of Access Services*, and *Journal of Interlibrary Loan & Document Supply*. She is the author of *Legal Solutions in Electronic Reserves and the Electronic Delivery of Interlibrary Loan* (The Haworth Press, Inc., Spring 2004).

[Haworth co-indexing entry note]: "Interlibrary Loan and Licensing: Tools for Proactive Contract Management." Croft, Janet Brennan. Co-published simultaneously in *Journal of Library Administration* (The Haworth Information Press, an imprint of The Haworth Press, Inc.) Vol. 42, No. 3/4, 2005, pp. 41-53; and: *Licensing in Libraries: Practical and Ethical Aspects* (ed: Karen Rupp-Serrano) The Haworth Information Press, an imprint of The Haworth Press, Inc., 2005, pp. 41-53. Single or multiple copies of this article are available for a fee from The Haworth Document Delivery Service [1-800-HAWORTH, 9:00 a.m. - 5:00 p.m. (EST). E-mail address: docdelivery@haworthpress.com].

KEYWORDS. Interlibrary loan, licensing contracts, copyright, databases, negotiation, model licenses

Interlibrary loan–the lending and borrowing of items between libraries at the request of a patron–is an extremely popular service. According to the statistics collected by the Association of Research Libraries, interlibrary loan borrowing has risen dramatically from an annual average of 4,806 items per member library in 1980, to 20,620 in 2000. Similarly, interlibrary loan lending by member libraries has more than doubled in the same time period, from an annual average of 12,442 items per library in 1980, to 27,065 in 2000 (see http://fisher.lib.virginia.edu/arl/index.html to generate statistics).

In the United States, for physical items owned by the lending library, interlibrary loan is a straightforward process supported by the right of "first sale" (U.S.C. Title 17, Section 109), which allows the owner of a copy of a copyrighted item to lend, rent, resell, or dispose of that copy as desired. For photocopied items, the interlibrary loan exception to a copyright holder's exclusive rights to copy and distribute a work is codified in the copyright law in U.S.C. Title 17, Section 108(d), governing reproduction by libraries and archives, and further defined and regulated by the CONTU Guidelines on Photocopying and Interlibrary Arrangements (both reproduced in the Copyright Office's Circular 21, http://www.copyright.gov/circs/circ21.pdf).

However, the "loan" of items from electronic formats is a practice still in flux. Should libraries be allowed to send a paper or electronic copy of an electronic item to another library to fulfill a patron request? More and more electronic items in the library catalog are not actually owned by the library, and therefore arguably not subject to the "first sale" doctrine. Instead of the library owning the item, the library signs a license or contract which permits access to items which are owned by a third party producer or publisher. George Pike points out, "Courts have consistently held that the licensing of software or databases is not a sale and consequently is not covered by the first sale doctrine" (Pike 2002). The major library associations, in their commentary on the Digital Millennium Copyright Act, tried to argue that first sale does apply to digital works, but were unsuccessful (Alford 2002).

Because these are not outright purchases, the use of these electronic databases and journals is governed by the contracts the owner and the library sign under state law, and not by federal copyright law. As a result, the producers of these products can limit or forbid uses we consider fair use, like interlibrary loan lending. If ILL is permitted, they can mandate that the lending library, rather than the borrowing library (as is required with print ILL), meet copyright restrictions they impose (for an example, see Croft and Murphy 2002, 7). As Duncan Alford states, "nearly all publishers have been uncomfortable with the interlibrary loan of digital materials" (Alford 2002, 625), and this is borne out by the variety of clauses by which producers seek to limit transmission to parties outside the licensed institution. We may find ourselves signing away our expected fair use exceptions (which we often see as our patrons' rights) when we sign a contract, and while "it is possible that licenses can be pre-empted by the federal courts if copyright is found to be violated, . . . most legislative and judicial arenas favor the freedom of contract over copyright" (Leiding 2000, 285).

Many producers specifically prohibit using their electronic databases to fill interlibrary loan requests, or include other language which forbids providing any copies from their product to anyone outside a clearly defined group of users. Donna Nixon examines the flaw in their understanding of library operations:

> Some publishing interests wish to restrict ILL of copyrighted materials because they feel it is a cheap, easy and fast way for libraries to subvert copyright. Nevertheless, that is actually not true. ILL is a slow, labor intensive, and costly process for libraries, in both personnel and monetary measurements. Each ILL transaction in a research library takes about ten days. . . . [T]he mean cost of each ILL transaction for research libraries in 1998 was approximately $28.00. (Nixon 2003, 57)

Not being allowed to lend something from our collections to another library conflicts with our deeply-held beliefs in interlibrary cooperation and patron service. We feel we have a responsibility to serve our own patrons better by building sharing relationships with other libraries; we gain access to wider collections by sharing our own. These ILL restrictions become more onerous as we replace print items with electronic formats to provide 24/7 access for our patrons and save money, time, and space, and as more and more resources are "born digital."

THE REACTIVE APPROACH

There are two approaches to dealing with licenses with restrictive terms: reactive and proactive. Of course, a library may also take an avoidance approach and simply not consider interlibrary loan requests for items they have only in electronic format (Croft and Murphy 2002, 9-10). As a working group of the RUSA Interlibrary Loan Committee discovered, "Many ILL librarians do not utilize electronic resources for lending because they are not sure of the legality of doing so" (Liaison to Licensing Entities Working Group 2003). One librarian commented,

> The mish-mash of licensing terms has simply made interlibrary loan of digital materials impractical for us to provide to the detriment of users around the globe with whom we otherwise share scholarly material. (quoted in Webster 2002)

The reactive approach involves developing tools and procedures which aid library employees in complying with licensing terms that differ from the copyright regulations under which the library normally operates–like interlibrary loan, electronic reserves, off-campus or multi-campus access, and so on. Many libraries develop simple in-house lists or more complex databases of licensing terms, to which the interlibrary loan department can refer whenever they receive a request which could be filled from an electronic resource. At its simplest, this might just be a list posted near the lenders' workstations saying, "Do not loan from these databases and journals." But as libraries acquire more and more electronic material, a list becomes awkward to use and too narrow in scope. As Nixon points out, "monitoring may become an overwhelming burden on library personnel and resources" (Nixon 2003, 70).

To solve this and other problems, the Massachusetts Institute of Technology developed an extremely sophisticated relational database, called Virtual Electronic Resource Access (VERA) and described by Ellen Finnie Duranceau in a 2000 article in *Serials Review*. VERA not only provides library staff with access to terms of use and tracks renewal, technical support, and budgeting information, but also controls which resources are available off-campus, allows patrons to search its publicly accessible fields, permits global editing of the database, and links to the actual scanned license itself for staff reference, among other features. However, as Duranceau points out, a cost-benefit analysis must show that designing such a database would "yield substantial labor savings in multiple areas, such as access, education, administration, and budget," or it is not worth the considerable amount of time required to create and maintain such a complex tool (Duranceau 2000). Additionally, workflow efficiency must be considered; if checking a request against a database requires an extra step, it may not be used to its full extent by busy ILL staff members.

Other libraries track licensing terms by entering them in their online catalogs, usually in a MARC field not normally seen by the public (for example, 500: general note, 590: local notes, or 856: electronic information and access, among others mentioned on different discussion lists). This has the advantage of requiring interlibrary loan staff to look in only one place to both confirm the item is owned and retrieve its call number, and to see if it can be loaned. However, new software which automates the process of checking incoming requests against the catalog is becoming more widely available. Before a library embarks on a massive retrospective project of entering ILL term information in the catalog for thousands or tens of thousands of individual titles (some available in multiple databases, to confuse the issue further), the way automated look up software works should be taken into consideration. Can the software recognize a "no ILL" code and go on to the next occurrence of the title in the catalog? Or will the location information presented to the lending staff include this information for multiple occurrences of a title, so they can choose the appropriate record from a list or manually search for another record?

There are several commercial products now available to help track and manage licensing terms. These management tools can easily store information on licensing terms, but either ILL workflow would have to include checking these databases, or the catalog would have to connect to the management software listing and not directly to the database containing the e-journal, if these products are to be useful to ILL staff. In addition to the products described below, some existing journal management products which do not specifically market themselves as license management tools may have customizable fields which would permit displaying the necessary information to the ILL staff, such as EBSCO's Electronic Journals Service (http://www.ebsco.com/home/ejournals/ejsintbro.pdf).

The Innovative Interfaces Inc. automation system has developed a new module, called Electronic Resource Management, which provides a template for storing all necessary information about electronic resources, including whether ILL is allowed (http://www.iii.com/mill/digital.shtml#erm). It can be used as a stand-alone module or integrated with the rest of Innovative's automation package, and is currently being implemented at University of Arizona, among other places. Other automation software producers are likely to follow III's lead in developing similar modules.

Another product is Gold Rush, which is produced by the Colorado Alliance of Research Libraries and is available in three different packages. Gold Rush is explored in detail in the Fong and Wicht article included in this volume.

TDNet has also developed a management system for electronic journal subscriptions; their Web site (http://tdnet.com/) gives insufficient detail, but several libraries have mentioned their product as an option for tracking licensing clauses. TexShare uses TDNet as an interface for public users to locate journal titles within its state-supported databases (www.texshare.edu/programs/academicdb/tdnet.html; a good place to test TDNet for yourself), and the University of Houston reports that the TDNet database they use includes a code in the Online Coverage column which indicates if ILL is permitted from the particular title or database. TDNet is also in use at Boise State University (http://tdnet.boisestate.edu/) and Oxford University (http://tdnet.bodley.ox.ac.uk/).

THE PROACTIVE APPROACH

The proactive approach challenges libraries to ask for what their patrons need from the start. If all contracts are negotiated under the same criteria, the interlibrary loan department (and other affected departments as well) won't have to deal with a long list of different terms for different resources. Ideally, all databases and electronic resources would operate under the same or very similar contracts, simplifying management across library departments.

But is it realistic to plan to refuse to sign a contract that prohibits using the product to fill ILL requests? Georgia Harper reassures and encourages us:

> These licenses are fully negotiable! Do not hesitate to ask for what you want. Vendors are willing to work with libraries to tailor their contracts to your needs. In fact, the really good news is that as more libraries ask for better terms, contracts are improving for everyone. This is the function of standard-setting. (Harper 2001)

Reba Leiding reports that panelists at an ACRL preconference on licensing exhorted librarians to "assert their free market role by negotiating licenses that maintain rights and norms established in the print realm, and incorporate relevant standards" (Leiding 2000, 285). And from the other side of the bargaining table, a license negotiator for a major database producer says, "we are happy to accommodate all reasonable requests" (Lawrence 2000, 150).

There may be some suppliers who refuse to negotiate their terms. Is it a disservice to your patrons to refuse to subscribe to these resources? It is a problem which must be judged on a case-by-case basis. In the short run, this can delay your patron's work while you attempt to obtain the item elsewhere. In the long run, this is good for all libraries and their patrons, as it forces publishers to acknowledge our needs or lose our business. As Lesley Ellen Harris states, "If you cannot obtain the access you need for your patrons, then the electronic product loses much of its value to you" (Harris 2002, 28), and in the interlibrary loan field one must apply this to patrons from other libraries as well as one's own local patrons.

All libraries need to realize they have the freedom to negotiate; and all producers should understand that we are willing to walk away if the terms are unsatisfactory. We are not trying to put them out of business; we simply expect full value for our money. Eileen Lawrence, currently with Alexander Street Press, wrote these reassuring words for publishers:

> Librarians are by nature protectors, defenders, and nurturers of information. We're not in a tug of war with each other, but rather on the same side of the table, working together to achieve practical and comfortable situations. And, despite all else, librarians do want publishers to survive and thrive, so that we can continue to provide the information that you need in order to do your job. (Lawrence 2000, 148)

At the University of Oklahoma, our negotiation team insists on certain terms being included in all licenses we sign, including: the ability to deliver ILL requests electronically; access to permanent archives of the licensed material; access by all OU campuses; access through IP address range; and Oklahoma jurisdiction (or no jurisdiction stated) for legal remedies. The state consortium is also developing similar standards, which include permission to use state-licensed databases for interlibrary loan.

TOOLS FOR PROACTIVE NEGOTIATION

The amount of material available to help librarians negotiate licenses has proliferated rapidly in recent years. Among the outstanding resources is Lesley Ellen Harris's book published by the American Library Association in 2002. This detailed guide to negotiation acknowledges that ILL from electronic resources is still controversial, and includes useful tips on defining what you need in the way of ILL functionality to vendors. As Harris says, "The bottom line is that if ILL is something your library requires, then ask for it in your agreement. . . . Try to negotiate an ILL provision that works best for your library" (Harris 2002, 51). Two shorter articles by Harris are good introductions to the topic of negotiation (Harris 2000a, 2000b).

A 1997 Association of Research Libraries SPEC Kit (*SPEC Kit 248: Managing the Licensing of Electronic Products* 1999) is an older but still very useful resource. Its checklists for the goals of license review, cost, location, ownership issues, and indemnification, are useful starting points, as are the questions on practical considerations such as user definitions, potential uses of the material, and access control. As the authors point out, "If users cannot do at least as much with electronic materials as they could with print equivalents, the license needs attention" (Brennan, Hersey, and Harper 1997, 17).

Useful journal articles include a lengthy piece by Duncan Alford in *Law Library Journal* (Alford 2002), which incorporates an excellent summary of UCITA issues and model and consortial licensing initiatives. Articles by Lawrence W. Bebbington and Fiona Durrant discuss licensing under British laws (Bebbington 2001; Durrant 2003); Rob Richards includes a discussion of licensing trends in other regions of the world in his chapter in *Publishing and the Law* (Richards 2001). Kim Guenther's "Making Smart Licensing Decisions" mainly deals with collection development issues to consider when evaluating licenses, but also touches on interlibrary loan and other utilization issues briefly (Guenther 2000). George Pike's article on licensing, copyright, and fair use includes his advice to change business-oriented language in contracts ("client," for example) to library-oriented terms like "patron" (Pike 2002).

One very useful online tool for negotiating licenses is the Software and Database License Agreement Checklist used by the University of Texas System (http://www.utsystem.edu/ogc/intellectualproperty/dbckfrm1.htm), which guides the user through the steps of analyzing a contract and provides suggested wording to insert in the contract if certain clauses are included. It is specific to the needs of the University of Texas system, but an excellent framework for developing a tool to analyze contracts for an individual library's requirements.

The LibLicense Guide to Digital Licensing software program, available for free download on the LibLicense site, is a sophisticated tool which allows the user to create draft licensing agreements or revisions to licenses under review (http://www.library.yale.edu/~llicense/download/liblicenseguidefaq.htm). The program can also be used to maintain a database of licensing agreements and their terms. Also available on the LibLicense site are extensive bibliographies of articles, books, and Web resources on all aspects of licensing (http://www.library.yale.edu/~llicense/bibliogr.shtml and http://www.library.yale.edu/~llicense/liclinks.shtml).

Another useful resource currently under development by LibLicense is the Interlibrary Loan Terms database (http://www.library.yale.edu/~llicense/ILLproject.html). In 2001, a working group of LibLicense list participants developed a publisher questionnaire and database format for collecting and organizing information on ILL terms offered by different suppliers and aggregators. At the time, this was conceived of as a centralized location where libraries could check their interlibrary loan requests to see if the provider of the database they planned to use allowed interlibrary loan. However, as more and more libraries find that negotiating terms is possible, its purpose has evolved. The database can now be used to find out a publisher's terms before negotiations begin, and to gather data about other providers' interlibrary loan terms to show reluctant providers that interlibrary loan from electronic documents is a viable option. The Interlibrary Loan Terms database committee hopes that, as more vendors enter their terms into the database and see what other publishers are doing about interlibrary loan, terms will become more standardized across the industry.

Online and face-to-face classes and workshops on license negotiation are frequently offered by national organizations (such as the Association of Research Libraries, which offers both introductory and advanced classes), regional networks (PALINET, AMIGOS), and other sources (such as EBLIDA in Europe or the Canadian Library Association). Workshops are particularly useful for practical exercises in license analysis and negotiation role-playing. Informative reports on conference workshops have been written by Trisha L. Davis (Davis and Rossignol 2000), Reba Leiding (Leiding 2000), Judy L. Johnson (Johnson 1999), Laurie Thompson (Thompson and Srivastava 2002), and Melissa Nasea (Nasea 2000).

Like the University of Texas and LibLicense license analysis tools, model licenses are highly useful for analyzing licenses and suggesting alternate wording to providers. Some models, like the John Cox Associates suite of licenses (http://www.licensingmodels.com), have been developed by librarians and publishers working together, and are therefore more likely to be viewed as acceptable sources of wording by producers than models developed by libraries alone. As Davis reminds us, "[I]t is very easy to lose sight of the fact that providers of information as well as other parties also have rights. . . . It is our responsibility to remember the rights of authors and disseminators of electronic information" (Davis and Rossignol 2000, 359). But in most cases, as Alford suggests, "license agreements currently in use are prepared by publishers and therefore favor their positions. . . . Librarians should therefore be wary of publisher agreements and scrutinize them carefully to ensure they do not restrict the needs of their users" (Alford 2002, 623).

A model license can help both sides understand what the other considers to be a fair use of the resource. A model license also reduces effort and confusion, and saves time during both negotiation and renewal. Model licenses protect both parties, and can be used to eliminate unenforceable clauses. It is possible that widespread use of model licenses could eventually lead to the "development of an equitable copyright code for electronic information" (Croft 2001, 167). Thomas A. Peters summarizes: "We all seem to be involved in a massive trial-and-error exercise to find pricing/terms models that are good, true, and beautiful–and viable for the new e-conditions of scholarly communication and scholarly publishing" (Peters 2003). Model licenses developed cooperatively between libraries and publishers are a step in the right direction.

Additionally, some libraries find it worthwhile to farm out license negotiation the same way they do journal subscriptions–and to the same companies, like Faxon or EBSCO. Taxpayer-supported libraries may or may not be able to take advantage of such arrangements, depending on the laws in their state about allowing other entities to negotiate and sign contracts on their behalf, but it is an option which could save a great deal of time and effort. Library consortia perform a similar service by consolidating negotiations for all their members.

CONCLUSION

In recent years, libraries seem to be doing more and more negotiating, if the number of books, articles, Web sites, and workshops now available is any indication. A 1999 SPEC Kit on managing licenses reported that 25% of all libraries polled did require that the product could be used to fill ILL requests before signing a contract (*SPEC Kit 248: Managing the Licensing of Electronic Products* 1999, 3), and it is likely that number has risen. In 2001, I did a quick informal survey of license management practices for ILL on the LibLicense discussion list. I found that, of six responding libraries, the majority took a reactive approach and kept a list or database of licensing terms or made a notation in an existing database like the online catalog. Only one library negotiated contracts on a regular basis, and that was a British institution which used model licenses as the basis for contract analysis. But in 2003, the same question was asked on the Great Western Library Alliance (GWLA) and national ILL-L discussion lists, and the results were quite different. Ten libraries reacted to licensing terms by keeping a list or database, entering the information in an existing database, or using a commercial license management product. But five libraries negotiated licenses that included ILL options, and all five were in the United States.

Some of this increase in proactive behavior may have been prompted by librarian anxiety about the Uniform Computer Information Transactions Act (UCITA), and a corresponding increase in awareness about licensing terms and their potential impact on library services. Even though the National Conference of Commissioners on Uniform State Laws (NCCUSL) has recently abandoned its efforts to have UCITA approved by the American Bar Association (Krause 2003), we need to remain vigilant and continue using our new-found negotiating power to ensure we get the fair use exceptions in our contracts that our patrons need and expect. In the end, each library must decide whether it will take a purely proactive approach and make permission to use the resource for ILL a deal-breaker, or weigh the benefit of local access to the material against both the practical problems of managing differing ILL clauses from different publishers, and the philosophical problems of restricting access to material against established fair use protocols applied to other media. Remember, "very rarely do vendors refuse to negotiate their terms" (Harper 2003). It is in the best interests of our patrons and our colleagues at other libraries to insist that interlibrary loan is a reasonable use which should be supported by the providers of our electronic information sources.

REFERENCES

Alford, Duncan E. 2002. Negotiating and Analyzing Electronic License Agreements. *Law Library Journal* 94 (4):621-44.

Bebbington, Laurence W. 2001. Managing Content: Licensing, Copyright, and Privacy Issues in Managing Electronic Resources. *Legal Information Management* 1 (2):4-12.

Brennan, Patricia, Karen Hersey, and Georgia Harper. 1997. *Licensing Electronic Resources: Strategic and practical considerations for signing electronic information delivery agreements.* Washington DC: Association of Research Libraries.

Croft, Janet Brennan. 2001. Model Licenses and Interlibrary Loan/Document Delivery from Electronic Resources. *Interlending and Document Delivery* 29 (4):165-168.

Croft, Janet Brennan, and Molly Murphy. 2002. Licensing and the Interlibrary Loan Workflow. *Journal of Access Services* 1 (2):5-14.

Davis, Trisha L., and Lucien R. Rossignol. 2000. Realistic licensing or licensing realities: Practical advice on license agreements. *The Serials Librarian* 38 (3/4): 357-361.

Duranceau, Ellen Finnie. 2000. License tracking at MIT Libraries. *Serials Review* 26 (3):69-73.

Durrant, Fiona. 2003. Negotiating an Online Contract. *Legal Information Management* 2 (1):10-12.

Guenther, Kim. 2000. Making Smart Licensing Decisions. *Computers in Libraries* 20 (6):58-61.

Harper, Georgia. 2001. *"Just Sign It and Send It Back": And Why Not?* University of Texas, 28 August 2001 [cited 10 October 2003]. Available from http://www.utsystem.edu/ogc/intellectualproperty/justsign.htm.

_____. 2003. *Acquisition Under Contract.* University of Texas, 6 February 2003 [cited 29 August 2003]. Available from http://www.utsystem.edu/ogc/intellectualproperty/l-cntrct.htm.

Harris, Lesley Ellen. 2000a. Deal-maker, Deal-breaker: When to walk away. *Library Journal* 125 (1):Net Connect 12-15.

_____. 2000b. Getting What You Bargained For. *Library Journal* 125 (7): Net Connect 20-21.

_____. 2002. *Licensing Digital Content: A Practical Guide for Librarians.* Chicago: American Library Association.

Johnson, Judy L. 1999. License Review and Negotiation: Building a team-based institutional process. *Library Collections, Acquisitions, and Technical Services* 23 (3):339-341.

Krause, Jason. 2003. See Ya, UCITA. *American Bar Association Journal (ABA Journal)*:20.

Lawrence, Eileen. 2000. Licensing: A publisher's perspective. *The Serials Librarian* 38 (1/2):147-153.

Leiding, Reba. 2000. Understanding the licensing landscape: Highlights of the ACRL preconference. *Library Collections, Acquisitions, and Technical Services* 24 (2): 285-287.

Liaison to Licensing Entities Working Group. 2003. *Committee Report.* Reference and User Services Association Interlibrary Loan Committee, 20 May 2003 [cited 10 October 2003]. Available from http://www.ala.org/Content/NavigationMenu/RUSA/Our_Association2/RUSA_Sections/.

Nasea, Melissa. 2000. The joy of license negotiation: Having fun and being careful. *Library Collections, Acquisitions, and Technical Services* 24 (3):436-439.

Nixon, Donna. 2003. Copyright and Interlibrary Loan Rights. *Journal of Interlibrary Loan, Document Delivery & Information Supply* 13 (3):55-89.

Peters, Thomas A. 2003. Was that the Rubicon, Lethe, or Styx we just crossed? Access conditions for e-content. *Library Collections, Acquisitions, and Technical Services* 27 (2):215-223.

Pike, George H. 2002. The Delicate Dance of Database Licenses, Copyright, and Fair Use. *Computers in Libraries* 22 (5):12-17.

Richards, Rob. 2001. Licensing Agreements: Contracts, the Eclipse of Copyright, and the Promise of Cooperation. In *Publishing and the Law: Current Legal Issues*, edited by B. Strauch: The Haworth Press, Inc.

SPEC Kit 248: Managing the Licensing of Electronic Products 1999. Association of Research Libraries, 24 September 1999 [cited 29 January 2001]. Available from http://www.arl.org/spec/248fly.html.

Thompson, Laurie, and Sandhya D. Srivastava. 2002. Licensing Electronic Resources. *The Serials Librarian* 42 (1/2):7-12.

Webster, Duane. 2002. *The Practical Realities of the New Copyright Laws: A Librarian's Perspective*. Association of Research Libraries 2002 [cited 11 February 2003]. Available from http://www.arl.org/info/frn/copy/WebsterMLA02.html.

Copyright Clearance Center: Providing Compliance Solutions for Content Users

Tracey Armstrong

SUMMARY. The digital revolution has been a boon to those who seek convenient, expanded access to information. It has dramatically increased the opportunity to share ideas and discoveries and disseminate information to ever-broader audiences. At the same time, it has raised concerns on the part of those responsible for ensuring that access to content remains within the guidelines established by copyright law. The challenge is to tap the unprecedented potential of digital technology while respecting the rights of those who create original works. Some of the most effective solutions capitalize on the very technology and attributes that gave rise to the digital marketplace. By automating the copyright permissions process, they seek to make copyright compliance as

---

Tracey Armstrong is Vice President, Transactional Services, Copyright Clearance Center. She has been with Copyright Clearance Center for 14 years, working across multiple departments to develop and implement a variety of services and solutions. In this role, Ms. Armstrong sets the overall direction and management of Copyright Clearance Center's transactional services group. She also oversees the customer relations group and the data management group, which manages the rights licensing for all products and services.

[Haworth co-indexing entry note]: "Copyright Clearance Center: Providing Compliance Solutions for Content Users." Armstrong, Tracey. Co-published simultaneously in *Journal of Library Administration* (The Haworth Information Press, an imprint of The Haworth Press, Inc.) Vol. 42, No. 3/4, 2005, pp. 55-64; and: *Licensing in Libraries: Practical and Ethical Aspects* (ed: Karen Rupp-Serrano) The Haworth Information Press, an imprint of The Haworth Press, Inc., 2005, pp. 55-64. Single or multiple copies of this article are available for a fee from The Haworth Document Delivery Service [1-800-HAWORTH, 9:00 a.m. - 5:00 p.m. (EST). E-mail address: docdelivery@haworthpress.com].

http://www.haworthpress.com/web/JLA
Digital Object Identifier: 10.1300/J111v42n03_04

convenient as accessing information–and increasingly, they are suc-
ceeding. Current permissions services are available both at the point of
content and as an integrated component of existing information management software. In many cases, they provide one-stop shopping for content and permissions, and a convenient way to comply with copyright
law. *[Article copies available for a fee from The Haworth Document Delivery
Service: 1-800-HAWORTH. E-mail address: <docdelivery@haworthpress.com>
Website: <http://www.HaworthPress.com> © 2005 by The Haworth Press, Inc.
All rights reserved.]*

KEYWORDS. Copyright, copyright compliance, copyright permissions, digital rights management, rights management, intellectual property,
licensing, rightsholder, copyright holder, Copyright Clearance Center,
Rightslink, permissions integration services

The fundamental issue at the heart of copyright compliance has remained the same since the dawn of publishing: how to balance the rights
of those who create original works with the need for access to the latest
information and discoveries. Today's technology shines a spotlight on
this issue as never before. The demand for information has expanded
exponentially in the digital arena, as has the amount of content now
available for mass-market consumption. Copyright permission procedures also have advanced, making it easier than ever to comply with
copyright law. Point-of-content licensing solutions allow information
users to request and receive permissions with the click of a mouse.
Rights management tools can ensure that such permissions reflect copyright holders' wishes. And the latest generation of electronic licensing
solutions, permissions integration services, expedite the permissions
process from start to finish by providing direct links between high-volume content users and rights databases.

Copyright compliance technology supports the primary objective
of copyright law, which seeks to encourage the creation of original
works by facilitating the lawful use of that intellectual property. The
law also acknowledges that continued access to information is crucial
to furthering the educational process and encouraging continued innovation. Therefore, copyright legislation does not protect ideas, procedures, principles, or discoveries that rightfully belong in the public
domain.

THE EVOLUTION OF U.S. COPYRIGHT LAW

The United States has focused on copyright issues since the earliest days of its history. The Constitution assigned to Congress the "Power to Promote the Progress of Science and useful Arts, by securing for limited Times to Authors and Inventors the exclusive Right to their respective Writings and Discoveries."[1] The First Congress used that power to enact the Copyright Act of 1790, which focused primarily on textual materials. In the years since then, citizens have litigated their rights and developed new technologies and ways of expressing themselves, and Congress has done its best to keep pace. Thus, during the 19th and early 20th century, copyright law was expanded to protect maps, charts, prints, music, dramatic compositions, and photographs, and to cover foreign citizens, as well as Americans. More recent amendments expanded protection to even newer technologies, including sound recordings, broadcasts, software, and other embodiments for creative works. Future amendments no doubt will address the technologies yet to come.

The most extensive revision of U.S. copyright legislation was the Copyright Act of 1976, which was the culmination of 18 years of work by Congressional staff, the Copyright Office, copyright holders, content users, and other interested parties. The new Act, developed through the 1960s simultaneously with the rapid advance of technology, including the reproduction of text, music, movies, and other copyrighted materials, sought to modernize copyright law, in part by addressing technology issues on a more generic basis than in the past. Among the many technology issues that Congress sought to address was photocopying, which had evolved from a new technology of the 1950s to relatively inexpensive copiers in every business and at copy shops everywhere by the 1970s. Publishers, authors, and high-volume users of photocopies of copyrighted materials had identified a need for a clearinghouse to provide all users with a centralized resource for legal access to photocopying copyrighted works. Congress's endorsement of that recommendation was published in the legislative history of the Act in the early 1970s. President Ford finally signed the new Act into law in 1976 with an effective date of January 1, 1978–the same day Copyright Clearance Center opened its doors for the first time. The new Act also brought the United States into conformity with world practice by extending copyright terms to "life of the author plus fifty years" (extended to "life plus seventy" in 1998).

THE ROLE OF COPYRIGHT CLEARANCE CENTER

The principal purpose of Copyright Clearance Center is to remove barriers to copyright compliance by making it convenient for content users to obtain permissions to lawfully use protected works. A not-for-profit, nongovernmental organization, Copyright Clearance Center acts as a clearinghouse through which copyright holders can voluntarily offer centralized permissions to use their text-based copyrighted works. Rightsholders register their works with Copyright Clearance Center, and the organization grants permissions on their behalf and collects and distributes royalties. To ensure that Copyright Clearance Center serves as a trusted intermediary for copyright holders and users alike, from the beginning its Board of Directors has included representatives of the publishing, author, and user communities.

Copyright Clearance Center obtains the rights for those works it represents through voluntary, non-exclusive contracts with publishers, authors, agents, collecting societies, and other copyright holders. This practice makes Copyright Clearance Center unique among copyright clearinghouses worldwide and initially was met with skepticism by those who felt voluntary licensing is not feasible. Twenty-five years after its founding, the organization has emerged as the world's largest licensing agent for text reproduction rights and the foremost provider of copyright licensing services. Copyright Clearance Center represents more than 1.75 million titles, and its repertory of works includes textual materials of all types, from scientific journals to books, newspapers, and magazines. Copyright Clearance Center's customers include more than ten thousand U.S. corporations, plus thousands of government agencies, law firms, document suppliers, libraries, academic institutions, copy shops, and bookstores. Its licensing systems cover electronic and print reproductions within the United States and abroad.

Like copyright law, Copyright Clearance Center's compliance solutions have evolved to keep pace with changing trends and technology. In 1978, at the time of Copyright Clearance Center's founding, photocopying was the principal means of reproducing printed works. Widely used in libraries and businesses, the photocopy machine was having a distinct effect on the rights of authors and publishers of text-based materials. Copyright Clearance Center's first service allowed copyright holders and users to exchange permissions and royalties for photocopying uses on a case-by-case basis. Over the years, that basic transactional service has been augmented by a full complement of compliance offerings designed to meet the growing needs of content users and copyright holders. Its services also reflect the needs of its various constituencies. Companies, for example, can opt for annual repertory licenses that cover in-house reuse rights for all employees, within the United States and abroad. Colleges and universities can request permission on a case-by-case basis for permissions to use copyrighted materials in the classroom and in distance learning.

Copyright Clearance Center has consistently adapted to the changing marketplace and, as a result, now offers services in keeping with today's digital environment and global economy. When new technologies created a demand for permission for digital reproduction and distribution, Copyright Clearance Center responded with licenses that cover uses such as e-mail, Internet and extranet postings, and PC-to-PC faxing. Similarly, when the Internet started becoming a preferred source of information, Copyright Clearance Center introduced rights management solutions that have earned the organization a place at the forefront of the content industry. More recently, it established partnerships with key vendors to integrate the rights permissions process into the routine workflow of high-volume customers.

TECHNOLOGICAL SOLUTIONS

Copyright Clearance Center was among the first to recognize the role that technology could play in facilitating copyright compliance. The organization's first forays into the digital arena focused primarily on ease-of-use. Each subsequent service has increased in sophistication and capabilities. As a result, today's digital offerings make it more convenient than ever to lawfully copy and share information beyond the scope of fair use. In some cases, they also provide data that can serve as a powerful tool for anticipating and meeting the needs of content users in the future.

www.copyright.com

Copyright Clearance Center began licensing through public electronic means in 1995 with the launch of its Web site at www.copyright. com. The site significantly streamlines the permissions process by providing a central location where users can request and obtain copyright permissions to reproduce portions of text works. The Web site walks users through a simple, step-by-step process that covers virtually every type of permitted use, from classroom, business and general uses, to electronic coursepacks, PowerPoint™ presentations, and CD-ROM/ DVD uses to republication in books, newsletters, newspapers, and magazines. Users can search by publication title, publisher name, or standard number and, within seconds, can determine if permission is available. They also can learn more about Copyright Clearance Center's service offerings, compare the costs and benefits of different licensing solutions, and decide which is best for their purposes. Fortune 500 companies and large multinational corporate users, for example, typically opt for annual "blanket" licenses that clear the way for lawful use of all registered titles, internally, by all company employees. Transactional or case-by-case permissions meet the needs of smaller companies and academic users for authorization of uses beyond fair use, as well as provide permissions for companies to lawfully share copyrighted materials with others outside their organization.

For publishers, authors, and other rightsholders, www.copyright.com offers one-stop management of the permissions process and the potential to earn royalty revenues by allowing use of their works in business, government, academic, and international markets.

Permission Integration Services

In response to the needs of high-volume, academic users such as libraries, information centers, and coursepack providers, Copyright Clearance Center has developed permission integration services that incorporate copyright licensing directly into content users' work flow. Application vendors, content aggregators, and publishers integrate their software with Copyright Clearance Center's unique rights licensing database, giving librarians and other content users one-stop, seamless access to copyright permissions and copyrighted works.

To deliver its permission integration services, Copyright Clearance Center has forged partnerships with companies, including most recently Ex Libris and XanEdu. They, in turn, pass on the benefits of this partnership to their customers, who generate significant requests for copyright permissions. Ex Libris is a worldwide supplier of high-performance applications for libraries, information centers, and researchers. It is perhaps best known for its flagship product, ALEPH (Automated Library Expandable Program), a fully-integrated library automation system that has been installed at over 800 sites in 50 countries. The partnership with Copyright Clearance Center involves Ex Libris' SFX product, which in 2001 earned The Charleston Advisor's "Best New Product" Award for electronic service to libraries. SFX allows context-sensitive linking between Web resources and the scholarly information environment. An SFX server facilitates the management of a library's interlinked electronic collection, including resources hosted by the library itself and by external information providers. Under its arrangement with Ex Libris, Copyright Clearance Center essentially becomes one of those external providers, allowing SFX customers to access the Copyright Clearance Center database to request and receive permission for the content they wish to produce. For most librarians, this direct link represents a dramatic improvement in the permissions process. Not only is it more convenient, but it also eliminates duplication of effort, reduces the potential for error, and increases overall workflow productivity.

XanEdu is reaping these same benefits, but through a different permission integration service: Copyright Clearance Center's Permissions Gateway. XanEdu is a leading publisher of online and offline course materials for the higher education market and boasts a content base that's the largest commercial archive in the world. Through its parent organization, ProQuest Company, XanEdu has access to the archives of journals, periodicals, newspapers, books, dissertations, primary literature works, and academic collections. In the past, XanEdu staff members lost valuable time exiting applications each time they sought reuse permission. With Permissions Gateway, they now have a direct link to Copyright Clearance Center's rights database, enabling them to quickly obtain copyright permissions as part of the normal production workflow. Permissions Gateway has eliminated the need for repetitive data entry, improved data accuracy, and expedited the entire rights licensing process.

Rightslink®

Copyright Clearance Center broke new ground in rights management with Rightslink digital licensing solution, a service specifically cited by EContent as a reason that Copyright Clearance Center made the trade publication's top 100 list for 2002 and 2003. Rightslink also provides a glimpse into the future of copyright compliance and rights management because it harnesses technology to enhance customer service immediately and for the long term. By gathering data on usage trends, the Rightslink service can help ensure that information users have access to the content that is most important to them. Works that are seldom accessed could be replaced with new offerings in subject areas for which there is significantly more demand. Information users then would have access to an expanded repertory of content that better meets their needs.

Rightslink was introduced by Copyright Clearance Center in 2000 in recognition of the growing prevalence of digital media and the challenges and opportunities it presents. In fact, digital media now accounts for 41 percent of all pages consumed by U.S. workers.[2] That exerts enormous pressure on publishers and other copyright holders to make their works readily available.

Through Rightslink, publishers and other rightsholders can provide information users with immediate, lawful, online access to digital works–at the point of content. To users, the Rightslink process is nearly seamless. They view digital content, determine that they need a copy either for themselves or to transmit to someone else, and simply click on the Rightslink icon, which is featured prominently on the rightsholder's Web site. Rightslink's technology automatically determines the licensing details, based on the type of content and the general terms and conditions specified by the content owner. Using a simple, e-commerce process, Rightslink then displays the licensing options, records the user's acceptance, grants the license on-the-spot, and either delivers the content or increases the level of Web site access granted to the user. The transaction takes just minutes, start to finish, with the user never leaving the rightsholder's Web site. It is advantageous for the information user, who avoids the inconvenience of having to search for the site again should he or she need additional information.

Rightslink currently is in use on more than 220 publisher Web sites representing new media and all key segments of the text publishing industry. Among them are many of the nation's largest newspapers and business and industry-specific magazines and journals, from *The New York Times*, *Wall Street Journal*, and MSNBC to Marcel Dekker, Inc., Reed Business Information, Thomson Media, and SAGE Publications. No two of them use Rightslink in precisely the same way. In fact, one reason for Rightslink's broad appeal is the ability to integrate Rightslink software into existing technology platforms and customize it for a broad range of publishers and their customers. For each article, publishers set the terms and conditions that best meet their needs and the needs of those who seek access to their works. They also choose from a variety of formats for distribution–hard copy and digital reprints; e-mail; Internet, intranet, or extranet postings; republication in print and digital media–again, to best serve the information users who are their primary customers.

One example is Marcel Dekker, Inc., an international publishing firm specializing in the scientific, technical, and medical fields, who signed on with Rightslink in early August 2003 to help streamline the copyright permissions and reprint ordering process for its content users. Dekker was seeking an end-to-end digital licensing solution that could be fully integrated with its own systems. The company chose to phase in several uses for Rightslink, beginning with processing orders for hard-copy reprints of journal articles and encyclopedia entries. Phase two involves using Rightslink to issue digital reprints and book chapter reprints, offer custom publishing, and fulfill copyright permission requests.

Dekker selects the specific ways its customers can use and distribute its content in various formats. It also gives customers the ability to obtain rights to copy and distribute its online material. Dekker even allows customers to decide how their reprints will be packaged, giving them choices of paper types and cover text. Before they place their orders, customers are given a price quote based on the finishing options that they select. Order details are automatically sent directly to the printer, who prints exactly the amount requested by the customer. In Dekker's case, Rightslink even allows reprint customers to check the status of their orders and track shipments online.

The Dekker case offers just one illustration of how Rightslink can facilitate convenient, lawful use of copyrighted works. The benefits of Rightslink can vary from publisher to publisher, depending on how they use the rights management tool. But without exception, the advantages to information users can be summed up in a single word: convenience. Rightslink provides automatic electronic delivery for those who opt for digital content, and automatically generates reprints and routing for printing and direct delivery of hard copy. In addition, its ability to track permissions and provide publishers with insight into the content most in demand better ensures that future content offerings align with users' needs.

LOOKING TO THE FUTURE

In simplest terms, the challenge for the future of copyright compliance is inevitable, for it will remain the age-old dilemma of balancing the rights of publishers, authors, and creators against the needs of information users. Far less predictable, of course, is what form that challenge will take, especially given the speed with which new technologies are introduced. In the near term, it's reasonable to assume that digital technology will continue to drive most of the changes in the way information is accessed, and the measures implemented to ensure that such access is as convenient as possible and in compliance with copyright law.

Unlike the publishing industry, which has been with us for centuries, the field of licensing solutions is still in its early stages. Despite this brief history, it offers valuable insights into the types of solutions that will be most welcomed by both users and rightsholders: solutions that eliminate what users perceive as barriers to copyright compliance and what rightsholders view as threats to their ability to control reuse of their content. In other words, future licensing solutions must provide maximum convenience, increasingly at the point of content, for information users. At the same time, through encryption and other security features, they must give publishers the ability to customize the access and use of each copyrighted work. In fact, this combination of customization and control has been a key factor in the success of Copyright Clearance Center's Rightslink licensing service.

The future also will require a more concentrated effort on educating information users not just about the provisions of copyright law and the penalties for violation, but also about the benefit of such laws to society. Such education already is underway at many of the nation's college campuses, in part in reaction to the widely publicized lawsuits against those who engage in illegal music sharing via the Internet. Ideally, copyright education will become a routine component of college and business orientation programs. Knowledge, combined with convenient licensing solutions, offers the best opportunity for a commitment to compliance.

Finally, there is one aspect of the future that is somewhat predictable: the role of Copyright Clearance Center in meeting the needs of rightsholders and content users. True to its mandate, Copyright Clearance Center will continue to refine existing licensing services and develop new solutions that address and incorporate technologies as they emerge. It also will continue to foster partnerships and other relationships that simplify the permissions process by offering licensing solutions at the point where content is consumed, and integrating them into the daily workflow. Regardless of the specific services it offers, Copyright Clearance Center's goal will remain much the same as it is today: to make copyright compliance so convenient that it becomes routine.

NOTES

1. U.S. Constitution, Article 1, Section 8.
2. Copyright Clearance Center Corporate Information Consumption Survey, 2003.

Using Model Licenses

Stephen Bosch

SUMMARY. The licensing of electronic resources has become a significant activity for all parties involved in the production, purchase, and delivery of these resources. During the early development of the licensing process, the industry as a whole had little experience with licensing as an integral part of the acquisition process. Licensing practice developed in a reactive state and the emerging process lacked standards and models. Since licensing was consuming greater resources and was becoming a distraction from the business of supplying resources to users, standards and model licenses were developed and used to bring some semblance of order to the process. Model licenses have not solved all problems associated with the licensing process, but they prevented the collapse of the process as licensing continues to see explosive growth. *[Article copies available for a fee from The Haworth Document Delivery Service: 1-800-HAWORTH. E-mail address: <docdelivery@haworthpress.com> Website: <http://www.HaworthPress.com> © 2005 by The Haworth Press, Inc. All rights reserved.]*

KEYWORDS. License/ing, electronic resources, model licenses, consortia

---

Stephen Bosch is Materials Budget, Procurement, and Licensing Librarian, University of Arizona Library, 1510 East University, PO Box 210055, Tucson, AZ 85721-0055 (E-mail: boschs@u.library.arizona.edu).

[Haworth co-indexing entry note]: "Using Model Licenses." Bosch, Stephen. Co-published simultaneously in *Journal of Library Administration* (The Haworth Information Press, an imprint of The Haworth Press, Inc.) Vol. 42, No. 3/4, 2005, pp. 65-81; and: *Licensing in Libraries: Practical and Ethical Aspects* (ed: Karen Rupp-Serrano) The Haworth Information Press, an imprint of The Haworth Press, Inc., 2005, pp. 65-81. Single or multiple copies of this article are available for a fee from The Haworth Document Delivery Service [1-800-HAWORTH, 9:00 a.m. - 5:00 p.m. (EST). E-mail address: docdelivery@haworthpress.com].

http://www.haworthpress.com/web/JLA
© 2005 by The Haworth Press, Inc. All rights reserved.
Digital Object Identifier: 10.1300/J111v42n03_05

INTRODUCTION

In today's environment most electronic resources from authoritative sources are commercially licensed for use. A vast majority of authors and publishers believe that current copyright laws do not effectively protect their intellectual property rights and have made licensing the process employed for protecting their interests. Unfortunately, the resulting license must be examined carefully to determine exactly which rights are granted and the license is revised and negotiated to include those rights commonly required for reasonable local use. This process is slow and resource intensive for all parties involved. From the perspective of library users, it is not a value-added activity.

The use of model licenses to streamline the process of purchasing electronic resources has been an appealing idea, but has this really been a successful activity or has it been just another distraction? For the purposes of this paper, a model license is defined as a formal written license that serves as the basis for all comparison with subsequent licenses and from which a final contract between a library and a vendor for the sale or lease of one or more proprietary (copyrighted) online products is to be made. As with most complex issues, the answer to questions concerning the success of model license programs lies between the two poles. Have libraries moved to an environment where all they need to do is hand their model license to a supplier and the process is done? No! Has the licensing process been improved and streamlined by the creation and use of model licenses? Yes! Maybe the ideal state has not been achieved but the use of model licenses provides many benefits even if the license is never fully accepted by a supplier.

THE HISTORY OF THE DEVELOPMENT
OF MODEL LICENSES

During the 1990s, licensing became a central feature of the acquisition process for nearly all electronic resources. Neither publishers, vendors, nor libraries had extensive experience with the creation, negotiation, and execution of licenses. There was little consistency in the industry, and there was a lack of mutual understanding within organizations. The language of licensing lacked consensual validation. The terms in licenses meant different things to different groups. The driving force behind the creation of model licenses (also commonly known as standard licenses) was the need for librarians to work in an environment in which standardized language can be found and used to expedite the process of license negotiation. In the licensing process both publishers and librarians had to define their requirements and establish policies. Publishers, uneasy with the idea of fair use in the electronic environment, had the most to lose and pushed licensing as a way to protect their interests. Publishers met this perceived need with a profusion of licenses that were similar in scope yet very different in the offered terms. This great variety of licenses had much that was in common in intent but used different terms to express that intent. These differences forced each license to be reviewed one by one, a time-consuming and expensive process. Consequently, suppliers and librarians were required to negotiate terms, prepare and review written agreements, and ensure alignment with legal requirements for each individual license transaction. Since much of the real content was the same, this expense seemed to have little value since it was primarily an unraveling process to get to, "Yes, that was what we meant."

In the latter part of the 1990s, efforts were made to bring some standards and structures to the licensing process. One of the first model licenses to appear was the UK's PA/JISC model license http://www.jisc. ac.uk/index.cfm?name=wg_standardlicensing_report, jointly developed by publishers and librarians from the UK's Publishers Association and the Joint Information Systems Committee of the Higher Education Funding Councils (JISC). JISC coordinates the development of the information technology infrastructure for higher education in the UK. The license provided a uniform set of definitions, standard terms for what is being agreed to, standard terms for use permissions, terms for prohibited uses, standard terms for obligations, guidelines for terminations, and standard general licensing terms. The Standard Licensing Arrangements working party was asked by the JISC and the Publishers Association to explore options for developing "umbrella" license models which individual publishers could employ. These generic tools were intended to cover different products and different types of use and would set out the more routine conditions of use, but leave a limited number of commercial issues (e.g., price per access, territory) to be added by different suppliers.[1] Soon after the PA/JISC's model was released, the Council on Library and Information Resources (CLIR), the Digital Library Federation (DLF) and Yale University Library, made available model terms on the Liblicense Web site http://www.library.yale.edu/~llicense/modlic. shtml. The Liblicense Standard Licensing Agreement is an attempt to reach consensus on the basic terms of contracts to license digital information between university libraries and academic publishers. Liblicense represents the contributions of numerous college and university librarians, lawyers, and other university officials responsible for licensing, as well as significant input from representatives of the academic publishing community.[2] The Standard License Agreement is not organized like the PA/JISC document. A major difference between the two licenses was that many terms of the earlier license were grouped under a broad heading of general terms; in the CLIR/DLF/Yale license terms were included as separate sections.

Neither of these licenses existed in a vacuum and important licensing concepts and provisions were found in the U.S. Principles for Licensing Electronic Resources (http://www.arl.org/scomm/licensing/principles.html) produced jointly by the American Library Association, the American Association of Law Libraries, the American Association of Health Sciences Libraries, the Association of Research Libraries, the Medical Library Association, and the Special Library Association. Another important initiative was the Statements of Current Perspectives and Preferred Practices for the Selection and Purchase of Electronic Information (http://www.library.yale.edu/consortia/statement.html) from the International Coalition of Library Consortia. Both of these documents codified elements that Libraries desired to see in licenses including: clear use of language, clear statement of usage rights, terms for obligations, terms for restricted uses, and clear legal rights and obligations.

In 2000, five subscription agents, including Blackwell's/Swets, Dawson Information Services Group, EBSCO, The Faxon Company, and Harrassowitz, worked with a group of librarians and John Cox, an international publishing consultant specializing in licensing and content management, to draft model licensing agreements. The outcome was a set of four licenses, one each for academic libraries, academic consortia, a public library license, and another one for both corporate and other special libraries. These model agreements were freely available for libraries or publishers to use at http://www.licensingmodels.com/. These models were clearly indebted to their predecessors, yet provided greater elaboration of previous ideas so that the resulting licenses were more useful to specific types of libraries. This enhanced their value to librarians. Trisha Davis (one of the contributors to the licenses) commented, "I know from experience that librarians will eagerly welcome standardized licenses that are clearly written, flexible, and succinct. Both publishers and librarians alike constantly search for methods to reduce the enormous (and expensive!) workload that licensing requires. It's time for all of us to focus more of our resources on the product development and the needs of our end users."[3]

Each of the four license models followed a standard format based on the PA/JISC model, starting with definitions and then defining what institutions can and cannot do with the licensed material. The models provide options and choices and there is normalized language that most libraries could employ. The licenses provide protection for the intellectual property rights of authors and publishers and provide libraries with the terms they need in order to be able to make the products available to their users.

CURRENT PRACTICE

At this time many national and international organizations, as well as individual libraries, have created and use model licenses. One model that is in common use in the United Kingdom is the National Electronic Site Licence Initiative (NESLI) model. It is available at www.nesli. ac.uk and is referred to by several publishers who model their licenses after it. State, provincial, and regional consortia may have adopted a particular model or have created a model of their own. An example of this type of model license is the Consortia Canada model. Consortia Canada gathered together consortia directors to promote national site licensing initiatives in Canada and their model was created through that initiative. The model is on their Web site at *Consortia Canada*. Other examples of groups that have adopted model licenses include the California Digital Library and the Northeast Research Libraries.

Today many publishers' licenses and libraries' model licenses reflect heavily the influence of the aforementioned efforts. Some licenses depart little from the original models, others bear great resemblance, but incorporate changes required by particular groups or publishers. All achieve one thing, they bring to the industry standard terms for licensing that are bringing a greater uniformity to the process. It is interesting to review licenses and see the models reflected in the document. There is much that is familiar, and the process and time involved in reviewing those licenses is considerably shorter than licenses that are not based on a standard model.

The use of model licenses or at least the use of model principle has essentially become a best practice for the process of licensing. Most licensing guides suggest that each library should have a prepared list of basic rights that must be included in a license. If those rights are not granted, the product should not be acquired. A second list of rights desired, but not mandatory, also should be created. If, after negotiation, these rights are not available, the library can decide on a case-by-case basis if the product should be acquired.

WHY IS THE USE OF MODEL LICENSES BENEFICIAL?

Model licenses were not created as part of a fad. Their creation was in direct response to the need to bring the licensing process under control. There was explosive growth in the number of electronic resources that users wanted to access. There was a potential that the process for reviewing and negotiating licenses would consume far more time than all parties were willing to invest. Model licenses were developed in this environment and provide many benefits. These include:

- Model licenses are powerful communications tools.
- The process for developing models improves understanding within an organization.
- Model licenses use a common language expressed in plain English.
- They provide efficiencies regarding the management of licenses.
- The review process is simplified.
- The editing of model documents is easier.
- Legal liability is reduced.

Model licenses are a powerful communications tool across the industry as well as within an organization. The widespread use allows organizations to inform the marketplace concerning what is considered to be important in the licensing process. This would apply to both suppliers and libraries. This is very valuable as it allows publishers to review what an organization has in a model prior to trying to sell into that organization. Experience shows that sales and especially consortial sales can be greatly slowed down or sometimes completely stopped by bringing a license to the negotiation that is far removed from the group's standard. The negotiation process gets bogged down on the wording in the document and discussions concerning how to get the product to the market are lost in the details. Suppliers who review models or even basic principle documents prior to attempting to sell into organizations, will know beforehand if the overall stated needs are what they are willing to offer in a product. If there is a large divergence, the sales attempt will be more costly in terms of time and effort since there will have to be more negotiation, and consequently more time before the sales can be completed.

If the models are in alignment, the process can go much quicker, less time is focused on the document, more effort is invested in getting the resource to users. Models are very effective at communicating priorities in the licensing process, and at reducing costs in getting a resource into a market. Even if a particular group doesn't have an established model license, internally their practices are not going to be far removed from national standards. By reviewing the existing models suppliers will come to see what the current best practices are from the librarians' viewpoint. If these terms are not what a supplier is willing to agree to, then there needs to be some hard questioning, since the marketplace will demand to know why the product is so different that terms accepted by many other publishers won't apply to this product. Most model licenses have been developed with input from publishers and other interested parties. Model licenses are dynamic documents and over the past few years have changed in response to the marketplace. Use of these models by all parties reduces costs for the industry as a whole. The less producers have to spend getting their product sold is savings for all. The less time licensees spend reviewing contracts, the more time they can devote to bringing content to their users.

The process for developing and adopting a model license forces an organization to review their needs, and then express these needs in the licensing document. Dialog and consensus must occur on what terms are required in the license to conform to internal legal standards. Dialog and consensus must occur to determine what rights are required in a license in order for the license to be approved. Dialog and agreement must occur to identify desired elements. Desired terms are those that can be left out of an agreement without breaking it. Elements required by internal legal standards can't be negotiated away. These terms must be clearly identified since these are automatic deal breakers. The other areas are sometimes less clear, since desired and required can be grey areas. A licensee may require that users be able to print and download portions of a product, but be willing to leave electronic ILL out of the agreement. The model licensing process forces a dialog on what should be agreed to, what can't be agreed to, and then encapsulates the outcomes in language that is understood by all affected parties in the organization. A normal process for developing a model license begins with discussions and then agreement on what the underlying licensing principles should be. A document is then crafted, probably based on other standard agreements, that conforms to these principles and includes the necessary terminology required by internal legal codes. The model is then reviewed by the necessary parties to insure conformance with internal standards. The final outcome is a common understanding of what is in the license and why it is there.

The use of model licenses provides for a common language that provides consistency across the industry. Publishers understand what librarians are describing when they refer to walk in users, and librarians use the terminology consistently in negotiations. Clear language describes ILL rights and the publisher's need for protection is understood. Important terms such as site, users, agents, commercial use, etc., are clearly defined from the beginning of the document and are used consistently throughout the document. The importance of common language cannot be understated. The goal of a licensing process should be to get a product to an audience. Having to spend a great deal of time trying to determine what is meant by site, users, etc., is not productive. By using language and definitions that have been seen many times before, the review process shifts from looking at words to the actual review of content, which is as it should be.

Management of licenses has become a major issue. Few systems exist that adequately provide a good mechanism for tracking and managing licenses and the information contained in them. The use of model licenses can reduce some of the burden by using standard terms and reducing the number of exceptions that have to be handled individually. If a particular license requires special terms for use, then these terms must be recorded and communicated to public areas in order to conform to the terms of the agreement. The use of standard terms reduces the need for special handling. It helps suppliers understand why such terms are a burden, and helps licensees to understand when nonconforming terms cause management problems further down the road.

Model licenses reduce the time it takes to review, edit, and negotiate license agreements. The use of a standard agreement allows a licensee to glance at a license and quickly identify those elements that are within the norms for acceptance, and those terms that need to be edited. Time is concentrated on a few areas instead of an entire document. Also, since standard language exists for those areas that may be questioned, the replacement language in all probability has been previously reviewed and accepted by other licensees and licensors. This results in reduced negotiation since it may not be necessary to spend time working on the language. Sometimes that is easily half the battle. Ideas can be agreed to quickly and the proverbial devil is in the details. Time is money in most organizations. Model licenses have been through legal, and once approved don't need costly review. This savings would be important to organizations that don't rely on in-house legal services, and must hire outside legal advice.

The process for updating the license document is made simpler by the use of model documents. Once it is known that a change is required, the change can be edited into the template and the change will be included in all future applications. Also, a document can be easily amended if there are needs for customization in a particular license. The model doesn't need to be rewritten each time there is a need for specialized wording, a document can be easily edited by the use of an addendum or memorandum of agreement. The basic document stays the same and the needed changes are appended in an appropriate addition. This is an accepted practice, and again reduces licensing overhead. There are always elements in the license that will have to be changed. The internal policies of an organization are never static, especially public institutions that are governed by state law. Without a model license, someone has to remember what the changes are to insure that the required changes are incorporated into future contracts. Model licenses make the process of editing and tracking needed changes much simpler.

Another important benefit of the model license process is the reduction in the possibility of "amateur oops." Most of the individuals who review licenses for libraries are not trained legal professionals. Legal terminology, especially in areas associated with liability, performance, and indemnification, is hard to unravel. Legal professionals are trained to recognize the meaning behind thick legalese. What may appear on the surface to be acceptable terminology to the untrained eye may in fact be wording that is highly detrimental to the licensee. The use of language that has been crafted in a model makes it much easier to strike the unfamiliar terms and replace with the familiar. If the model language has been reviewed by legal, this further reduces the risk to the organization that unacceptable terms slip into a license. It is much simpler to recognize a liability clause, strike the offered wording, and replace with wording that has a proven track record. Model licenses also help reduce "amateur oops" by using simple English to express the required terms instead of using thick legalistic jargon. Lay people can read the model license and understand the terms, whereas some documents crafted in legal departments are unintelligible to anyone not in the legal profession. Since the model license is based on common language and terms, there is no need to qualify and specify every term with thick legal ramblings.

WHAT PROBLEMS CAN BE ASSOCIATED WITH THE USE OF MODEL LICENSE AGREEMENTS?

The use of model licenses is not without drawbacks. Any tool can end up bringing unexpected results to a process. These negative results are few and can easily be avoided, but without awareness of the possible problems it is easier to have negative outcomes. Potential problems include:

- Inflexibility during negotiations
- License terms that can meet multiple situations
- Potential increase in legal liability
- Routine, leading to failure to maintain an agreement

One of the greatest problems involved in the use of model licenses is the undue reliance on a model or a set of principles that leads to a high number of failed negotiations due to an unwillingness to discuss proposed changes in an agreement. The use of models can lead to the creation of a "safe" place where there is a high level of comfort. The inertia is to stay in that place, consequently a participant may not be actively listening to their counterparts during negotiations. Again, the overall goal for suppliers and licensees is to bring needed information resources to their users. If a mentality develops that relies on "these are our terms, take them or leave them" as a negotiating stance, the number of failed negotiations increases. Models are a tool, and the goal of a negotiation is to get a good product for users, not to get the other side to accept the license. There may be good reasons why a supplier needs different terms. The licensee needs to be able to negotiate with the supplier and determine when it is in the users' best interest to step outside the framework of the model license and agree to non-conforming terms.

A related issue is the ability of the model license to address many licensing situations without requiring significant editing. Is the document flexible enough to be useful in many situations? A model license can only be as good as it is made. If a model is too rigid in its approach and requires large amounts of editing in many situations, the model is not meeting the needs of the users and is too inflexible to be of real value. Just as the person using the model needs to be able to negotiate, the model itself needs to be flexible to accommodate many different licensing situations.

By using a process where a librarian may present a model license to a supplier, the licensing process is somewhat reversed. The licensee (normally the library) becomes for all intents the licensor. Instead of we agree to sell . . . the document is we agree to buy. There must be an awareness that this approach does carry with it a potential (however slight) for an increase in liability since the license becomes "their" license. Anything can be litigated. The proactive approach makes the one offering the license the owner of the license. Not to say that this is a major concern, but there still needs to be the awareness that there is the potential of unexpected surprises that can result from taking ownership of the license.

Complacency is a threat to any process, but can have a very negative impact on the use of model licenses. The document, if not kept up to date, will become a flawed tool. As changes occur in the environment the document needs to be updated. This is a strength of the model license, as well as a weakness. If not edited to address changes in the environment, the model soon will loose its ability to serve as a viable licensing tool. The document needs to be kept up to date and should include all necessary changes required to meet internal policies, as well as maintain currency with changes in the external environment.

Complacency, as regards the overall process, is also a potential downside. The licensing process might be going well with the use of a current model, but if changes and advances in the marketplace are not monitored and incorporated into the process, problems, or at least missed opportunities, will arise. Licensing is a dynamic activity. There are numerous changes that arise from many sectors that must continually be reviewed to determine their impact on licensing. For the process to remain effective, these changes must be incorporated into the document and the process.

Complacency during the actual review is also a downside of the model license. If an offered license resembles model "X," the reading of the license may not be as thorough as compared to the reading a non-standard license would receive. This may lead to lazy review habits. There will always be a tension between a streamlined process that reduces the review time by using model licenses and a process that cuts too many corners and misses important content in a license. Any license must be reviewed even if it is based on a standard format. Ninety-nine percent of the document may conform to local norms but that last 1% could be a real problem. The use of model licenses doesn't mean that it is unnecessary to read licenses anymore.

USING MODEL LICENSES

The benefits of using model licenses outweigh the negative aspects. Obviously, model licenses should be used. That leads to the question of what are the standard approaches to using model licenses. Some organizations may be large enough or influential enough that they really can offer their model license as the starting point in negotiations, but that scenario is probably the exception and not the rule. That does not diminish the value of a model agreement. Even if a supplier does not work from the document, the model will make the work go more easily.

The ideal use for a model license is to be able to fill in the blanks, (normally what product is being purchased, for how long, and who is selling the product for how much) send the signed license to a supplier who then agrees to the document, countersigns it, returns it, and initiates access to the licensed product. This ideal state is not a normal occurrence, but this does not diminish the value of the model license. Continued use moves the industry closer to this state. Many publishers have adopted the use of model licenses and their costs are reduced compared to other publishers that continue to negotiate non-standard licenses.

One of the valuable outcomes of creating a model license may not be the actual use of the license but the use of the process of creating the license to develop understanding of licensing in the organization. That may be particularly true of consortia. Developing the license forces the group to really think about what is important, and needs to be in their license. Dialog and discussion occurs and the group begins to see that there are some things that must go into the document and they will know why they must be in a license. The most valuable use of a model license may be that it forces an organization to review what terms are truly important and must be part of a license.

A model should be used as a tool for communicating your desired terms to publishers as well as educating the organization concerning what is important in the licensing process. If a model license exists, don't keep it secret but make it freely available to external and internal customers. Put it on a Web site. Publishers can see what is expected in the way of a license, and staff will be able to see what goes into a license. The model license is an important tool for communication and education.

Even if using a publisher's license, the model license provides a template that can be used to assess the content of the license. Does the license contain all the terms that were in the model document? Does the license use the same definitions? Are the required terms included? Are the desired terms included? Does the license contain language that is not acceptable within local legal frameworks? A model license may never be accepted by a publisher, but could still be very valuable as it would have provided a checklist that could be used to review any other license. The creation of model licenses forces an organization to determine what it needed in a license. The comparison of an offered license to the approved template goes much quicker than working without a template.

SUMMARY OF THE COMMON ELEMENTS FOUND IN MODEL LICENSES

The following section outlines and summarizes information that can be typically found in model licenses. This section is not inclusive, and is meant to be an example of what is often included in a model license. It is not a template. A well-written model license agreement will begin with a set of definitions of terms to be used consistently in the license. The following list represents the most common terms that are defined in licenses. Not all of these must be defined for each license, but it is important to note common use and have an understanding of their meanings.

Agent	Authentication System
Authorized Site	Authorized Users
Commercial Use	Course Packs
Database	Effective Date
Electronic Reserve	Fee
Intellectual Property	Library Premises
Licensed Materials	Licensed Software
Managing Agent	Publisher's Representative
Remote Access	Secure Network
Server	Service Date
Subscription Period	Walk-in Users

After a section on definitions, a model license then outlines the terms used in the agreement. This normally includes the following:

1. Who is participating in the license, both the licensee and licensor
2. What is being licensed, its cost, and the timeframe for the license

3. Basic required rights. Remembering that all rights must be specifically included in the contract, the license should include a list that would allow users to:

    i. Access the product
    ii. Search the product
    iii. Retrieve search results
    iv. Review and download information from the search results
    v. Print in hard copy information from the search results
    vi. Store search results in electronic format for a temporary period
    vii. Share search results with other authorized users
    viii. Include limited portions of the search results in subsequent works as long as authorship and copyright are noted

4. The license should include terms for rights that could be considered "desired." Some of these areas may be considered mandatory by some librarians, although few insist that every one of these terms are required rights:

    i. Continuing access to subscribed materials or archiving, if not supplied by the publisher or an intermediary source
    ii. Interlibrary loan
    iii. Electronic reserves
    iv. Electronic course packs
    v. Remote access to distance learners

5. Prohibited uses, being those types of use publishers tend to forbid, protecting their rights to the licensed materials. These prohibited uses could deny the user the ability to:

    i. Load the Licensed Materials on its server or anywhere else
    ii. Systematically make local electronic copies of the Licensed Materials, whether temporary or permanent. Temporary copies made as a result of caching activities will be removed from local systems and will not be permanently stored
    iii. Remove or alter the authors' names or the Publisher's copyright notices or other means of identification or disclaimers as they appear in the Licensed Materials

iv. Make print or electronic copies of the whole or a significant part of the Licensed Materials for any purpose
v. Mount or distribute any part of the Licensed Material on any electronic network, including without limitation the Internet and the World Wide Web
vi. Use all or any part of the Licensed Materials for any Commercial Use
vii. Use all or any part of the Licensed Materials to develop or market a database, infobase, or other information resource for resale, reuse, or sublicense
viii. Alter, abridge, adapt, modify, translate, modify or make a Derivative work, or make any other changes to the Licensed Materials

6. Obligations or undertakings. A normal function of a license agreement is to obligate either party to specific activities. Both parties should consider these obligations as significant and be prepared to comply with the terms as they are written. Potential obligations on the part of the library or licensee could include:

   i. Registration of authorized users in a manner approved by the licensor
   ii. Notification of changes to the Registered Patrons or Authorized Users lists
   iii. Notification of additions and deletions to the IP range
   iv. Retention of ILL, electronic reserve, course pack records for licensor review
   v. Removal of licensed content from e-reserves or course pack after the end of the course
   vi. Immediate notification of any breach of the license
   vii. Timely notice of termination of the contract or notice of financial exigency

7. Potential obligations on the part of the licensor could include:

   i. Provider should have the right to market the products as advertised and the provider needs to be sure that their activity doesn't violate the rights of copyright holders.
   ii. How will the information be provided to the licensee?
   iii. If online access is provided which site(s) will be available?

   iv. If you are receiving a CD-ROM or some other physical object, will it be in working order and free of defects?

   v. Up-time. If you are accessing the supplier's server, what is acceptable performance? Will the information supplier maintain back-up servers/mirror sites?

   vi. Will technical support be provided? Which browsers, Web tools, etc., are supported?

  vii. How often will the content be updated? Monthly? Weekly? Daily? Will the licensee be notified of content changes and is there recourse for significant changes in content?

 viii. Can the provider change the terms of the contract after the sale and after the receipt of the product and electronically block use of the product for security reasons without interaction with the licensee?

8. General terms. This section contains terms for the license that may include:

   i. The process for amending the license

  ii. The process used to terminate the license

 iii. Dispute resolution

 iv. Governing law

  v. Procedure for assignment in case of sale of the supplier

 vi. Failure of performance

CONCLUSION

Licensing has become a significant activity for all parties involved in the acquisition of electronic resources. Licensing developed as a reaction on the part of publishers to the spread of electronic resources and the publishers' fear that current copyright laws did not protect them in the electronic environment. The new process of licensing lacked standards and models. Since licensing was consuming greater resources and was becoming a distraction from the business of supplying resources to users, standards and model licenses were developed and used to bring some semblance of order to the process. Model licenses have not solved all problems associated with the licensing process, but they prevented the collapse of the process as licensing continues to see explosive growth. The use of model licenses has streamlined the process of purchasing electronic resources. We have not moved to an ideal environment where all that is needed is to hand a model license to a supplier and the process is done. Despite that fact, the licensing process has been improved and costs reduced by the creation and use of model licenses. According to Lesley Ellen Harris, editor of *The Copyright & New Media Law Newsletter: For Librarians & Information Professionals*, "When drawn up professionally, model licenses or standard agreements, can be very complex yet still be accessible and flexible. These agreements may also provide a checklist for negotiating a license, and help in clarifying the rights and responsibilities of each party to the agreement, while saving an organization both time and money."[4] Maybe the ideal state has not been achieved but the use of model licenses provides many benefits even if the license is never fully accepted by a supplier.

NOTES

1. JISC, The Joint Information Systems Committee. "Standard Licensing Report." January 21, 1999. http://www.jisc.ac.uk/index.cfm?name=wg_standardlicensing_report. (October 21, 2003).

2. LIBLICENSE: Licensing Digital Information for Librarians. "CLIR/DLF Model License." April 1, 2001. http://www.library.yale.edu/~llicense/modlic.shtml (October 21, 2003).

3. Cox, John E. "Model Generic Licenses: Cooperation and Competition," *Serials Review* 26, no.1 (2000), pp. 3-9.

. 4. Harris, Lesley Ellen. "Are Model Licenses the Answer?" http://copyrightlaws.com/articles/armodel.html (October 21, 2003).

Where the Giants Stand:
Protecting the Public Domain
in Digitization Contracts
with Commercial Partners

Richard Fyffe
Beth Forrest Warner

SUMMARY. Digital dissemination of public-domain works of historic, literary, and artistic value increases the intellectual value of those materials; repositories that license digitization rights to commercial agencies should seek the greatest possible availability for these works on the open Internet. As with copyright law, a balance must be struck between society's legitimate interest in maximizing access to and use of the work and society's equally legitimate interest in encouraging capital investment in digitization, dissemination, and long-term sustainability. This paper proposes that the open-access movement and efforts to "reclaim the public domain" provide a theoretical framework for evaluating prospective

Richard Fyffe is Assistant Dean, Scholarly Communications, University of Kansas Libraries, 1425 Jayhawk Boulevard, 351 Watson Library, University of Kansas, Lawrence, KS 66049 (E-mail: rfyffe@ku.edu).

Beth Forrest Warner is Director, Digital Library Initiatives, University of Kansas; Information Services, 1450 Jayhawk Boulevard, 223 Strong Hall, University of Kansas, Lawrence, KS 66049 (E-mail: bwarner@ku.edu).

[Haworth co-indexing entry note]: "Where the Giants Stand: Protecting the Public Domain in Digitization Contracts with Commercial Partners." Fyffe, Richard, and Beth Forrest Warner. Co-published simultaneously in *Journal of Library Administration* (The Haworth Information Press, an imprint of The Haworth Press, Inc.) Vol. 42, No. 3/4, 2005, pp. 83-102; and: *Licensing in Libraries: Practical and Ethical Aspects* (ed: Karen Rupp-Serrano) The Haworth Information Press, an imprint of The Haworth Press, Inc., 2005, pp. 83-102. Single or multiple copies of this article are available for a fee from The Haworth Document Delivery Service [1-800-HAWORTH, 9:00 a.m. - 5:00 p.m. (EST). E-mail address: docdelivery@haworthpress.com].

http://www.haworthpress.com/web/JLA
Digital Object Identifier: 10.1300/J111v42n03_06

partnerships between non-profit repositories and commercial digital publishers, and recommends practical guidelines for developing digitization contracts that both uphold the value of the public domain and meet the needs of the marketplace. *[Article copies available for a fee from The Haworth Document Delivery Service: 1-800-HAWORTH. E-mail address: <docdelivery@haworthpress.com> Website: <http://www.HaworthPress.com>]*

KEYWORDS. Public domain, digitization, contracts, licenses, open access, commercial vendors

If I have seen further it is by standing upon the shoulders of Giants.

–Isaac Newton to Robert Hooke, 5 February 1675

[. . .] I find that principles have no real force except when one is well fed. . . .

–Mark Twain, *Extracts from Adam's Diary*

INTRODUCTION

Two rapidly growing movements are reshaping scholars' expectations for the availability in digitally networked form of intellectual works created or curated with public support. One is a movement to "reclaim" the public domain, or protect it by limiting measures that seek to extend copyright protection to works that could otherwise be freely copied and modified by all users. The other is a movement to assure the universal cost-free availability of peer-reviewed scholarly articles.

In this paper, we will argue that these movements create a new context within which libraries, archives, and other repositories of intellectual and cultural heritage should evaluate their strategies for providing digital access to their holdings of literary, historical, and artistic works in the public domain. For such public-domain works, the institution's ownership of the tangible medium in which the work is instantiated gives it a limited set of property rights, but not the *exclusive* right to disseminate the intellectual property or use it to create new works.[1] Although many successful digital projects have been publicly or privately funded and then disseminated without direct cost to users,[2] partnership with a commercial publisher is naturally seen as an attractive way of covering the costs of digitization, dissemination, and marketing while extending access to these objects and safeguarding them from the damage that may result from direct use. In such partnerships, a repository licenses (for some form of compensation) to the commercial partner the right to digitize from its holdings, and the commercial partner in turn licenses access to paying subscribers, expecting a fair financial return on its investment and its risk—and therefore restricting access to those subscribers.[3] The fact that subscription-based licensing is becoming a primary mode of information provision for many libraries and other repositories increasingly gives such an arrangement an appearance of business-as-usual. Such partnerships with commercial publishers may appear to be an attractive way for the repository to gain access to capital, specialized equipment, and trained personnel, and to share (or even eliminate) the financial risk of digitizing materials that may turn out not to have a large audience.

The open-access and public-domain movements, we will argue, call into question (we do *not* argue that they invalidate) the propriety of library/commercial partnerships in creating and disseminating digital collections of public-domain materials. Our paper has two parts. In the first, more theoretical, part (section II) we will briefly review the arguments associated with both of these movements and note the ways in which they do and do not apply to the case of libraries and archives that hold public-domain materials that they wish to digitize and disseminate. Throughout this paper we will use the term "repository" to cover the various kinds of institutions that may hold materials to which the concept "public domain" applies, including libraries, historical societies, and archives. It should be noted that although the materials targeted by academic libraries for digitization are often held in their rare book or special collections units, we will not be concerned with the special administrative issues that may apply there.[4] Public-domain material of great intellectual value may also be found in the general or circulating collections of most libraries, and the arguments we advance here apply to both closed-stack and open-stack collections.

In making these comparisons, we will acknowledge the economic constraints facing repositories, the costs associated with successful and sustainable digital projects, and the legitimate role that may be played by commercial firms seeking profit in return for capital investment in these projects. We will also recognize that subscription-restricted access to digital copies of public-domain works does not change the copyright status of these works; the works themselves and the originals of which the digital objects are copies remain available to the public for copying, publishing, and using them to create derivative works. Nevertheless, we will argue for the growing importance of the world-wide digital commons created by the Internet, and suggest that the "opportunity cost" of restricting access to digitized versions of the materials of intellectual heritage must be factored into a decision to use a subscription model to defray the costs of conversion and dissemination. In this respect, we will argue, digital dissemination differs essentially from traditional forms of publication for reformatted materials like microform publication.

In the second part of the paper (section III), we will apply this perspective by suggesting some considerations that should guide libraries and other repositories in a decision to license digitization rights to a commercial partner (these considerations may apply as well to a repository that chooses to use subscription fees to defray the internal costs of digitization and dissemination); and we will recommend terms that should be incorporated into a digitization license.

TOWARD THE DIGITAL COMMONS: THE PUBLIC DOMAIN AND OPEN-ACCESS SCHOLARSHIP

Article I, Section 8 of the United States Constitution empowers Congress to "promote the progress of science and useful arts, by securing for limited times to authors and inventors the exclusive right to their respective writings and discoveries." This language is traditionally interpreted as calling for a balance between the rights of authors and inventors to be fairly compensated for their intellectual labors and the rights of society at large to use the products of those labors for the creation of new knowledge and new technology. For a prescribed period of time, authors and inventors hold the near-exclusive right to disseminate their works and create derivative works, but after that period has elapsed those works may be freely disseminated and used by anyone (they enter the public domain). Moreover, even during that period of copyright protection, society at large enjoys certain limited rights to use the work, under conditions defined as "fair use."[5]

Statutory and case law define the period during which a work may enjoy copyright protection and the kinds of uses of copyright-protected work that will be considered "fair." A growing number of legal scholars, artists, and activists are expressing concern over the effect of a long series of extensions to the period of copyright protection. The duration of copyright protection was originally set at 14 years, with the possibility of renewal for another 14 years if the author was living. The period was extended by legislation in 1831 and 1909. In 1976, the Copyright Revision Act further extended protection (for works created after January 1, 1978) to 50 years after the death of the author. In 1998, Congress passed the Sonny Bono Copyright Term Extension Act (CTEA), extending the term of all existing copyrights by an additional 20 years. CTEA thus extended the term of most existing copyrights to 95 years and that of many new copyrights to 70 years after the author's death.

In a suit filed in 1999, Eric Eldred challenged the constitutionality of CTEA. Eldred argued that the effect of this series of copyright extensions has been to render copyright protection "perpetual," thus contravening Article I, Section 8, of the Constitution. The United States Supreme Court, in an opinion delivered on January 15, 2003, ruled against Eldred, finding that "Congress acted within its authority and did not transgress constitutional limitations."[6] However, Justices Breyer and Stevens separately delivered sharply worded dissents from this verdict. In Justice Breyer's words, "The economic effect of this 20-year extension–the longest blanket extension since the Nation's founding–is to make the copyright term not limited, but virtually perpetual. Its primary legal effect is to grant the extended term not to authors but to their heirs, estates, or corporate successors. And most importantly, its practical effect is not to promote, but to inhibit, the progress of 'Science'–by which word the Framers meant learning or knowledge."[7]

Despite the failure of *Eldred v Ashcroft* to void the Copyright Term Extension Act, a growing movement of judges, legal scholars, artists, and activists is drawing national attention to the importance of public domain works as the foundation for the creation of new knowledge and creative work. A petition campaign, Reclaim the Public Domain, argues that serial extensions of copyright protection "unnecessarily threaten the public domain without any corresponding benefit to copyright holders" and calls on Congress to enact new legislation, the Public Domain Enhancement Act, that would

> require American copyright owners to pay a very low fee (for example, $1) fifty years after a copyrighted work was published. If the owner pays the fee, the copyright will continue for whatever duration Congress sets. But if the copyright is not worth even $1 to the owner, then we believe the work should pass into the public domain. This legislation would strengthen the public domain without burdening copyright owners. It would also help clarify rights

over copyrighted material, which in turn would enable reuse of that material. The law could thus help restore balance to the protection of copyright, and support the public domain.[8]

Similarly, Stanford University law professor Lawrence Lessig has argued in his best-selling book *The Future of Ideas* that "always and everywhere, free resources have been crucial to innovation and creativity" and that "without them, creativity is crippled."[9] In the digital age, he continues

> the central question becomes not whether government or the market should control a resource, but whether a resource should be controlled at all. Just because control is possible, it doesn't follow that it is justified. Instead, in a free society, the burden of justification should fall on him who would defend systems of control.[10]

In his book, Lessig analyzes the social and economic conditions that foster creativity and innovation. Economic incentives–the right and the ability to profit financially from one's innovations–are one necessary component, he says. Equally necessary, however, is the right and the ability to use the works of one's predecessors: "Free content," he notes, "is crucial to building and supporting new content."[11] Quoting Judge Alex Kozinski of the Ninth Circuit Court of Appeals, "Creativity is impossible without a rich public domain"; "Overprotection stifles the very creative forces it's supposed to nurture."[12]

Alongside the movement to protect the domain of commonly held intellectual works against restrictions on *use*, a parallel movement is focused on protecting or expanding *access* to scholarly literature. According to proponents within this movement, peer-reviewed research papers are a public good that should be made as widely available as possible. Moreover, Internet-based technologies make it possible to remove print-based barriers to access:

> An old tradition and a new technology have converged to make possible an unprecedented public good. The old tradition is the willingness of scientists and scholars to publish the fruits of their research in scholarly journals without payment, for the sake of inquiry and knowledge. The new technology is the internet. The public good they make possible is the world-wide electronic distribution of the peer-reviewed journal literature and completely free and unrestricted access to it by all scientists, scholars, teachers,

students, and other curious minds. Removing access barriers to this literature will accelerate research, enrich education, share the learning of the rich with the poor and the poor with the rich, make this literature as useful as it can be, and lay the foundation for uniting humanity in a common intellectual conversation and quest for knowledge.[13]

Although not (or not yet) the predominant model for disseminating scholarly literature, open access is gaining momentum. The *Lund Directory of Open-Access Journals*, for example, indexes over 550 peer-reviewed subscription-free journals in a wide range of disciplines.[14] The Public Library of Science, which started as a petition drive signed by over 30,000 scientists world-wide calling on conventional subscription-based journals to open their backfiles to cost-free access, was awarded a $9-million grant in December 2002, to develop a competing suite of new open-access journals in the biomedical sciences.[15]

The arguments of the proponents of open access generally turn on three key features of this literature.[16] In the first place, they note, creation of much scholarly literature is funded through taxpayer support either directly or indirectly. Much of the research in question is directly funded by federal agencies such as the National Science Foundation and the National Institutes of Health. Moreover, the salaries of many of these researchers (if not covered directly by public grants) and of the researchers who provide peer-review services are paid by universities and other institutions that enjoy tax-exempt status as charitable organizations. It is wrong, these proponents argue, that the host institutions that provide the research and review services should have to pay again for access to this literature through subscription fees. It is especially problematic that commercial journal publishers should realize high profits through ownership of the intellectual property represented by these papers.

Within the open-access movement, proponents differ with respect to the proper copyright status of such publicly funded works. Signatories of the Budapest Open Access Initiative expect *authors* to retain copyright to their works and call on journals to "no longer invoke copyright to restrict access to and use of the materials they publish" but instead to "use copyright and other tools to ensure permanent open access to all the articles they publish."[17] Under this regime, authors will not transfer copyright to journals but instead will grant specific, limited licenses to publishers for the right to disseminate their papers. By contrast, legislation introduced by Rep. Martin Sabo (D-Minnesota) in June 2003 (the "Public Access to Science Act") and endorsed by the leadership of the Public Library of Science directs that copyright protection will not be available "for any work produced pursuant to scientific research substantially funded by the Federal Government." "It is the sense of the Congress," according to this Act, "that any Federal department or agency that enters into funding agreements [for scientific research] should make every effort to develop and support mechanisms for making the published results of the research conducted pursuant to the agreements freely and easily available to the scientific community, the private sector, physicians, and the public."[18]

Second, according to the proponents of open access, scholarly literature is intended by its authors to be given freely to the journals that will publish it. The authors seek compensation from their institutions in the form of salary increases, promotions, and other recognition, but they do not seek (and do not receive) compensation from the publishers of these journals.

Finally, the goal of an author of this kind of literature is to maximize its scholarly impact (typically measured by citations from subsequent papers), and this is accomplished by assuring its widest possible availability. Access to literature that is intended to generate royalties (for example, textbooks, novels, cookbooks) must be restricted to paying customers, but to restrict access to literature intended only to be read and not to generate revenue defeats its purpose.

The public-domain literary, historical, and artistic works that are the subject of this paper share some of these features of scholarly research papers and to that extent are susceptible to the same claims for cost-free digital access, but they also differ in important respects. We will examine the similarities and the differences in turn.

The repositories that hold these works typically enjoy public support, directly or indirectly. The repositories are often tax-exempt charitable organizations. They may receive a portion of their operating revenue from public sources, and they may receive special grants from public sources (such as the National Endowment for the Humanities or the Institute for Museum and Library Services) for the acquisition or care of these materials. And, if the grants or gifts are from private foundations, those foundations may themselves be tax-exempt charitable organizations.

Moreover, the tax-exempt network within which these repositories operate enlarges the support available for these holdings at public expense: taxation of the repository or its benefactors would reduce the total amount of support available for acquiring or curating the holdings, and exemption of these institutions from taxation requires that other members of society pay a larger portion of taxes in addition to the tax-support directly supplied to the repositories. These institutions enjoy public support because they are considered to provide a significant public benefit. It diminishes this benefit to restrict access to the holdings of these institutions, especially when a commercial business is permitted to profit through subscriptions or sales that restrict public access.

Furthermore, the works in question have passed from copyright protection into the public domain because society considers the authors to have had ample time and opportunity to realize profit from their intellectual labor. (Some works lack copyright protection even at the moment of creation. Under United States law, works created as part of federal employment are in the public domain.) For these works, the profit-making period has ended.

These considerations should cause a repository of public-domain materials to study carefully any plan to license digitization rights to a profit-making firm that will restrict access to the digital copies. Is such an arrangement consistent with the public support the repository may enjoy? Should digital access to works in the public domain, works in the custody of tax-exempt and tax-supported institutions, be restricted to paying subscribers? Is the move to profit-based partnerships contrary to the movements to maintain a rich and diverse domain of copyright-free works and to open access to recent works of original scholarship? In Section III of this paper, we will suggest some practical ways to help assure that digitization partnerships respect the spirit of open access and preservation of the public domain.

However, works in the public domain differ from current works of original scholarship in some important ways, and the parallels just adduced require some important qualifications.

Unlike the majority of contemporary works of original scholarship that are the target of the open-access movement, historical works in the public domain do not enter the world in digital format. As the best-informed proponents of open-access scholarship recognize, digitization and digital dissemination are neither cost-free nor cheap. A decade of experience has demonstrated that the practices necessary to digitize a collection of tangible works and then render the collection discoverable, interoperable with related collections, and capable of being migrated forward to new technologies require time, highly trained personnel, and specialized software and equipment.

Moreover, public support for repositories is not total support. Most repositories that hold primary-source collections (and for which licensing of rights to a commercial partner is permitted) do not receive their whole operating budget from public funds. Society expects them to generate revenue independently, and partnerships that transfer resources (financial or in-kind) to the repository should, all other things being equal, be encouraged.

Finally, public-domain status for a work does not mean that profit on that work is forbidden, only that an exclusive right to profit from the work cannot be claimed. After all, traditional re-publication of public-domain works like those of Shakespeare and Dickens is a thriving business.

Given these differences from the scholarly literature that is the focus of the open-access movement, it might therefore be argued that digital dissemination of public-domain material does not differ substantially from the traditional practice of selling microform copies either directly or through a licensing agreement with a commercial microform publisher. Under such arrangements, it might be argued, access is expanded, not diminished. In the first place, distribution of microform copies to repositories across the world lessens the financial burden on scholars who would otherwise have to travel long distances to examine rare or unique artifacts. The cost to the repositories that purchase the microfilm is small compared to the collective savings enjoyed by users. Subscription-based digital distribution accomplishes the same thing in principle, with greater practical benefits such as improved searchability, accessibility from remote locations, etc.

Second, distribution of microform copies reduces handling of the original documents, preserving them for use by those few scholars (in present and future generations) who might need access to details not captured by the reproduction. The total revenue derived from these sales could not replace the collection of originals if they were to be lost through mishandling. The same argument applies to subscription-based digital distribution. Finally, neither microform sale nor fee-based digital distribution changes the public-domain status of the individual works. They remain available for copying and for use in the creation of derivative works, as the foundation for new knowledge and new creative works.

These arguments overlook the critical difference between analog reproduction and digital reproduction in a networked environment. The emerging digital commons represents a new phenomenon, one that raises the stakes for repositories that are considering digitization of public-domain material. "The critical feature of the Internet that sets it apart from every other network before it," Lessig writes, "is that it could be a platform upon which a whole world of activity might be built. The Internet is not a fancy cable television system; the Internet is the highway system, or the system of public roads, carrying bits rather than trucks, *but carrying them in ways no one can predict.*"[19] Moreover, Lessig points out, "Where we have little understanding about how a resource will be used, we have more reason to keep that resource in the commons."[20]

The Internet has created unprecedented potential for *unpredictable* discovery and use of texts and other expressions, and this potential is enriched with each addition to the commons. The enrichment is in the form of a network effect, and it is this effect that creates a greater "opportunity cost" when digitized public-domain material is restricted to paying subscribers than is seen when the same material is distributed in microform. In economics, a "network effect" is defined as an increase in the benefit that an agent derives from a good when the number of other agents consuming the same kind of good increases. Having an e-mail account or a telephone, for example, becomes more valuable as more people have accounts or telephones. At the same time, under conditions that display a network effect the purchase of a good by one individual indirectly benefits others who own that good—for example, by purchasing a telephone a person makes other people's telephones more useful.[21]

A similar analysis applies to the effect of posting open-access digitized texts, based on the Web's ability to collocate texts in unexpected ways and to yield unexpected materials through keyword and other kinds of searches. The intellectual value of every text already openly available is exponentially enhanced with each new addition, and the cost of the opportunities lost when one group of public-domain works cannot be accessed alongside other groups of such works is greater than it was under an analog regime (like microform). This cost should be factored into a repository's digitization strategy.

BUILDING THE DIGITAL COMMONS:
LEVERAGING THE POWER OF LICENSES

We have argued that digital dissemination of public-domain works of historic, literary, and artistic value increases the intellectual value of those materials, and that repositories that license digitization rights to commercial agencies should seek the greatest possible availability for these works on the open Internet. As with copyright law, however, a balance must be struck between society's legitimate interest in maximizing access to and use of the work and society's equally legitimate interest in encouraging capital investment in digitization, dissemination, and long-term curation.

The terms of a partnership between a repository and a commercial publisher should be defined in a contract by which the repository licenses to the publisher certain rights regarding its tangible property (the books or other materials that it owns) for specific compensation, and each party sets expectations for the other. The contract is an important instrument by which a repository can help to assure that the digital commons is enriched–both through terms that maximize access over the short and the long term and (of equal importance) through terms that give the commercial partner fair opportunity to realize a return on its investment. Thus, the terms we recommend for digitization contracts must be evaluated in the context of the specific circumstances of the repository, the works under discussion, and the publisher or agent. They must also be grounded in a clear understanding of the digitization process and the costs involved in converting, disseminating, and sustaining the resulting digital collection. And finally, projects should operate within the basic principles outlined in *A Framework of Guidance for Building Good Digital Collections* from the Institute for Museum and Library Services and the Digital Library Federation.[22]

The Business Model: Assessing a Prospective Commercial Partnership

As a first step in arriving at a balanced contractual arrangement, it is important for the repository to understand the basic business approaches and requirements of the publisher. For example, the SPARC *Declaring Independence* program for the reform of scholarly publishing calls on editors of scholarly journals to become more knowledgeable about the finances of the publications for which they provide services. If the publisher's pricing and licensing terms prove to be impeding access to their journal, SPARC urges these editors to demand that the publisher make changes or to switch to a lower-priced publishing platform.[23]

Similarly, repositories that are considering a commercial digitization partnership should understand the finances behind the deal. Repositories should request from prospective commercial partners a statement of costs expected to be incurred for the project. In addition, they should consider any costs *they* may incur as well. Depending on the project, these overall costs may include the selection and preparation of originals; metadata creation and indexing; preservation and conservation of originals; production of intermediates; digitization; quality control of images and data; system/network infrastructure; on-going maintenance of digital materials; and marketing, sales, and support.[24]

Over the past decade, the number and variety of digitization projects has begun to provide a clearer picture of the associated costs. A recent symposium of the National Initiative for a Networked Cultural Heritage (NINCH) on cost models for digitization provides several case studies of projects done by educational institutions and a breakdown of general costs from an outsourcing vendor.[25] However, even with this growing body of information it is evident that digitization is still not a uniform or straightforward process and that the repository must have a clear understanding of the procedures and trade-offs involved that can affect the project's cost.[26] For example, a recent examination of average costs by Steven Puglia, of the U.S. National Archives and Records Administration, showed that

> on average, roughly one third of the costs are related to digital conversion, one third for cataloging and descriptive metadata, and one third for administration, quality control, etc. [. . .] an average cost, over three years of data, of $29.55 per digital image (but with a range of between $1.85 and $96.45). Within that, itemized average costs come to $6.50 for digitizing; $9.25 for cataloging; and $13.40 for administration. Adjusted for unrealistically high or low costs, the figures came to $17.65 overall (digitizing $6.15; cataloging $7; and administration $10.10).[27]

Given these wide-ranging cost figures, it is important to know the publisher's per-item cost estimates and justifications when evaluating any project proposal.

In addition to the direct costs of the project, the repository should also know the profit margin that is built into the proposal. Commercial partners will not engage in this work without profit, but the repository should expect to negotiate reasonable margins. Although hard-and-fast rules for profit margins are difficult to determine, some benchmarks to consider are general publishing industry profit margins, online information industry profit margins, and the Consumer Price Index.

Compensation Schedules: Planning for Independence

The contract should set a specific term during which the publisher will have exclusive rights to market the digital files created by the publisher. The term should be sufficiently long that the publisher has a reasonable opportunity to recover its investment and generate profit. To help determine the length of any exclusive distribution term, the repository should discuss marketing plans and sales projections for the collection. At the expiration of the exclusive distribution term, the repository should have the right to disseminate the files without restriction. The publisher, too, should be able to continue selling access to the collection, but it will then be competing on the basis of its platform (search engine, presentation, and any copyrighted works it may have created as supplementary to the collection), rather than through exclusive access rights for the content.

Most commercial digitization contracts will include a royalty payment to the repository based on a percentage of the net receipts.[28] Repositories should keep in mind that royalties can only be generated from sales revenue and that, all other things being equal (i.e., the publisher's costs) the higher the royalty is the higher the subscription price must be–and therefore the more restricted the access. A repository may choose to negotiate a lower royalty rate, but should get contractual assurance that the lower cost will be passed along to purchasers/subscribers.

Part of any profit derived from the commons should be returned to the commons. The long-term sustainability of the digital commons will require a steady stream of funding and we recommend that repositories use royalty payments to create reserves or endowments for the support of open-access digital collections. These endowments may be used to purchase and maintain systems that will host the digital collection after the commercial contract expires, to support the migration of the digital files into new formats or onto new platforms as technology changes, or to support digitization of other public-domain works held by the repository (assuming that the sustainability of existing files is provided for). For more detailed information on sustainability models, see the section on "Sustainability: Models for Long-Term Funding" in *The NINCH Guide to Good Practice in the Digital Representation and Management of Cultural Heritage Materials*[29] and the CLIR report *Building and Sustaining Digital Collections: Models for Libraries and Museums.*[30]

Copyright, Licensing, and Subscribers' License: Retaining Control

Before beginning any digitization project the copyright status of the original materials should be established. In the case of the materials discussed in this article, the repository should verify that they are currently in the public domain[31] or specifically spell out in the contract responsibilities for obtaining copyright permission for digitization.

Once materials are in electronic form, additional copyright considerations come into play:

> In order for a database to warrant copyright protection, its author must have made some original effort in the collection, selection, and arrangement of material (e.g. by indexing terms or adding keywords). This protection is irrespective of whether the individual contents of the database are original and therefore copyrightable in themselves or include factual data (where the database protection will not prevent an individual from extracting them, short of copying the selection and arrangement of the database as a whole). Currently in the U.S., if the database is unprotected by copyright law, the contents of the database may be copied unless such acts are prohibited by contract or license.[32]

Digitization agreements with the publisher should clearly indicate who owns the copyright to the digital files, individually and in aggregated form, as well as the rights licensed to the other party. It is important to clarify that any exclusive marketing right enjoyed by the publisher pertains to the digital files and not to the original collection that was digitized. The public-domain status of these works and the repository's tax-exempt status suggest that proposals of competing publishers should be honored.

The contract should stipulate that as soon as the digital collection is ready to market, the repository will receive (and/or be given access to) a set of the files, either for immediate use by the repository, to be held in escrow by a third party, or embargoed for a specified amount of time. The repository should also retain the right to provide access to the collection from its own server(s) to a restricted community of users, or stipulate a cost-free subscription from the publisher's server. In the case of an academic library, this community would be the faculty, students, staff, and other users typically authorized under contracts for licensed resources (including walk-in users); in the case of a museum or archival repository, this may be the staff of the institution and any other on-site users.

In addition, the repository should stipulate key terms for the license the publisher will establish for subscribers to the digital collection, or else negotiate substantive involvement in crafting that license when the time comes. Subscribers' licenses should follow the best practices outlined in the statements of the Association of Research Libraries,[33] the International Coalition of Library Consortia,[34] the Digital Library Federation,[35] and the Creative Commons.[36] Many libraries already have experience with licenses as subscribers; they should apply this experience to the construction of good licenses in their new role as publishing partners. Perhaps one of the most important issues to consider in this process will be determining how the responsibilities for providing archival access for subscribers will be addressed–whether this will be the on-going responsibility of the publisher, whether the subscriber will get copies of the digital files, whether the repository will be responsible for providing access, etc.

Getting It Done Right: Standards and Work Schedules

We have argued that the digital commons grows more valuable as more open-access work is made available over the network. It is therefore vital that the integrity of the commons be protected over time. In addition to the establishment of endowment funds to help ensure the financial sustainability of the collection, another critical consideration is its technical sustainability. Technical sustainability is directly related to the standards and best practices followed when creating the digital files; applicable standards and best practices should be stipulated in the contract. Following good practices and open standards for digital file creation will help ensure the interoperability and migration of these files over the long run. In addition, consideration should be given to the availability or creation of metadata (descriptive, structural, and administrative) describing the digitized files; these requirements should be outlined or referenced in the contract. Sources for information on appropriate standards and best practices include the Digital Library Federation, the Research Libraries Group, the Northeast Document Conservation Center, NINCH, and the Colorado Digitization Program.[37] Publications from these organizations cover topics such as acceptable file formats and image resolutions for various types of materials, text scanning (both marked-up and "dirty"), and metadata formats and standards. Repositories should ensure that the contract stipulates that copies of master files (image, audio, video), marked/unmarked text, display files, and meta-data be made available by the publisher to the repository either during or at the end of the contractual period, and what media will be used.

The schedule for digitization of materials should be laid out in detail in the contract, and should include stipulations that failure to meet a minimum amount of progress or specific project milestones will result in the repository taking possession of whatever digital files were created and making them openly accessible. This provides incentive to the publisher, assures that the investment is not altogether lost (the publisher will take a tax write-off), and ensures that collection digitization rights are not tied up indefinitely (if exclusive rights were granted).

The contract should also specify that scanner operators with demonstrated training and experience in the proper handling of original materials will be hired, and give the repository some role in selection of scanning personnel. Finally, the contract should also specify requirements for handling original materials. More details on digitization project planning and considerations can be found in materials from the Research Libraries Group, the Northeast Document Conservation Center, and NINCH.[38]

Assigning Responsibility: Legal Terms

The contract should assign to the publisher responsibility for compliance with all copyright and legal requirements applicable to the distribution of the digital collection and for obtaining all consents, permissions, licenses, and other instruments as may be necessary for such compliance. In return for accepting that responsibility, the publisher will need to reserve the right to eliminate any items from the digital collection where, in the publisher's opinion, reproduction of the item would violate copyright law (or other laws of libel, obscenity, etc.), or in cases where clear copyright cannot be established. The publisher should also agree to indemnify the repository and hold it harmless from any costs, including attorney's fees, resulting from any claim of a violation of any rights of a third party arising out of the reproduction, publication, and sale of the digital collection.

CONCLUSION

We have argued that digital dissemination of public-domain works of historic, literary, and artistic value increases the intellectual value of those materials and that repositories that license digitization rights to commercial agencies should seek the greatest possible availability for these works on the open Internet. As with copyright law, however, a balance must be struck between society's legitimate interest in maximizing access to and use of the work and society's equally legitimate interest in encouraging capital investment in digitization, dissemination, and long-term sustainability. By proactively working with vendors to contractually ensure access terms, distribution rights, and digitization standards, while at the same time recognizing the economic realities of the marketplace, repositories can provide digital access to their holdings of literary, historical, and artistic works in the public domain in a manner responsive to the broad needs of long-term open access.

NOTES

1. "Ownership of a copyright, or of any of the exclusive rights under a copyright, is distinct from ownership of any material object in which the work is embodied. Transfer of ownership of any material object, including the copy or phonorecord in which the work is first fixed, does not of itself convey any rights in the copyrighted work embodied in the object; nor, in the absence of an agreement, does transfer of ownership of a copyright or of any exclusive rights under a copyright convey property rights in any material object"–17 U.S.C. 202.

2. For example, *Making of America* is a joint project of the University of Michigan and Cornell University funded by the Andrew W. Mellon Foundation. Cf. http://www.hti.umich.edu/m/moagrp/about.html. The *American Memory Project* (http://memory.loc.gov/) is a collaborative project with the Library of Congress, partially funded by the Ameritech Corporation.

3. Examples include the microform and digital research collections offered by ProQuest/UMI, Primary Source Microfilm, and other companies.

4. For guidelines specific to administration of library rare book and special collections units, see Lisa Browar, Cathy Henderson, and Michael North, "Licensing the Use of Special Collections Materials," *RBM* 3, no. 2 (Fall 2002), 124-144.

5. Intellectual property laws that govern invention–patents–differ from intellectual property laws that govern expressions of ideas–copyright. This paper is concerned exclusively with copyright.

6. *Eric Eldred, et al., Petitioners v. John D. Ashcroft, Attorney General*, 239 F.3d 372 (2003), affirmed.

7. *Eric Eldred, et al., Petitioners v. John D. Ashcroft, Attorney General*, 239 F.3d 372 (2003), affirmed. (*Breyer*, J., dissenting).

8. "Reclaim the Public Domain," http://www.petitiononline.com/eldred/petition.html.

9. Lawrence Lessig, *The Future of Ideas: The Fate of the Commons in a Connected World* (New York: Vintage Books, 2002), 14.

10. Lessig, 14.

11. Lessig, 50.

12. Quoted in Lessig, 204.
13. Budapest Open Access Initiative, http://www.soros.org/openaccess/read.shtml.
14. *Directory of Open Access Journals*, http://www.doaj.org/; accessed 30 October 2003.
15. "Public Library of Science to Launch New Free-Access Biomedical Journals with $9 Million Grant from the Gordon and Betty Moore Foundation," http://www.plos.org/news/announce_moore.html.
16. Cf., among others, Stevan Harnad, "For Whom the Gate Tolls? How and Why to Free the Refereed Research Literature Online Through Author/Institution Self-Archiving, Now," http://www.ecs.soton.ac.uk/~harnad/Tp/resolution.htm.
17. Budapest Open Access Initiative, op. cit.
18. Public Access to Science Act, H.R. 2613, (108th).
19. Lessig, 174, our emphasis.
20. Lessig, 88.
21. *The New Palgrave Dictionary of Economics and the Law*, ed. Peter Newman (New York: Stockton Press, 1998), s.v. "Network effects and externalities."
22. *A Framework of Guidance for Building Good Digital Collections*, November 6, 2001, http://www.imls.gov/pubs/forumframework.htm.
23. "Stage 1, Diagnosis: Does Your Journal Meet Its Primary Goal–To Serve Its Community?" in: Scholarly Publishing and Academic Resources Coalition, *Declaring Independence*, http://www.arl.org/sparc/di/stage1.html.
24. Steven Puglia, "Revisiting Costs" in: *The Price of Digitization: Cost Models for Cultural and Educational Institutions*, NINCH Symposium, New York, April 8, 2003, http://www.ninch.org/forum/price.report.html.
25. *The Price of Digitization: Cost Models for Cultural and Educational Institutions*, op. cit.
26. "Project Planning (Cost Models)" in: Humanities Advanced Technology and Information Institute, University of Glasgow, and the National Initiative for a Networked Cultural Heritage, *The NINCH Guide to Good Practice in the Digital Representation and Management of Cultural Heritage Materials*, October 2002, http://www.nyu.edu/its/humanities//ninchguide/index.html.
27. Steven Puglia, "Revisiting Costs" in: *The Price of Digitization: Cost Models for Cultural and Educational Institutions*, op. cit.
28. Net receipts should be calculated based on payments received by the publisher from purchasers, subscribers, and distributors for access to all or any portion of the digital collection, adjusted for returns, customer and agency discounts and credits, and less sales tax, if any.
29. *The NINCH Guide to Good Practice in the Digital Representation and Management of Cultural Heritage Materials*, op. cit.
30. *Building and Sustaining Digital Collections: Models for Libraries and Museums* (Washington: Council on Library and Information Resources, August 2001), http://www.clir.org/pubs/reports/pub100/pub100.pdf.
31. D. Zorich, "Why the Public Domain Is Not Just a Mickey Mouse Issue," NINCH Copyright Town Meeting, Chicago Historical Society, January 11, 2000, http://www.ninch.org/copyright/2000/chicagozorich.html; and Laura Gassaway, "When Works Pass into the Public Domain," September 18, 2001, http://www.unc.edu/~unclng/public-d.htm.
32. "Rights Management" in: *The NINCH Guide to Good Practice in the Digital Representation and Management of Cultural Heritage Materials*, op. cit.

33. Association of Research Libraries and others, *Principles for Licensing Electronic Resources*, http://www.arl.org/scomm/licensing/principles.html.

34. International Coalition of Library Consortia, *Statement of Current Perspective and Preferred Practices for the Selection and Purchase of Electronic Information: Update No. 1: New Developments in E-Journal Licensing* (December 2001 update to March 1998 Statement), http://www.library.yale.edu/consortia/2001currentpractices.htm.

35. The Liblicense Model Licensing Agreement, http://www.library.yale.edu/~llicense/modlic.shtml.

36. *Creative Commons*, http://www.creativecommons.org.

37. Digital Library Federation Benchmark Working Group, *Benchmark for Faithful Digital Reproductions of Monographs and Serials,*Version 1, December 2002, http://www.diglib.org/standards/bmarkfin.htm; Anne R. Kinney and Oya Y. Rieger, *Moving Theory into Practice: Digital Imaging for Libraries and Archives* (Mountain View, Calif.: Research Libraries Group, 2000); *Guides to Quality in Visual Resource Imaging*, (Research Libraries Group and the Digital Library Federation, July 2000), http://www.rlg.org/visguides/; *Handbook for Digital Projects: A Management Tool for Preservation and Access*, Maxine K. Sitts, ed., (Northeast Document Conservation Center), http://www.nedcc.org/digital/dighome.htm; *The NINCH Guide to Good Practice in the Digital Representation and Management of Cultural Heritage Materials*, op. cit.; Western States Digital Standards Group-Digital Imaging Working Group, *Western States Digital Imaging Best Practices*, Version 1.0, January 2003, http://www.cdpheritage.org/resource/scanning/documents/WSDIBP_v1.pdf.

38. Anne R. Kinney and Oya Y. Rieger, *Moving Theory into Practice: Digital Imaging for Libraries and Archives*, op. cit.; *The NINCH Guide to Good Practice in the Digital Representation and Management of Cultural Heritage Materials*, op. cit.

Producer Concerns
in Licensing Content

Andrea Ramsden-Cooke
Priscilla McIntosh

SUMMARY. This article addresses the issues in licensing content from the perspective of the database producers/aggregators. The producers of aggregated databases must balance the needs and interests of the publishers whose content they license, along with the interests and concerns of the library customers. Topics addressed include the publishers' desire to protect revenues and subscriptions; publishers' interest in maintaining control over how content is built and displayed; royalty and pricing issues; miscellaneous other contractual issues between publishers and database producers; difficulties in licensing premium content and in licensing content from large inter-governmental organizations; and the growing number of exclusive agreements between publishers and data-

Andrea Ramsden-Cooke is Director of Licensing & Business Development, LexisNexis Enterprise & Library, 4520 East-West Library, Suite 800, Bethesda, MD 20814 (E-mail: andrea.ramsden-cooke@lexisnexis.com).

Priscilla McIntosh is Account Executive, LexisNexis Academic & Library Solutions, 4520 East-West Library, Suite 800, Bethesda, MD 20814 (E-mail: priscilla.mcintosh@ lexisnexis.com).

[Haworth co-indexing entry note]: "Producer Concerns in Licensing Content." Ramsden-Cooke, Andrea, and Priscilla McIntosh. Co-published simultaneously in *Journal of Library Administration* (The Haworth Information Press, an imprint of The Haworth Press, Inc.) Vol. 42, No. 3/4, 2005, pp. 103-111; and: *Licensing in Libraries: Practical and Ethical Aspects* (ed: Karen Rupp-Serrano) The Haworth Information Press, an imprint of The Haworth Press, Inc., 2005, pp. 103-111. Single or multiple copies of this article are available for a fee from The Haworth Document Delivery Service [1-800-HAWORTH, 9:00 a.m. - 5:00 p.m. (EST). E-mail address: docdelivery@haworthpress.com].

http://www.haworthpress.com/web/JLA
Digital Object Identifier: 10.1300/J111v42n03_07

base producers. The article seeks to engender greater understanding among librarians about the licensing issues faced by producers of aggregated databases and advocates some radical rethinking of business models among publishers, aggregators, and library customers. *[Article copies available for a fee from The Haworth Document Delivery Service: 1-800-HAWORTH. E-mail address: <docdelivery@haworthpress.com> Website: <http://www.HaworthPress.com>]*

KEYWORDS. Licensing, aggregators, publishers, database producers

INTRODUCTION

Producers of aggregated databases are the quintessential "middlemen" between publishers who license their content for inclusion in these databases and libraries that purchase aggregated databases to access that content. In an increasingly complex environment, producers of aggregated databases must deal with issues emanating from the publishers whose content they are licensing and yet must address the concerns of their library customers as well. This article attempts to foster a better understanding among librarians of the licensing concerns and issues faced by producers of aggregated databases and ends by seeking new ways forward.

Topics covered include numerous publisher concerns that of necessity are also concerns of database producers: fear of loss of subscriptions that are the publishers' primary revenue streams; the desire to impose embargoes on publications as a means of protecting subscriptions; desire to control the ways that the publisher's content is built and displayed; royalty and pricing concerns; and the many contractual issues which arise between the publishers and the database producers.

Additionally, there are other concerns that database producers must address, particularly in the academic market. These issues include the difficulty of licensing certain premium publisher content due to the relatively low revenues generated from academic online products; the difficulties in dealing with the many layers of bureaucracy to license content from large inter-governmental organizations; and perhaps most importantly for libraries, the growth of exclusive agreements between publishers and a particular database producer.

PROTECTING REVENUES–
THE PUBLISHERS' GREATEST CONCERN

While there are many publisher interests that of necessity also become interests of database producers, the most important of these must be the publishers' fear of cannibalization of their own primary revenue streams. Put more directly, publishers ask the aggregators, "If we license this content to you for inclusion in your database, will our current subscribers cancel their existing subscription to our journal or online product?"

Tenopir discussed this threat of "disappearing databases" in *Library Journal*:

> In the interest of providing access to the most journals with limited funds, libraries sometimes cancel subscriptions if they receive the articles through full text aggregators. . . . But what benefits libraries can be disastrous to primary publishers. Sage Publications became the first major scholarly publisher to remove its journals from aggregator services. . . . According to Carol Richman, director of licensing and electronic publishing, and Blaise Simqu, executive vice president, Sage Publications, this withdrawal is a direct result of library cancellations. They claim there is a clear relationship between the availability of Sage content in aggregated databases and subscription cancellations. "The royalties earned from the database aggregators is very small, and Sage journals cannot sustain themselves without subscription revenue," they said. "Content in the aggregated databases literally threatens the long-term future of every journal we publish." (Tenopir 2002, 38)

Publishers and librarians can have differing views on the issue of journal aggregation. At the 22nd Annual Charleston Conference in 2002, the topic was extensively discussed. As *Library Journal* reported, "No one loves journal aggregators–except the users, who by all accounts appreciate the 'one-stop' shopping the big databases provide. Publishers complain that aggregators generate little income and worry about aggregation's impact on institutional subscriptions. . . . Librarians had mixed reactions, acknowledging that aggregation may not work for all publishers but fearing that "disaggregation" may snowball" (Kenney 2002, 18).

One means by which publishers attempt to address this concern about loss of existing subscription revenues is by imposing time embargoes on database producers. These embargoes create a varying time lag between when the latest issue of a publication appears in print and when those issues are available online through the various database producers. In a *Library Journal* roundtable with the aggregators, Audrey Melkin, Vice President, Publisher Relations at Ingenta, explained the publisher rationale behind these embargoes, stating that publishers "can put an embargo if they're concerned about the current year's content. It may be an incremental market for them, and [embargoes] let them feel at least in the short term that they protect their subscription revenue" (Albanese 2002, 36).

This approach, however, may only be viable in the academic market. Other markets, including the business school market, have time critical needs and if they have to wait seven days until after a report is published to gain access via an aggregator, it lessens the value of the aggregation.

Another solution that sometimes satisfies publishers is for the aggregator to offer a limited archive of content or a limited selection of articles. This is a frequent request, particularly from publishers of academic journals. However, neither of these solutions satisfies the library customer with deep research needs.

Looking to the future, there is increasing evidence that online usage of some content can drive up or stimulate print subscriptions. There are creative ways in which traditional print publishers, for example, are partnering with aggregators to bundle access to print and online. We need to identify those models and develop this concept.

WHO IS IN CONTROL?–
PUBLISHERS' DESIRE TO MAINTAIN CONTROL
OVER THEIR CONTENT

Another publisher issue that database producers must address is the desire of publishers to control the ways in which the publisher's content is built and displayed in the database. This can include placing restrictions on what formats the data can be displayed in. Many publishers require greater than average control over their data, such as only allowing content to be reproduced in PDF format so that the data retains its integrity, its look, and cannot be manipulated or distorted by the aggregator or by the customer. The difficulty for aggregators with central search engines is that this renders the content much less searchable and thus much less accessible by the customer. Also customers are asking for the data contained within tables to be downloadable to spreadsheets–something again which would be prohibited by several significant publishers wishing to protect the integrity of their data.

Issues such as these can only be addressed by building greater trust into the publisher-aggregator relationship in the interests of fulfilling customer needs.

SPIRALING COSTS OF BUILDING DATABASES– WHO IS RESPONSIBLE?

Data format issues between publishers and aggregators can exacerbate delicate relationships and can escalate database build costs far beyond what either party could foresee. Aggregators spend a lot of time and money analyzing, designing, converting, and building third-party data into an integrated, searchable database to suit their own customers' needs. This is particularly difficult when building archives because data formats from individual publishers can vary greatly not only between titles but also within a single title over the years, with each data format change requiring a new database conversion design and build. This is important for customers to bear in mind when they are constantly asking for wider and deeper archives. These are costly to build and only receive limited usage.

Publishers frequently change formats in the middle of a publication cycle, thus requiring a new design and the rebuilding of a database. Publishers need to work more closely with aggregators to minimize or share these costs.

ROYALTY AND PRICING ISSUES

How are licensors remunerated for their content? It is not difficult to imagine that this is an important issue for both publishers and database producers.

"Every man has his price"–unfortunately this is true in the world of content licensing. Above, we spoke of the Sage Publications situation that caused them to withdraw their content from aggregators. Later, however, Sage managed to conclude a deal with ProQuest to license a limited number of business journals and Blaise Simqu quite openly agreed that it was a matter of price. If an aggregator can offer an amount of money, via a guaranteed annual royalty, which the publisher feels will comfortably cover any loss of subscription revenue (and in this case it was six times the projected subscription revenue loss), then almost any deal can be done. The tricky part comes when the aggregator has to cover those high guarantees. What price will customers pay for the convenience of having a large amount of good content in one place, searchable via one query? The answer to that question varies hugely according to the market sector. A large part of the academic market, with its ever shrinking budgets, by necessity has to draw the line a lot sooner than corporate, federal and legal markets.

Royalty expenses are the second largest cost many aggregators have after staffing costs–in other words, it's a very substantial amount! The need to keep royalties at a reasonable level and maintain parity amongst similar content types is paramount. Many publishers new to the aggregation model approach a licensing deal as they would a redistribution or reselling deal and they can start with extremely unrealistic expectations. They tend to think of aggregators as simple resellers of their content, ignoring the value added in aggregating similar content sets and human and automatic indexing.

CONTRACTUAL ISSUES

The fine print is a part of most facets of business today and the licensing of content for inclusion in databases is of course no exception. Increasingly, publishers want shorter contract terms–i.e., 12 months is a common request. Not surprisingly, publishers want to test the water and if it doesn't work for them, they want a quick exit. Unfortunately it's not as easy as that. For some of the reasons mentioned above in regard to costs, the ramp up time for a new database build can be much longer than 12 months.

Another stumbling block in negotiations is the question of warranties and indemnities–generally aggregators ask publishers to warrant that the data they are providing is free from litigious risk and to indemnify them against any such risk. Small publishers in particular have great difficulty with accepting this and feel very exposed. On the other hand, aggregators feel it is only fair that the publisher stands by his content and that if he is prepared to accept royalties for use of his content on a database, then he must accept responsibility arising from the use of that content. Aggregators cannot be reasonably expected to accept liability for the accuracy and valid copyright status of over 30,000 different content sources. Now that is exposure!

LICENSING PREMIUM CONTENT–
SPECIFIC ISSUES IN THE ACADEMIC MARKET

Another issue that is specifically challenging for database producers in the academic market is the difficulty of licensing premium content because of the relatively low revenues generated for the publishers from inclusion in academic online products.

Most aggregators sell content into the academic market at a hugely discounted price to value ratio. This leads to the vicious circle in which publishers do not want to license their content when they feel it is being undersold. Of course aggregators use the usual arguments about greater exposure, reaching markets they would not normally be able to penetrate with their smaller sales forces, the value-added aspect that aggregators offer, etc. Increasingly, these arguments fall on unreceptive ears, particularly those publishers of business intelligence type content who somehow conjure up a fascinating picture of corporate executives rushing off to their nearest public or academic library to access the publishers' premium content for free via the LexisNexis™ services. What's the answer? Aggregators are constantly searching their souls (and their pockets) for new models that will revolutionize the content licensing world–surely there must be some way of keeping publishers, aggregators, and customers happy? Transactional pricing has always been rejected in the academic market but it is still a constant request from publishers of business intelligence content before they will allow their content into the academic arena. One publisher once compared the academic subscription fees to an all you can eat buffet with his content being filet mignon and said to us–"You're not gonna offer them as much of my steak as they can eat for $5.99!"

NEGOTIATING
WITH LARGE INTERNATIONAL ORGANIZATIONS–
PARTICULAR CHALLENGES

In a world where we are all conditioned to want and expect instant responses and action, negotiating to license content from large intergovernmental organizations can be a lesson in maintaining equilibrium and patience. The substantial numbers of committees and layers of bureaucracy can create very time-consuming negotiations. One particular organization pushed all its decision making through a publishing committee that met only three times per year. If you missed one of the cycles or a meeting was cancelled, you literally had to wait eight months for a decision–and if the committee came back with a simple question to which our answer was "Yes we can do that" you then had to wait another four months for that response to go up the line.

And whilst all this is happening (or not happening, as the case may be), frequent changes in personnel at these organizations led to the constant restarting of negotiations.

PUBLISHER EXCLUSIVES WITH PARTICULAR DATABASE PRODUCERS

The recent growth in exclusive licenses between publishers and a particular database producer is certainly an issue for database producers, but is also a very important issue for libraries as well.

In 2001, Krumenaker examined the issue of exclusive licenses as it relates to EBSCO, Proquest, and Gale. Krumenaker outlines the arguments made by executives from ProQuest Info and Learning and the Gale Group against these types of exclusive licenses being signed by EBSCO in this way:

> EBSCO is making outlandish offers to publishers to move all their titles to EBSCO host, paying three, four, 10, even 100 times as much as the usual fees. Often the money paid exceeds revenues publishers receive now from all sources. Many publishers simply can't pass up a windfall like this. It protects their bottom lines in shaky times. Meanwhile, there's an embargo on the new holdings so those publishers can maintain print products, causing libraries to continue print subscriptions and not go wholly digital. And the contracts extend from 1-5 years. This also protects the publishers, though some publishers undoubtedly don't want to play this game, believing in the current model of spreading themselves around to have a variety of inbound cash streams. . . . Both executives of the competing aggregators believe that this policy of EBSCO's will cause (1) publishers to have higher expectations in the future for money they can get from any of the three players when existing contracts come to an end, (2) initiate a bidding war for exclusives that will ultimately raise the costs that libraries and end users have to pay, (3) that libraries choosing just one service because budgets are too tight will be unable to get access to all the titles they need for their patrons with the missing titles unavailable anywhere else. (Krumenaker 2001)

Exclusives do not generally benefit customers. They reward publishers and give leverage to aggregators, but with the trend toward users wanting fewer sources from which to access all their information needs, one hopes the market pressure will be sufficient for the industry to move away from exclusives.

CONCLUSION

Radical rethinking of business models is necessary between all parties involved, including the customer. It should not just be a case of the publishers and the aggregators struggling to maintain their own respective viabilities. We need customer buy-in to develop sustainable models for effective information dissemination, search, and retrieval. These will probably vary between markets. On the publisher-aggregator side, it's fairly common knowledge that current business models and various licensing restrictions are at worst preventing, and at best hindering, the achievement of true customized solutions. On the customer side, there really is no point in saying "we want it all but we don't want to pay very much for it" or the even more curious, "information should be free." Most of the world's information currently exists in unstructured format and if we want to make that available to more people by easier means then we will all have to work together via partnerships and alliances to bring it about.

REFERENCES

Albanese, Andrew Richard, 2002. An LJ roundtable with the aggregators. *Library Journal* 127 (5): 34-38.

Kenney, Brian, 2002. More bytes than books in Charleston. *Library Journal* 127 (20): 18.

Krumenaker, Larry, 2001. A tempest in a librarian's teapot: EBSCO, ProQuest, Gale exclusive and unique titles [online]. *Searcher*, July/August 2001, 9 (7). Available at: (http://www.infotoday.com/searcher/jul01/krumenaker.htm).

Tenopir, Carol, 2002. Disappearing databases. *Library Journal* 127 (20): 38-40.

Licensing E-Books:
The Good, the Bad, and the Ugly

Emilie Algenio
Alexia Thompson-Young

SUMMARY. As e-books settle into the academic market, the relationship between publishers, vendors, and libraries grows more complex. This article highlights how licenses, which govern this business affair, are no exception. From aggregators to individual publishers, from large STM companies to small societies, e-book enterprises must acknowledge library values in order to remain economically viable. For the benefit of all parties involved, new and better ways of balancing the profit-driven goal of selling e-books and the educational benefit of lending e-books need to be negotiated. In an environment where communication is encouraged, flexible licenses and subscription models can balance these issues. *[Article copies available for a fee from The Haworth Document Delivery Service: 1-800-HAWORTH. E-mail address: <docdelivery@haworthpress.com> Website: <http://www.HaworthPress.com>]*

Emilie Algenio is Assistant Licensing Coordinator (E-mail: algenio@mail.utexas.edu); and Alexia Thompson-Young is Licensing Coordinator (E-mail: atyoung@mail.utexas.edu), both at Digital Library Services Division, The General Libraries, University of Texas at Austin, First Floor Dock, Austin, TX 78713-8916.

The authors wish to acknowledge Dennis Dillon's expertise and exemplary e-book examinations.

[Haworth co-indexing entry note]: "Licensing E-Books: The Good, the Bad, and the Ugly." Algenio, Emilie, and Alexia Thompson-Young. Co-published simultaneously in *Journal of Library Administration* (The Haworth Information Press, an imprint of The Haworth Press, Inc.) Vol. 42, No. 3/4, 2005, pp. 113-128; and: *Licensing in Libraries: Practical and Ethical Aspects* (ed: Karen Rupp-Serrano) The Haworth Information Press, an imprint of The Haworth Press, Inc., 2005, pp. 113-128. Single or multiple copies of this article are available for a fee from The Haworth Document Delivery Service [1-800-HAWORTH, 9:00 a.m. - 5:00 p.m. (EST). E-mail address: docdelivery@haworthpress.com].

KEYWORDS. E-books, electronic books, licensing, subscription models, digital content standards

An ever-increasing number of e-book offers, as e-mail announcements, web page advertisements, and even brightly colored postcards, are making their way from publishers to librarians. "Highly authoritative," "exceptionally usable," and "easily accessible" are among the descriptions listed in these offers. Underneath these pretty features, items that both publishers and librarians can agree on, are the e-book's business model and license, points where publishers and librarians are likely to disagree. Some may view e-book business models and corresponding licenses as *ugly* realities, but through earnest discussion *bad* models and licenses can be worked with.

The meaning of the term e-book can range from electronic copies of a book's printed form, to marked up text and figures that enhance the content of an e-book, to electronic content that offers online services beyond those of an individual book. Many e-book articles have investigated e-book formats, e-book reading devices and the general public's reading of popular e-books, such as author Stephen King's experiment in 2000. However, this article will focus on the e-book business models with online web access for academic libraries. Examining e-book publishing merits, such as the digitization cost, platform development, archiving mechanisms, marketing and pricing considerations, and internal content rights management, as well as external customer account management is highly complex. E-books are still in their infancy, and many aspects of the business have yet to become standard practices. Considering this, the instability of the content and medium, and the continuum of time, the authors are analyzing only a segment of the present to better predict the future. Examining library merits, such as licensing intellectual property rights, archival access, technological choices and maintenance, budget considerations, administrative reports, and accessibility issues is also highly complex. In practice, when it comes down to the details, no two e-book business models will be evaluated and subscribed to in the same way by any library. Therefore, this article will be generalizing e-book and library values for the sake of discussion.

Publishers want to sell books to customers and libraries want to lend books to users. E-books challenge both of these goals, since one e-book could be accessed by multiple library users at a time or could be protected by software that requires payment per view. Early e-book business models sought to avoid these revenue issues by digitizing older content that no longer had a substantial market share, such as the Early English Books Online (EEBO) collection. This collection has close to 100,000 online versions of books and other printed materials published in the English language from 1475 through 1700, and in many instances duplicates the print titles already held by academic libraries. The online benefit of greater accessibility to users with a web browser coupled with the timing of when EEBO was first offered for subscription, encouraged many libraries to purchase this content. As Dennis Dillon wrote in 2001, "After positive experiences with Web-based e-journals, full-text aggregators, and indexing and abstracting services, e-books were the obvious next step in our attempts to bring a full line-up of Web-based basic library resources to our clientele."[1] Now in the fall of 2003, libraries are dealing with shrinking budgets and are not as ready to purchase the same content in multiple formats. In this article we will review some current e-book proposals, recognize divergent e-book and library values, and suggest what *good* e-book business models and licenses the future may include.

E-BOOK MERITS IN LIBRARY MARKET

The e-book market is highly complex. Gone are the expectations that an e-book is just a book in electronic format that will be cheap to produce. This electronic format is being influenced by a number of factors such as the author's ability to enhance the content, the rethinking of the publishing supply chain, and the use of the e-book format with reading devices. Two very influential factors on the e-book market are the music industry's reaction to shareware, and the slightly more mature e-journal market. Like popular songs shared by Internet users, publishers are sensitive to the fact that e-books could be disseminated electronically to users without payment, unless e-books are protected with rights management software. This means that publishers must spend money upfront for computer programming and hardware, or pay for these services from an aggregator or other third party. At this point, an aggregator may successfully license a publisher's e-book content into an exclusive business deal, ensuring that libraries must gain access to the aggregator's e-book platform to access the desired content. The favored O'Reilly "nutshell" technology books are a good example of this. At one time, O'Reilly e-books were offered through one online platform that licensed access to academic libraries, but have since made their content available through other platforms.

E-book business models will continue to evolve, but there are some broad categories that can be described. The more common business models include one e-book/one user, fees for simultaneous users, free with print purchases, and annual fees based on a library or institution's characteristics. These models can be tailored to fit any one library, or multi-library consortia, and generally are.

The one e-book/one user model is unofficially referred to as the netLibrary model, since netLibrary was one of the first aggregators to employ it. The netLibrary model allows a subscribing library to purchase an e-book close to the print price plus any quantity discounts, presents two options for a fee to cover netLibrary's online platform service, includes MARC records, and permits only one patron at a time to view or check out an e-book. This model resembles how print books are purchased with one-time fees, and how only one patron at a time can check a print book out. A crucial component of the model is that netLibrary's platform ensures that only one user at a time can view an e-book, and has built in safeguards to keep the e-book from being systematically disseminated to non-authorized users. This same platform provides statistics to libraries so they can see how their e-book titles are being used. This type of model, one e-book available to one user, is appreciated by publishers that are concerned that one e-book available to an unlimited number of users would decrease their sales. However, many libraries have grown to expect unlimited users with their electronic resources and consider models that are priced per user as behind the times. As a variation on the netLibrary model, Ebooks.com permits multiple users to simultaneously view one e-book.

Certain e-book genres–dictionaries, encyclopedias, directories–may also be freely accessed online by libraries that buy the print versions, hence the free with print purchase model. Since the current usefulness of these traditional print reference resources has a limited shelf life, online access to updated content is desirable. However, libraries usually will not be gaining long term access to the online content, nor will they have archival rights to the online version, but since the print version is already in their collection this may not be of consequence.

Specific genres lend themselves well to the e-book format, "bibliographies, abstracting and index guides, citation indexes, dictionaries, encyclopedias, directories, product catalogs, maintenance manuals . . . [have] succeeded because [they are] not literal translations of their predecessor print products."[2] These genres benefit from frequent content updates, something that is more easily done with e-books than with print books. Since these e-books are updated, online publishers use the annual fee model for these evolving monographs. These annual fees are usually based on institutional characteristics such as FTE or degrees granted, library characteristics such as Carnegie classifications, and/or a multiple library consortial discount. Libraries recognize the benefits of up-to-date content and have been willing to pay annual fees, especially if the fees are inexpensive. However, an inexpensive designation is a subjective concept, unique to each library.

Recently, many science, technology, and medical (STM) publishers have come out with their own e-book offers marketed directly to libraries instead of making their content obtainable through an e-book aggregator. These e-books may be considered to be reference materials, but they will generally contain more research content than the reference materials cited above. Most of these publishers are using e-book models that resemble their e-journal offers in that annual subscription fees are required. One of the reasons cited for an annual fee is that unlike their print predecessors, these electronic editions are updated online regularly, instantly available to users. Publishers will certainly view these e-books as more weighty in content than a mere index and will set the fees accordingly. Many libraries are not looking to add another annual fee to their subscription budgets, yet they might be willing to buy this research content and forgo the updates in favor of a one-time purchase. There is anecdotal evidence that some publishers are willing to offer this one-time purchase option for e-books which are normally advertised as annual subscriptions.

Finding new ways to provide access to e-books with a sustainable revenue is a challenge publishers and aggregators are accepting. A unique e-book model from Ebrary requires a free plug-in, and when once installed users may read e-books from more than 100 publishers online at no cost. Printing and downloading of content will require users to purchase the e-book, or these activities will be covered under prepaid library fees to Ebrary. Another upcoming experimental model from eBooks Corporation, announced at the Fall 2003 International Coalition of Library Consortia (ICOLC) meeting, will support "non-linear lending." E-books will be accessible to a subscribing library for a fixed number of days per year, and these days can be used concurrently depending on user demand. Experimental business models are needed to find new and perhaps better ways to balance the publisher's goal of selling books and the library's goal of lending them.

While a standard business model and license for e-books would be nice, such as the taken for granted standard of buying and using print monographs, the truth is that this utopia would be impossible. As new technologies develop, e-books will continue to evolve along with their business models and licenses. Publishers and librarians are well aware that licenses reflect more than the business model agreed to. Many states have licensing language that by law state-supported institutions must include in their contracts, and there are always institution and library specific language that should be included as well. The publisher also has specific language that will need to be addressed in their contracts. The licensing process is quite demanding, since all parties want to make sure that the license manifests the best e-book model possible. Noted by Ian Jacobs, with Palgrave Macmillan, in the context of licenses between publishers, "One might think that once the first one or two contracts have been negotiated then the third and fourth would take much less time. Unfortunately, this turns out not to be the case."[3] Licenses will probably never be completely standardized for either publishers or libraries.

LIBRARY MERITS IN LIBRARY MARKET

Librarians have gained experience with subscribing to e-journals and certain subscription functionalities should now be expected for e-books. Bibliographers use statistics for their collection development efforts, and vendors oblige. Knowing the numbers is critical in gauging the utility of online resources, regardless of whether the vendor conforms to ICOLC's or the Counting Online Usage of NeTworked Electronic Resources' (COUNTER) guidelines. The time-honored Association of Research Libraries' statistics currently include guidelines on how to count e-books within the larger context of the collection <http://www.arl.org/stats/arlstat/arlstatqa.html>.

Recently, a few new offerings of e-books from publishers have been using the subscription model. Unlike buying a book, these models are built upon yearly fees like a journal subscription. A steady revenue stream for publishers is desirable, but libraries have to make hard choices about their online subscriptions. Many a subscription budget is being consumed with e-journal package fees, and when a library has to make a choice between an established, non-cancelable by license, peer reviewed e-journal and an e-book that also collects updated, edited articles from authors with an annual license fee, the library will most likely choose the e-journal.

As a business customer, libraries tend to purchase a single title, and a single title covering infinite subjects, as opposed to buying one title in bulk, and within a select subject range. As a whole, libraries' purchasing power has not reached a critical mass, at least not in the eyes of e-book publishers and not for the current output of e-book titles. For this reason, publishers have the advantage to push certain prices and licensing terms. Within the current legal landscape for libraries, e-books are governed by licenses, and are protected federally by the Digital Millennium Copyright Act (DMCA) and literally by digital rights management systems (DRMs). What rights does the library have, if any? The answer, in true lawyer fashion, depends on the rights granted in the license. If archiving and preservation are excluded, then libraries bear the entire burden, in theory and in practice, to sustain content that will need to be migrated to a new medium within a decade. Clifford Lynch articulated this sentiment well: "Forced obsolescence of content–the need to repurchase it over and over again for changing technologies, to hope that the content will be made available in the new format and that money can be found to acquire it again–is only one threat to the cultural and intellectual record."[4] The business of technological controls and the legislative activity around those controls are on parallel courses, and no reprieve is in sight.

What about works in the public domain? One side of the argument is the cost could be less because copyright permissions are not incurred. On the other hand, publishers could increase the price because of value-added features–e.g., XML markup for full-text searching capabilities. Another possibility for high cost is the need for a source of income.

LICENSES:
INTERSECTION OF VALUES

So, what happens during the convergence of the library, the publisher, and the law? The exchange of a print license tends to be initiated by the vendor. Since it already reflects the vendor's business model, it is up to the library to negotiate for the terms that meet the library's requirements. Librarians are entitled to strike and reword at will. It is becoming more common for libraries to add language to the license that addresses their local requirements, such as state mandated clauses, but more importantly, libraries can insert language that addresses fair use, ILL, reserves, coursepacks, MARC records or another patron discovery tool, and archival rights.

There are a few rare times when an e-book business model will not require a license, and as long as a library is satisfied with their archival rights, avoiding a license is preferable. Generally, a license will be necessary, and there are some very good model licenses from the library community that can be used with e-book, as well as e-journal, licensing. An excellent example of a model license is the Council on Library and Information Resources/Digital Library Federation Model License <http://library.yale.edu/~llicense/modlic.shtml>. While negotiating the license, it is the perfect time to let each party know what issues are important to them, even if it is not possible to include them in the license itself. The license will spell out how the subscription will be handled and should contain values that are important to each of the parties. Especially now, librarians need the license to have language that addresses the ability of the library to cancel or pare back subscriptions as necessary. Additionally, if e-books are bought with one-time money, then the license should cover archiving rights and the ability to find a mutually acceptable technology platform when it becomes necessary to migrate the content. Not all licensing language need be explicit; generalized language will sometimes be preferable to both parties, especially when speaking of the future. For example, licensing language can be used to further the interoperability of assistive technology with e-book formats or platforms, and one would want to mention the need for cooperation between systems and not specify software in the license.

The realm of fair use is, perhaps, the most polarizing force between libraries and publishers. Academic libraries, by virtue of their location, are both the beneficiaries and conduits of this privilege. As information providers, libraries' missions are about unfettered access for educational advancement. Publishers, in the other corner of the boxing ring, are determined to control and protect their intellectual property. In their world, "perfect protection would allow that all uses of a copyrighted work be accounted for: fair use and piracy would be virtually eliminated."[5] They fear unauthorized duplication and reproduction. Although DRMs are not innovative enough to distinguish patrons' legal and illegal uses, publishers could use this as an incentive to build features that limit how content is manipulated.

E-journal subscriptions are now including as a matter of course intellectual property rights such as interlibrary loan, library reserves, and coursepack rights. For example, with a one-e-book/one-user model, a library consortium will share a collection of e-books, which means each institution's user can view any of the available e-books, but a library cannot interlibrary loan one of the e-books to an institution outside of the consortium. When e-journals were first being licensed to libraries, they placed restrictions on library functions such as interlibrary loan and reserves. Now e-journal licenses routinely grant these traditional library rights, and e-book licenses should follow suit. Librarians want e-book publishers to either provide these functionalities now or plan for their future inclusion in their e-book business model.

When electronic books are purchased, libraries need to be assured that they are also buying archival rights. Since many of these titles are not being duplicated by print purchases, library values such as fair use, archival access, ILL, and library reserve rights must be addressed in an e-book license. Lucia Snowhill addresses the finer details between various disciplines, "The ability to manipulate an e-book collection easily to eliminate older editions is attractive where currency matters. In other disciplines where long-term research is essential, assurance of perpetual access will be vital."[6]

In terms of distribution models, libraries are accustomed to the mobility and ease of use of circulating print monographs. Is this possible with an electronic book? Again, the answer is it depends. Publishers have to be willing to market e-books in a manner that can be circulated like a print book; otherwise, a library's ability to rely on the doctrine of first sale is useless.

In the absence of specific clauses, language in the contract needs to cover the following issues: standards, technology access, authorized users, subscription models, withdrawn material, statistics, selection/deselection, company solvency, archiving/preservation, continued access, and planned content obsolescence. Since the authors are not proffering legal advice, critical questions will be raised. This list is not comprehensive and not in an order of importance, but grouped more by logical relationships with each other.

Standards. Given the aforementioned infancy of the e-book business, is this possible? The following content standards are in the inceptive stages:

> *Open eBook Validator.*
> < http://www.stg.brown.edu/service/oebvalid/>

> This allows publishers to test whether or not a publication is compliant with the Open eBook Publication Structure Specification. Librarians can request that vendors utilize this measure.

Open eBook Forum (OeBF).
< http://www.openebook.org/about.htm>

The web site notes "[OeBF] is a trade and standards organization dedicated to the development and promotion of electronic publishing." In 2000, the American Library Association joined the OeBF, which lends the singular library presence to the process of developing standards. Critics point to their failure to address non-Roman character sets, and mathematical and scientific notation. Librarians can, at the very least, inquire if a vendor is a member.

Online Information Exchange (ONIX) for Books.
< http://www.editeur.org/>

ONIX is the international book industry's metadata standard for books and serials, and is maintained by EDItEUR, an international group of publishers managing the progress of the standards infrastructure for electronic commerce. Librarians can insist that vendors use the latest release. The caveat is the inclusion of a digital rights management system.

There are no standards, yet, for management–i.e., how content can be manipulated, distributed, and preserved. Librarians' partnerships with publishers and technology developers are critical in the development of standards. Taking a back seat will have serious social, cultural, and economic repercussions.

Archiving/Preservation. Libraries need to bargain for the right to a hard copy. Their relationships with publishers must include agreements for the safe, opportune, and dependable deposit of content, and to secure the rights necessary to archive the material. This demands a proactive approach; "libraries must take control of their own fate and get the actual printed book to ensure that e-books do not destroy libraries."[7]

Technology Access. Libraries are sensitive to patron access and the Americans with Disabilities Act, and are justifiably concerned with the limited audio capabilities of current e-books. On the other hand, publishers, taking their cues from the 2001 court case *A & M Records v. Napster*, are worried about patrons stealing their content. On the legislative front, the Library of Congress addressed this problem. As reported in an October 28th article, their recent review of the Digital Millennium Copyright Act clarified one exception to circumventing protections, "e-books that do not allow disabled-access tools such as screen readers to function."[8]

Authorized Users. The definition for authorized users for e-book licenses should be the same definition used within e-journal licenses. The interests of distance education students are assumed to be taken into account. Academic libraries are leaning toward the distribution model of networked e-books because of their distance education capabilities.

Statistics/Usage Monitoring/Privacy. Vendors currently track usage via Internet Protocol addresses; this practice should continue. If the e-books are not on a networked system, how will privacy be maintained? Will vendors be entitled to track user behavior without compromising privacy, or without making privacy an issue at all?

Subscription Model. Licenses need to clarify how monetary figures are calculated, but not necessarily the actual cost price. Do they charge a per book maintenance or access fee? The contract should also accurately reflect how the technology will work in practice.

Company Solvency. Harking back to e-book commerce as young, a clause should be included about contingency plans if a vendor goes out of business. Libraries learned this lesson from the serial agent Faxon, their filing bankruptcy, and the fallout. Clifford Lynch asked the important questions:

> Do you have the right and the ability to reformat an e-book or a digital book in response to changes in standards or technologies or do you need to repurchase it? What happens when you upgrade or replace your e-book reader with another one? What happens when you replace the PC that might house your "library"? What happens if you replace one brand of e-book reader with another, perhaps because your reader vendor goes out of business?[9]

The license could say something to the effect–"Licensor will deliver any bought content in a tangible form to the Licensee if the Licensor becomes insolvent." This situation was imminent with netLibrary, which occurred in late 2001, until the Online Computer Library Center bought them.

Content. Does the contract address what will happen to withdrawn titles? Will an alternative format be provided? Will that format be one that can be migrated? What are the terms, and how will notification and "consent" occur? What about the continuation of access to material, if the vendor does go out of business? What are the penalties, if any, for canceling titles? Can titles be cancelled at all?

CONCLUSION–GOOD, BAD, AND UGLY

The *ugly* truth is that libraries cannot afford to sustain more annual subscription fees. The distinguishing characteristics between academic e-journals and e-books are fading. They both have content that is updated online, they have editors and review processes, they have annual subscription fees, and libraries are making hard subscription choices. Generally, the limited funds in recurrent accounts are being spent on licensed e-journals, e-journals that have high impact factors and e-journals that may be part of consortial library packages gathered into shared title collections far larger than what one library could pay for. These licensed consortial library packages, sometimes referred to as the Big Deal, have taught libraries that ever increasing annual fee business models are not sustainable without the ability to contain costs. Lately e-journal subscriptions have risen 7-10% annually[10] at a higher percentage than many library budgets. As noted by Van Orsdel, "More than 40 states report serious budget deficits. Endowed institutions are losing investment income, and library spending is being cut just about everywhere. Academic libraries face perhaps the most widespread budget losses in decades."[11] For example, Dennis Dillon, Associate Director for Research Services at The University of Texas at Austin, evaluates subscription e-book fees against the one-time cost for print books by calculating the e-book price for ten years. Even when an e-book business model is attractive, such as when a library gains unlimited user access to more research content on the Web than they would have with a print copy of a title, libraries are wary to begin another annual subscription cost. Libraries need the flexibility to choose the content that is important to their users in order to be fiscally responsible with their budgets.

Libraries are at odds, philosophically, with both publishers and the current legal framework. Libraries, as institutions, are the physical embodiment of the cultural and intellectual record. The conversion of the United States' literary heritage into e-book form is not going to be quick, cheap, occurring in leaps and bounds, nor methodical, and with the publishing industry holding all the copyright permission cards, so to speak, they can stack the deck as they please. Regarding the future, "Libraries, which make systematic, institutional investments in content on behalf of society as a whole, must be particularly vocal and articulate advocates of the need for preservation."[12]

There would be a *bad* future for e-book business models and licenses if the interested parties did not communicate with each other. This will not be the case because publishers recognize the benefits of communication, "One advantage of entering the e-content business is that we publishers have much more contact with our customers and receive much more user feedback. Through this dialogue I am sure we will develop better e-content and enhanced services,"[13] and librarians do too:

> Those of us who occupy the existing links in the traditional chain of scholarly information need to find ways to transfer the inherent strengths, as well as the checks and balances of the traditional arrangement into the new environment. Ultimately it is to no one's advantage if the actions of libraries financially squeeze authors, publishers, and distributors; and it is not to the advantage of authors, publishers, and distributors to forgo the reliability and predictability of the library market for the uncertainties of selling scholarly materials directly to consumers.[14]

Concurrent with our business model and license discussions, the e-book industry is in a state of flux. A cursory view of any literature reveals the following words in many of the headlines: bankruptcy, mergers, and acquisitions. As long as fear, fear of illegal sharing of content and fear of no content to share, does not dictate the discussions, e-books will succeed in the library market.

The first e-books mirrored their print counterparts' content, and in some cases their graphical presentation. E-books have continued to evolve, such as The New Grove Dictionary of Music and Musicians into grovemusic.com, and so do their business models. It is a *good* time to be working with electronic content and intellectual property. Just as publishers and librarians have made great strides in constructing how e-journals will work in the library environment, the same foundation is being built for e-books right now.

AN ALTERNATIVE:
A DIGITAL LENDING RIGHT

James Foley, taking his lead from the Europeans, suggests a Digital Lending Right (DLR). In his words, it is "a publicly-funded, collectively-administered, blanket licensing scheme for the noncommercial, private use of digital works."[15] The courts, passing judgment in the 1994 case *American Geophysical Union v. Texaco Inc.*, suggested a licensing design that was supported by private resources and governed by a copyright collective. He analyzes the benefits from an economical perspective, noting that the more copyright transactions there are, the lower the price for each transaction. So, in the abstract sense, "a single, unified administration of a copyright collective would be the most economically efficient."[16] How does the library fit into this scheme? He explains it thus:

> The Library of Congress could act as an independent arbiter of usage, while consolidating the accounting to one entity, or by contracting out facets of the administration to collectives that are then regulated. As with the [Public Lending Right] schemes, sampling could be used to estimate use in a fair and impartial way, open to public inspection. Libraries are uniquely situated to sample use. There would be no discrimination between major label (or any major publisher) and independent artists, as there would be no pecuniary incentive to do so.[17]

One possible obstacle to the backing of a DLR is the issue of assignability. Once a DLR plan was centralized and nationalized, it could attain reciprocity with foreign countries' authors and publishers. This could pave the way toward building a shared intellectual commons. In the words of Lawrence Lessig, "Our past had a commons that could not be designed away; that commons gave our culture great value. What value the commons of the future could bring us is something we are just beginning to see."[18]

NOTES

1. Dillon, Dennis. "E-Books: The University of Texas Experience, Part I." *Library Hi Tech* 19, no. 2 (2001): 113.

2. Lynch, Clifford. "The Battle to Define the Future of the Book in the Digital World," *First Monday* 6, no. 6 (June 2001), <http://firstmonday.org/issues/issue6_6/lynch/index.html>, (accessed September 30, 2003).

3. Jacobs, Ian. "E-Books and Online Publishing: A Publisher's Perspective." *The Charleston Advisor* 4, no. 1 (July 2002): 60.

4. Lynch, Clifford. "The Battle to Define the Future of the Book in the Digital World," *First Monday* 6, no. 6 (June 2001), <http://firstmonday.org/issues/issue6_6/lynch/index.html>, (accessed September 30, 2003).

5. Foley, Joshua H. "Enter the Library: Creating a Digital Lending Right." *Connecticut Journal of International Law* 16, no. 369 (Spring 2001).

6. Snowhill, Lucia. "E-Books and Their Future in Academic Libraries."*D-Lib Magazine* 7, no. 7/8 (July/August 2001), <http://www.dlib.org/dlib/july01/snowhill/07snowhill.html>, (accessed September 29, 2003).

7. Cohen, James. "Endangered Research: The Proliferation of E-Books and Their Potential Threat to the Fair Use Clause." *Journal of Intellectual Property Law* 9, no. 163 (Fall 2001).

8. Borland, John. "Feds Grant DMCA Exceptions." CNET News.com, (October 28, 2003): <http://news.com.com/2100-1028-5098639.html>, (accessed November 1, 2003).

9. Lynch, Clifford. "The Battle to Define the Future of the Book in the Digital World," *First Monday* 6, no. 6 (June 2001), <http://firstmonday.org/issues/issue6_6/lynch/index.html>, (accessed September 30, 2003).

10. Van Orsdel, Lee; Born, Kathleen. "Big Chill on the Big Deal?" *Library Journal* 128, no. 7 (April 15, 2003): 56.

11. Ibid.

12. Lynch, Clifford. "The Battle to Define the Future of the Book in the Digital World," *First Monday* 6, no. 6 (June 2001), <http://firstmonday.org/issues/issue6_6/lynch/index.html>, (accessed September 30, 2003).

13. Jacobs, Ian. "E-Books and Online Publishing: A Publisher's Perspective." *The Charleston Advisor* 4, no. 1 (July 2002): 60-61.

14. Dillon, Dennis. "Digital Books: Making Them Work for Publishers and Libraries." *College and Research Libraries News* 61, no. 5 (May 2000): 391-393.

15. Foley, Joshua H. "Enter the Library: Creating a Digital Lending Right." *Connecticut Journal of International Law* 16, no. 369 (Spring 2001).

16. Ibid.

17. Ibid.

18. Lessig, Lawrence. *Code and Other Laws of Cyberspace.* New York, New York: Basic Books, 1999, p. 141.

REFERENCES

Borland, John. "Feds Grant DMCA Exceptions." CNET News.com, (October 28, 2003): <http://news.com.com/2100-1028-5098639.html>, (accessed November 1, 2003).

Cohen, James. "Endangered Research: The Proliferation of E-Books and Their Potential Threat to the Fair Use Clause." *Journal of Intellectual Property Law* 9, no. 163 (Fall 2001).

Dillon, Dennis. "Digital Books: Making Them Work for Publishers and Libraries." *College and Research Libraries News* 61, no. 5 (May 2000): 391-393.

Dillon, Dennis. "E-Books: The University of Texas Experience, Part I." *Library Hi Tech* 19, no. 2 (2001): 113-124.

Foley, Joshua H. "Enter the Library: Creating a Digital Lending Right." *Connecticut Journal of International Law* 16, no. 369 (Spring 2001).

Jacobs, Ian. "E-Books and Online Publishing: A Publisher's Perspective." *The Charleston Advisor* 4, no. 1 (July 2002): 60-61.

Lessig, Lawrence. *Code and Other Laws of Cyberspace.* New York, New York: Basic Books, 1999.

Lynch, Clifford. "The Battle to Define the Future of the Book in the Digital World," *First Monday* 6, no. 6 (June 2001), <http://firstmonday.org/issues/issue6_6/lynch/index.html>, (accessed September 30, 2003).

Snowhill, Lucia. "E-Books and Their Future in Academic Libraries."*D-Lib Magazine* 7, no. 7/8 (July/August 2001), <http://www.dlib.org/dlib/july01/snowhill/07snowhill.html>, (accessed September 29, 2003).

Van Orsdel, Lee; Born, Kathleen. "Big Chill on the Big Deal?" *Library Journal* 128, no. 7 (April 15, 2003): 51-56.

Consortial Licensing Issues:
One Consortium's Viewpoint

Anne E. McKee

SUMMARY. Although library consortia are thought to be relative new-comers to the library field, in actuality consortia have existed for several decades. As consortia have become much more complex (multi-type versus single; "buying club" focused versus those with a focus on impacting scholarly communication), it becomes a daunting process to effectively meld the needs of each member institution. This article will briefly discuss the history of consortia as they relate to the library marketplace and examine the issues and trends facing consortia today. Negotiation tools which can help in obtaining fair and equitable content agreements will be highlighted. *[Article copies available for a fee from The Haworth Document Delivery Service: 1-800-HAWORTH. E-mail address: <docdelivery@haworthpress.com> Website: <http://www.HaworthPress.com> © 2005 by The Haworth Press, Inc. All rights reserved.]*

KEYWORDS. Consortia, Greater Western Library Alliance, history of consortia, licensing, negotiation

Anne E. McKee is Program Officer for Resource Sharing, Greater Western Library Alliance, Glendale, AZ (E-mail: mckeea@lindahall.org).

[Haworth co-indexing entry note]: "Consortial Licensing Issues: One Consortium's Viewpoint." McKee, Anne E. Co-published simultaneously in *Journal of Library Administration* (The Haworth Information Press, an imprint of The Haworth Press, Inc.) Vol. 42, No. 3/4, 2005, pp. 129-141; and: *Licensing in Libraries: Practical and Ethical Aspects* (ed: Karen Rupp-Serrano) The Haworth Information Press, an imprint of The Haworth Press, Inc., 2005, pp. 129-141. Single or multiple copies of this article are available for a fee from The Haworth Document Delivery Service [1-800-HAWORTH, 9:00 a.m. - 5:00 p.m. (EST). E-mail address: docdelivery@haworthpress.com].

http://www.haworthpress.com/web/JLA
© 2005 by The Haworth Press, Inc. All rights reserved.
Digital Object Identifier: 10.1300/J111v42n03_09

INTRODUCTION

While some may regard the emergence of library consortia as a late-comer to the library marketplace, consortia in some form have actually been around for decades. However, just as libraries have become adept at adapting and transforming themselves due to the available technology and trends in the library world, so too have consortia become agile in altering and converting themselves to best suit the needs of their members. This article will examine the current consortial trends in regard to licensing issues.

DEVELOPMENT OF CONSORTIA

A consortium develops when a group of libraries join together to work cooperatively. While there are as many type of consortia as there are libraries (i.e., "buying club," multi-type, user focused [as in health sciences or corporate], geographic, etc.), a consortium usually begins when a group of libraries decide that their individual missions, objectives and services to users could be enhanced by working together cooperatively. As early as the 1880s articles were published in *Library Journal* on library cooperation and encouraging libraries to work together. Thereafter interest remained high in working cooperatively.[1]

Geographic relationship was one of the earliest methods to creating a consortium.[2] Like institutions in the same geographic area (primarily if they were within the same state and subject perhaps to the same guidelines in fiduciary responsibilities) were easiest to create and maintain. Some of the earliest consortium cooperative projects were (and may remain) shared cataloging and interlibrary loan reciprocity agreements. As technology changed, consortia were able to mold and adapt their guidelines and cooperative agreements to embrace the functional aspects of the technology. Library consortia, for example, were "the first to take advantage of networked computing."[3] With the advent of available non-print mediums (beginning with microforms and quickly morphing into digital information), as well as static or rapidly declining budgets, library consortia have really come to the forefront.

As the informal or casual policies of interlibrary loan or reciprocal borrowing agreements have turned into cohesive, established missions and policies for established consortia, "libraries [began] taking the consortia to which they belong with a great deal more seriousness. . . ."[4] As the economy worsened, the Internet was employed to become the publishing medium for many forms of scholarly communication.[5] Publishers, both scholarly and for-profit, began to realize the possibilities of electronic publishing, the bundling of journal packages–either by publisher or topic–began to appear. The offers made to libraries for this electronic information became much more complex and very time-consuming for each library to keep updated. Libraries learned that there was strength in numbers.[6] Libraries quickly determined economies of scale could also work in the electronic environment and turned to the library consortia they belonged to for a way of getting the most "bang" for their rapidly shrinking buck. In turn, publishers and content providers as well as vendors began to realize that consortial purchasing could also be advantageous.[7] Landesman and Van Reenan state it well "[Libraries] are able to expand the reach of titles that otherwise would have a small audience by bundling them with titles in higher demand, thus making the more specialized (and sometimes weaker) titles attractive to the consortium."[8]

A good example of how a consortium can evolve is demonstrated by the Greater Western Library Alliance (GWLA). GWLA (formerly the Big 12 Plus Libraries Consortium), is a consortium of 30 research institutions located in 15 states as far east as Illinois and as far west as Washington State. It began several years ago as a regional group interested in ILL reciprocity. From these beginnings, the consortium (which has gone through at least four name changes) has evolved, grown, and matured. While there was some membership restriction, more stringent membership criteria has been enacted over the past few years and it is interesting to note that some of the very early members who left the consortium years ago are no longer eligible for membership. Requirements include:

1. Must be an ARL institution and
2. A Doctoral/Research–Extensive category under the new Carnegie classification or
3. A Principal land grant institution.

A prospective member must first send a formal letter of application to the GWLA Board. A review process has been formalized whereby two designated members of the GWLA Board of Directors (of which one is usually the current Board Chair), as well as the two GWLA administrative staff, visit the institution requesting membership for a day long meeting with campus and library administration as well as pertinent departments within the library (Collection Development and Interlibrary Loan/Resource Sharing). If the site team feels the institution requesting membership should be endorsed, it is forwarded to the GWLA Board for approval. If the board approves the application, the issue is then sent to the full membership and 3/4ths of the current membership must vote affirmatively to accept the new member.

Today GWLA has a paid Executive Director and a Program Officer for Resource Sharing. GWLA's strategic plan encourages and promotes new avenues for scholarly communication (they are one of the founders of BioOne) as well as a robust Resource Sharing/Document Delivery program and licensing program.

LICENSING ISSUES

Although libraries realized the potential of working through consortia for subscribing to or purchasing information, other issues arose almost as quickly. Some have been resolved by evolving accepted practices within the marketplace but other issues still remain that must be continuously confronted and dealt with on a case-by-case basis by libraries, consortia and commercial entities.

It is widely known and accepted that many academic libraries belong to more than one consortium and many if not most belong to several at the same time. Some of these are politically motivated (state legislature mandated, for example), some are the result of the library "shopping around" to obtain the most products by the cheapest package possible, and others are the result of institutions making permanent alliances with other like-minded institutions that have same general goals and missions. Other consortia are formed only for a specific transaction and then disband almost as quickly.

Consortia managers are increasingly encountering members who maintain memberships in larger groups that may offer good discounts on basic services while maintaining membership in smaller consortia that focus on specialized services or needs.[9] There are significant inherent problems and challenges when working with any group and consortia are no exception. As each institution has its distinct rules, regulations and personality, licensing products can sometimes be a daunting prospect.

Another factor that must be weighed is the fact that many consortia (either formally or informally) allow for "associate" members to join. In some cases, the associate or affiliate member role may actually be formalized with a Memorandum of Understanding (MOU) or contract. These affiliates may even pay [lower] membership dues. Other consortia may allow non-members registration privileges for only a certain product. In these cases, the commercial entity must agree to allow these non-members into the agreement and the consortia agrees that these "affiliates" receive the rights and privileges of consortia membership for this specific transaction. Some consortia will affix a surcharge on each licensing agreement for the participation of each non-member. Some publishers are very open to this idea as it helps gain access to new markets, other publishers will not allow it, and still others decide on an institution-by-institution basis.

The daunting process, however, of trying to meld every institution's needs can be problematic at best and almost discouraging at worst. Not only must consortia deal with these problems and in some cases, establish institution-by-institution work-arounds, but the publisher/vendor must also institutionalize processes for each consortium. This is done with the realization that the process could change from year to year as participants join in or leave an agreement.

How should a consortium proceed? Quite simply, they need to establish working policies that help support the goals and objectives of the consortium and the institutions within its membership. Such policies lay a firm foundation for future trends. These policies must also be widely articulated so that the commercial entities understand the intent and needs of the members. Some of these policies may remain static and others may change according to the stipulations of different agreements. Establishing policies on which all members must agree is not something that can be done quickly and quietly. It is often a time-consuming, sometimes almost painstaking process and each step of the process must be continuously communicated to all members. However, if a successful outcome is the expectation and all members mutually agree upon the policies developed, then the time spent is well worth the final outcome.

ISSUES TO CONSIDER

When presented a proposal for information, the first question asked should always be "Does this product help foster the ongoing policies of the consortium's institutions?" If a product is determined to have only peripheral information relevant to the mission of the institutional members, the proposal most often ends up dying a quick and painless death. These types of packages usually are never even forwarded to the consortium members for their consideration.

The question as to whether to forward a proposal to the rest of the consortium can be a difficult decision in and of itself. This is yet another example of why consortium policies are so important to have in place and agreed on by all members. Some consortia have a "first refusal" committee that receives all new proposals and ascertains (based once again on the missions and policies of the consortium and its members) if the proposal should be forwarded to the membership as a whole. Other consortia may wish to have all proposals automatically forwarded with no value statement attached. It is also fairly common for consortia to have a consortial staff member (whether paid administrative staff or volunteer) act as liaison between the publishers and the consortium. This consortium staff member would then either make the judgment whether or not to forward a proposal further depending on the specific policies of his/her organization.

A second challenge is the inundation of publisher's special offers. On an almost daily basis, consortia (especially the larger consortia) find an almost dizzying array of new offers filling up their e-mail inbox or fax machine. This makes it difficult to separate the "wheat from the chaff" and focus on those proposals that offer a greater benefit to the consortium.[10] While it is difficult enough for consortium staff to receive the onslaught of proposals, it is even more difficult if there IS no paid administrative consortial staff but instead dependency on a volunteer librarian or group of librarians. These volunteers must juggle the responsibilities of their day-to-day jobs with the ever-increasing workload of consortial agreements. Regardless of position, neither a paid consortium officer nor a volunteer from a member library finds it easy to understand the many and varied ways publishers and content providers price their products.

A challenge faced almost daily is the attempt to decipher the complex pricing structures that are affixed to the electronic product packages. As Baker states, "consortia are overwhelmed with pricing models that need detailed instructions for interpretations."[11] So intricately priced are many products that it may involve much face, phone, and e-mail contact with the sales representative to fully understand the complicated pricing scheme. Consortia need and should demand easily understood pricing information that can be quickly and easily disseminated among the consortial members. This price must apply to those consortia that may have mixed-type libraries as members. A hotly debated topic of pricing continues to be FTE versus simultaneous users.

Pricing by FTE has become the preferred method by the commercial sectors but it may pose many problems to academic consortia. One question that must always be asked is "Just WHAT does the publisher consider FTE?" All too frequently, FTE is considered not just "full-time enrollment" but rather "full-time employment" as well. Some publishers and content providers are determined to include not only the faculty and students of an academic institution but to attempt to include *all* employees of the institution. This is done with the thought that perhaps all institutional employees may want to access the information some day and in some format. While this is slowly changing, thanks to the ongoing efforts that consortia have worked on in partnership with publishers and content providers, it is not uncommon to still receive proposals where the FTE on the publisher's/content provider's behalf counts all faculty, students, and employees of an institution.

This obviously can serve as a negotiation item. It can also help to educate publishers and content providers on who will most likely utilize the electronic information they are marketing. If the product offers more general information that may appeal to a wider user base, FTE pricing might make sense. However, one must ensure that the institution's FTE is being utilized and *not* the FTE as quoted by the publisher/content provider. For those subject-specific products that would appeal to a smaller, finite group (i.e., faculty and declared majors), FTE should only be considered for those faculty and students in that specific discipline.

While many publishers/content providers and even some consortia prefer FTE, simultaneous users (SU) may be the preferred method to other consortia. A consortium or academic library must carefully consider what is the realistic number of users who want to access this material. If a consortium estimates too low, there could be frustrating turn-aways for the users. Estimate the number too high and more money was spent than needed to be. The full number of SUs may go unused.

A compromise (backed up with an institution's prevailing statistics) may be to start with a conservative number of simultaneous users and then write into the license an agreed upon sliding scale of SU units that can be automatically upgraded to the maximum number imposed by the institution. Some publishers and content providers actually allow you to choose between FTE pricing and SU units. It may also be possible to begin with one type of pricing and then alternate to the 2nd pricing scheme depending upon the parameters set forth by the consortium and content providers.

Once the pricing has been decoded and a decision has been made on FTE versus SU units, it is imperative to closely examine the proposal and licensing language. As important as it is for each consortium to have their collection development policies in place, it is also, if not more so, imperative for the consortia to have established policies on the language terms that are and are not acceptable.

One stipulation that usually elicits groans is the publisher imposed "benchmark." The benchmark requirements add yet another complicated level to an already convoluted process. Not only must a consortium decide if an offer meets the established goals and policies of the group, and decipher and determine if the proposed pricing structure is fair and equitable, the consortium must also distribute the process to the group and spend an inordinate amount of time polling members to see if there is enough interest to meet the benchmark. Invariably, there are members who are "really interested" but do not want to make a commitment either way until the benchmark has been met. This continuous back and forth, give and take, between the designated consortium negotiator and the individual members involves expending twice as much energy and time as a normal proposal would. All too frequently, the benchmark is not made and all the liaison work was done in vain. While some publishers will at least consider letting a number less than the benchmark target still go forward, it is almost always at a higher price, which may cause the other interested parties to withdraw as well.

There are, however, some positive signs that at least some publishers or content providers understand the complexities and problems of setting benchmarks. More of the marketplace needs to follow the example of Alexander Street Press, L.L.C. Former executives of the former Chadwyck-Healey group founded Alexander Street Press in 2000. Their specialty is publishing electronic works in the humanities and they sell the complete set of a specific work or offer paid, annual subscriptions to the material. They have a rather novel approach to licensing and consortia that is fair and equitable for both sides.

Alexander Street Press discounts primarily to consortia and offers for those institutions that may want to purchase the material outright, excellent, well-reviewed products at good prices. They do not set a benchmark on how many libraries need to be involved but instead offer a base discount to a consortium's members (whether one or many). The base discount rises during the fiscal year as more products are purchased. A unique feature of Alexander Street Press is that they will proactively credit back the difference in purchase price for those members who may have purchased earlier in their selling year. Even better, they willingly send a refund check back to the institution rather than a credit if the institution so desires. This allows the institution to use the refunded amount for other information and not be forced to use it on Alexander Street

Press products. Additionally, their licenses are user/library friendly, short and to the point. As this model is one of convenience and ease to the consortium, more publishers and content providers should attempt to pattern their offers in this manner.

Invoicing or how to invoice is always another important factor for the consortium to raise with the content provider/publisher from the very onset of discussions. Quite simply, most content providers want to cut one invoice and bill centrally through the consortium. (The consortium will receive one invoice, issue one check in payment, and will in turn invoice each participant individually.) Publishers and content providers feel this practice is justified as the consortium is getting a price break to assume some of the cost of the work. It saves the publisher/content provider time and money to only cut one invoice and book one payment in return. This practice can be an outright daunting prospect for those consortia that use only librarian volunteers or for those consortia that may have a very small number of paid administrative staff.

A related aspect of central invoicing is the cash flow issue. This is of primary concern for those consortia that do not have a central purchasing fund upon which to draw. While most consortia have some operating reserves that could be utilized for very short periods of time (between needing to pay an invoice to the publisher and waiting for the funds to come in from each member), it is not sound business practice to continually dip into operating reserves. This has forced some consortia to be innovative in how they operate the cash flow.

The Greater Western Library Alliance (GWLA) is an example of a consortium which does not have a central acquisitions fund from which to purchase electronic products. Member institutions must pay for any new products out of their acquisitions budgets. Desiring to head off any potential cash flow problems in the future, GWLA's Finance Committee studied the issues and instituted new guidelines within the past year. These include ascertaining a firm price for a product and proactively invoicing a member PRIOR TO receiving the publisher's/content provider's official invoice. This practice helps the consortium receive the payments in time to pay the official invoice. This is the preferred model so operating reserves would not have to be dipped into even for a few weeks, possibly resulting in realized lower interest. Another cash flow procedure instituted was changing the issuance of the annual membership dues invoices, thus allowing GWLA to capitalize on more "banked" money at the end of the calendar year. Lastly, as GWLA's shared electronic purchases have increased, a cost-recovery surcharge has been assessed for non-member participants in GWLA agreements.

Another unpleasant truth about central invoicing and cash flow considerations is the sometimes-necessary evil of needing to "chase" down payment for consortial agreements. While this is fortunately not a large problem for consortia, institutions that lag in prompt payments could impact negatively on a consortium's cash flow. The problem almost always lies OUTSIDE the library at a central office responsible for cutting checks for the entire institution or state. Academic institutions all have their own financial plans and cash flow policies. Some institutions and states privately admit that they realize more revenue in keeping the money in their funds until the last possible moment than they lose in having to pay "late" fees!

Some of the largest challenges that consortia face in licensing, however, are the stipulations required by the content providers and publishers in agreements and licenses. Gone are the heady days of budgetary growth (or at least budget maintenance). Instead libraries and consortia are faced with ever-decreasing budgets. It was just a few years ago that libraries were quick to license "big ticket" items and at least (reluctantly) agree to stringent publisher requirements as the increased access to information was considered a fair trade-off. Some of the more common restrictions in contract licenses included: no cancellation of print or electronic titles during the length of the agreement; non-allowance of utilizing the material for ILL; bundled packages–whether the library needed all information in the package or not. These restrictions severely limited the creativity of the consortia or library in how they could institute cutbacks. Having to protect these large collections of very expensive journals had the unpleasant effect of forcing libraries to cancel many of the lower (and fairer) priced titles that were not included in the electronic packages.[12]

Today with annual and even semi-annual budget reductions, libraries are beginning to declare emphatically that no package is now off limits when it comes to saving money. As the larger electronic packages reach the end of their agreements, many libraries are re-negotiating the terms of the offer. They are steadfastly refusing agreements that have a non-cancellation clause. They are exerting their rights to cancel paper and retain electronic only and they will refuse any proposal that does not allow ILL in any format. More and more libraries are insisting on "blow up clauses." These stipulate that the agreement between publisher/content provider and consortium/library may be terminated or re-negotiated for better terms by either side in cases of financial exigency. Consortia and their members have become very savvy negotiators and are not afraid any longer of walking away from a deal or canceling some core journals.

NEGOTIATING TOOLS CONSORTIA CAN USE

While librarians have shied away from hard-nosed negotiations in the past, it is simply good business practice to obtain the best agreement possible for all sides involved. In the following (but by no means exhaustive) list, are some salient, matter-of-fact points that consortia and libraries could utilize when negotiating an agreement.

A. From the very first meeting with your sales or publisher representative, always inquire as to when their fiscal year ends. This is some of the most powerful information you can know about a publisher or content provider. The publishers and content providers understand that year-end money sometimes appears in a library's coffers needing to be spent immediately (though this phenomenon has become almost a thing of the past). It is important to understand that consortia have greater bargaining power nearer the end of the publisher's fiscal year. If the sales representative or company/publisher itself has had a rather lackluster selling year, they may feel more inclined to deal more aggressively. These circumstances could also aid the consortium in re-opening negotiations for a wanted but never purchased product.

B. Ensure from the outset the main consortium negotiator knows exactly who is the decision maker on the publisher's/content provider's side for approving packages and discounts. If it is known at the beginning that the sales representative does not have authority to make discount approval, insist that the person who *does* have that authority be present at all negotiation meetings. This effectively eliminates the down time that can occur when a sales representative must go back to his/her employer and consult about discounts.

C. It is also very helpful to ascertain immediately who on the publisher's/content provider's side has final authority for approving licensing terms. Request that this person sit in on all license negotiation meetings as this also eliminates down time. Another interesting option to request is that the commercial entity reads any and all documents the consortium has produced stating their required and preferred licensing language. Ideally, this information would be located in an easy-to-find file on the consortium's web page. These can help to considerably shorten the negotiations on licensing.

D. Negotiate for agreements that do not carry a required "benchmark." These require many staff hours in contact time between the consortium and its members. Negotiate instead on discounts that increase as more members join in.

E. A negotiating point that the Greater Western Library Alliance is trying to now place in new agreements is for the publisher/content provider to provide one free print copy for each title in the agreement. These can then be placed in an archive for use by all consortium members. If the publisher or content provider balks at this request, try to obtain a very deep discount for the paper copies.

F. Depending on your consortium's guidelines, negotiate permission to extend the offer(s) to libraries outside your membership. A good bargaining tool is to demonstrate to the content provider the possible increased penetration of his/her material to a wider audience. These agreements also provide great public relations marketing for the consortia.

G. Lastly, a small but important negotiation point: try to arrange for the content provider to be the responsible party for mailing out the final licenses to all participants. It is a greatly-appreciated timesaver for the volunteer or paid consortial staff member and also saves the consortium mailing costs.

CONCLUSION

Consortia fill a very real, basic need for both their members and for the publishing market. Through consortia, resource sharing and new trends in scholarly communication have been instituted, and libraries and publishers realize that utilizing consortia can be a win-win situation for all. Through ethical negotiations, both consortia and publishers gain a trust and admiration for the other side. As Alberico succinctly stated, "an effective consortium becomes the center of a constellation of trust relationships."[13]

REFERENCES

1. Sharon L. Bostick and Robert E. Dugan, "The History and Development of Academic Library Consortia in the United States: An Overview," *Journal of Academic Librarianship* 27 (March, 2001): 128.

2. Ralph Alberico, "Academic Library Consortia in Transition," *New Directions for Higher Education* no.120 (Winter 2002): 63.

3. Ibid.

4. Margaret Landesman and Johann Van Reenen, "Creating Congruence," JEP the Journal of Electronic Publishing v.6 (December, 2000) www.press.umich.edu/jep/06-02/landesman.html.

5. Alberico, " Academic Library in Transition," p. 64.

6. Scott Carlson, "Libraries' Consortium Conundrum," Information Technology, *Chronicle of Higher Education*, p. A30, October 10, 2003.

7. Landesman and Van Reenan, "Creating Congruence."

8. Ibid.

9. Carlson, "Libraries' Consortium Conundrum," p. A30.

10. Angee Baker, "The Impact of Consortia on Database Licensing" *Computers in Libraries* 20 (June 2000) 46.

11. Ibid.

12. Landesman and Van Reenan, "Creating Congruence."

13. Alberico, "Academic Library Consortia in Transition" p. 69.

Software
for Managing Licenses and Compliance

Yem S. Fong

Heather Wicht

SUMMARY. As more collection dollars are allocated to the purchase of electronic content, the management of these resources continues to challenge libraries. In order to streamline this activity, and to improve compliance with license terms and conditions, libraries are exploring a number of software solutions. These range from tracking data in spreadsheets or developing local databases to buying software from commercial vendors. This article reviews the progress of e-resource software development, such as the Colorado Alliance's Gold Rush software, Innovative Interfaces' Electronic Resource Management module, EBSCO's journal management services and others, and explores what these products are designed to do. *[Article copies available for a fee from The Haworth Document Delivery Service: 1-800-HAWORTH. E-mail address: <docdelivery@haworthpress.com> Website: <http://www.HaworthPress.com> © 2005 by The Haworth Press, Inc. All rights reserved.]*

KEYWORDS. Electronic resources, licenses, use permissions, electronic journals, serials, subscription management, aggregator databases, OpenURL, link resolvers

Yem S. Fong is Associate Professor and Faculty Director for Electronic Resources Development and Information Delivery (E-mail: fongj@colorado.edu); and Heather Wicht is Assistant Professor and Electronic Resources Librarian (E-mail: heather. wicht@colorado.edu), both at the University of Colorado at Boulder Libraries.

[Haworth co-indexing entry note]: "Software for Managing Licenses and Compliance." Fong, Yem S., and Heather Wicht. Co-published simultaneously in *Journal of Library Administration* (The Haworth Information Press, an imprint of The Haworth Press, Inc.) Vol. 42, No. 3/4, 2005, pp. 143-161; and: *Licensing in Libraries: Practical and Ethical Aspects* (ed: Karen Rupp-Serrano) The Haworth Information Press, an imprint of The Haworth Press, Inc., 2005, pp. 143-161. Single or multiple copies of this article are available for a fee from The Haworth Document Delivery Service [1-800-HAWORTH, 9:00 a.m. - 5:00 p.m. (EST). E-mail address: docdelivery@haworthpress.com].

INTRODUCTION

Statistics in the literature report that the growth in electronic resources–full-text journals, databases, annuals, electronic books, and other digital material–continues to consume larger percentages of libraries' collection budgets, often over fifty percent of new serials funds.[1] The increased availability and popularity of electronic content is further complicated by new publishing and subscription models from both commercial and scholarly publishers. Adding to this is the growing trend for libraries to participate in consortia purchases with complex licensing agreements for online bundled subscriptions, back-files, and databases.

As a result, significant organizational shifts are taking place to facilitate the process of negotiating, purchasing, tracking, and providing access to these resources. One of the most important activities is keeping track of the conditions, terms, and use permissions specified in each license. This article reviews the progress of electronic resource management systems that are in various stages of development. Since it is difficult to assess these products solely in terms of licensing, this article will also include some coverage of key e-resource management functions. The authors will also briefly consider e-journal management products, such as EBSCO's A-to-Z, and will explore more fully the functionality of the Colorado Alliance's Gold Rush product, and Innovative Interfaces' Electronic Resource Management module.

Software products currently in use for managing e-resources fall into three primary categories: (1) e-journal management software–used to identify and update local journal holdings from print and electronic subscriptions, including titles in aggregator databases, and to provide linking; (2) locally developed databases–created to track license terms, order and renewal information and collect administrative data such as URLs, administrator passwords, vendor contacts, etc.; (3) commercial e-resource management software–developed as a stand-alone product or as an integrated library system (ILS) module that may utilize data already existent in the library's other ILS modules. Many libraries also rely on their local acquisitions system for noting important license details in their order records. In addition, many institutions track e-resource information in spreadsheets, e-mails and attachments, paper files, and often in the brain cells of over-burdened librarians. Depending on the organization, the process of acquiring, managing, and supporting electronic collections may require substantial time and resource commitments from staff in several departments. It is not surprising then that libraries are searching for guidance in best practices, and looking for software tools to facilitate the management of e-resources and licenses.

In 2000, the Digital Library Federation (DLF) conducted a comprehensive survey and analysis of locally developed systems (existent at the time) as part of a larger study on practices related to the selection and presentation of commercially available electronic resources.[2] Recognizing that many libraries are on the same path in search of solutions for managing electronic resources, Tim Jewell identified functions and data elements supported in varying degrees by these systems. They are listed in detail in the appendix of the 2001 report.[3] In summary the report identifies eight broad functional and operational areas: (1) listing and descriptive functions; (2) descriptive/bibliographic data elements; (3) license related data elements/display and reporting; (4) financial/purchasing data; (5) process/status information; (6) systems/technical/access information; (7) contact and support information; (8) usage information. As expected, similarities and differences in recording and displaying information emerged among the systems reviewed.

In the area of license terms and conditions, the systems were more different than alike. Information on licenses included data elements such as date signed, duration, license terms, and use permissions–interlibrary loan, e-reserves, course-packs, downloading, copying, printing, walk-ins, remote access, and restrictions on commercial use. Other data tracked included: user guidelines, confidentiality, special terms, archival rights, links to scanned images, location of paper license, and active or inactive status. As a result of this in-depth investigation, Jewell observed that it could be feasible " . . . to devise common functional and data definitions and standards that could be used as the basis for future design and implementation work–by libraries working individually or collectively or by vendors."[4]

Following the publication of this study in 2001, DLF sponsored public forums, workshops, and American Library Association meetings to address the issue of developing these standards. The DLF Electronic Resource Management Initiative (ERMI), working cooperatively with the National Information Standards Organization (NISO), assembled a working group of representatives from libraries with local systems and representatives from vendors and publishers such as EBSCO, Ex Libris, Innovative Interfaces, Serials Solutions, and others. An overview of the work of the ERMI, along with drafts and reports, as released, on system specifications, standards, architecture elements, and best practices, can be found on the project Web site, http://www.library.cornell.edu/cts/elicensestudy/. The group's mission and goal is stated as follows: "This project will develop common specifications and tools for managing the license agreements, related administrative information, and internal processes associated with collections of licensed electronic resources."

E-JOURNAL MANAGEMENT SOFTWARE

Since the late nineties, libraries have struggled with the problem of identifying and locating serials holdings, whether in print or online, and whether e-journals are provided via publisher Web sites or found in aggregated multidisciplinary databases. As a result, a number of commercially developed products are available to assist in identifying and managing electronic serials collections. In addition, several institutions have developed in-house e-journal access and management systems, such as the University of North Carolina, Greensboro's Journal Finder product (http://journalfinder.uncg.edu/uncg/).[5]

Products such as Serials Solutions (www.serialssolutions.com) and TDNet (www.tdnet.com) have been available for several years. New enhancements and features continue to be offered by these companies, such as greater searching capabilities, OpenURL linking, and MARC records for journal titles. However, these services are not intended to function as tools for tracking and managing license terms and use restrictions. Since the focus of these products is e-journal management and they have been evaluated elsewhere in the literature, this article will consider more recent trends regarding these types of services.[6]

The latest entrants into the marketplace are subscription agents and vendors with products such as SwetsWise (https://www.swetswise.com/) and EBSCO's A-to-Z and EBSCOhost Electronic Journals Service (EJS) (www.ebsco.com/). Similar to Serials Solutions and TDNet, these products offer a Web-based interface as a single entry point for locating serials titles. Both products offer access to large databases of full-text titles and publishers. A-to-Z provides basic and advanced searching by title, publisher, ISSN, and subject with coverage of 40,000 unique titles from more than 530 database and e-journal packages from around 100 publishers and vendors. SwetsWise offers Boolean searching and cites a database of more than 7,800 full-text publications from 300 publishers. Both products track usage for titles searched within the database. The SwetsWise product also offers a decentralized subscription ordering and management component, while EBSCO's subscription management product is a separate package, the EBSCOhost Electronic Journals Service (EJS). EJS also offers management functions such as tracking the registration status of e-journals, authentication assistance to facilitate both on-campus and remote access to e-journal content, and automatic management of e-journal URLs. These vendor-created products are intended to utilize the subscription information that these agents already hold related to an institution's local holdings and related to publishers' title lists. By offering URL management and title tracking features, subscription agents are looking to enhance the value of their services in a marketplace where libraries are no longer tied to a handful of agents. The question is, do these e-journal management systems provide sufficient functionality for a library's electronic resource management needs, or are they pieces of the larger puzzle for handling access, use, and discovery of e-content.

LOCALLY DEVELOPED LIBRARY SYSTEMS

Many libraries began using spreadsheets to track e-resource budget and license information, then moved to database software such as Microsoft Access, FileMaker, and Request Tracker when the amount of data to be maintained grew too unwieldy. A number of institutions are sharing the experiences they encountered in developing these systems to meet local needs. Some of these reports and articles are listed on the DLF ERMI Web site cited above, and others can be found in the recent literature and attached references.[7] What is striking about these reports from the field is that many libraries, since the late nineties, have already gone through various iterations of a locally developed system, and some are on to the second, third, or fourth enhanced version of their product.

With the building of any networked system, librarians inevitably see multiple applications for the data that is tracked and maintained. What may transpire is that different audiences begin to have divergent needs for data originally collected to meet a few specific goals. For electronic information resources, this is especially true when attempting to track even a subset of information such as license terms. Since license information affects many library departments, such as technical services, acquisitions, collection development, and public services, any database intended for tracking e-resources will require constant updating to stay current. Some libraries report that the reality of finding time to populate these in-house databases prevents the systems from being fully utilized.

Duranceau, in an article on license tracking, succinctly describes the problem faced by large, decentralized operations that seek in-house solutions.[8] She notes that creating local databases and maintaining them can only be successful if there is a significant labor savings. If a system requires substantial staff resources for updating information, the costs in time and labor may outweigh the desired benefits of an online solution. Based on MIT's experiences, such a system would need to "track only the minimum essential data, nothing more and nothing less."[9] As a result, MIT developed a single, integrated Web interface using FileMaker that tracks license details, links to scanned licenses, has the ability to display use restrictions, and provides public and administrative access points to a larger database of information on electronic titles and subscriptions.

Once a database is developed, it needs to accommodate different levels of authorizations for different users. Acquisitions and technical service staff may require deeper levels of access than those in public services. Concurrently, public displays and interfaces for meeting library user needs often drive the development of some system features, such as URL linking and electronic journal title lists. In a review of the literature, several needs, attributes, and functional requirements for electronic resources management systems stand out.

Electronic resource management system criteria:

1. Must provide a dynamic unified Web-based tool for viewing, updating, reporting, and administering licensed electronic information resources.
2. Must be interoperable with existing and future library systems and technology; i.e., ILS system, portal, URL linking functionality, authentication software, and other applications.
3. Must track essential data such as: license terms, use permissions, archival rights, access and authentication, status of current and pending orders, status of negotiations, etc.
4. Must provide real-time, online global updating of records and batch uploading of relevant e-resources metadata.
5. Must provide access to information displays for different levels of users, including library patrons, with appropriate authorization levels and security mechanisms.
6. Must provide time and labor savings; i.e., automatic notification (e-mail alerts) to appropriate staff of changes of status and scope in orders, renewals, cancellations, licensing and vendor dead-

lines, financial data, and other data related to subscriptions and contracts.

7. Must provide real time custom report generation.
8. Must provide linking functionality–linking to scanned licenses and linking management including centralized updating of URLs in ILS, proxy tables, and library Web sites.
9. Must provide journal title holdings (electronic and print runs) or easy uploading of information from publishers for content held in aggregated databases and subscriptions.
10. Must offer the ability to customize interfaces, and to be able to add new fields to capture relevant data for local needs.

The DLF project "Web Hub" lists a number of local e-resource management systems in planning or development at more than fifteen libraries, such as the California Digital Library, Johns Hopkins, University of California, Los Angeles, and many others. One of the early library e-resource systems was developed at The Pennsylvania State University (Penn State) in 1999 using Microsoft Access.[10] This system, ERLIC (Electronic Licensing and Information Center) is evolving into a second generation of the product, ERLIC2, for a number of reasons. According to Robert Alan, Head of Serials, this is chiefly due to transitioning from a cumbersome, somewhat static system to a real-time Oracle database and adding a scanning platform and other enhancements. In addition, at the fall 2003 Charleston conference, Alan reported that a significant amount of staff time was still required to maintain the data in the system.[11] While the next version of ERLIC will continue to support management and licensing of e-resources, Penn State is also looking at vendor solutions to facilitate an A-Z list, provide MARC records, and support open URL linking to meet broader staff and patron needs.[12]

The experience at Penn State, moving from an Access database to a more robust Oracle database, may mirror paths being taken at other institutions with their in-house software. As these libraries share their experiences, these insights will help others learn about pitfalls and strategies. The work of the DLF ERMI in developing data and functional standards will also contribute to finding tools for managing e-resources. Currently, two products, Gold Rush, developed by a non-profit consortium, and the Electronic Resource Management system, developed by an ILS vendor, are showing promise in the search for software solutions. In addition, several other vendors are reportedly developing e-resource modules, including Dynix, Endeavor, Ex Libris, and Sirsi.

ELECTRONIC RESOURCE MANAGEMENT SYSTEMS

Gold Rush (GR)

The Colorado Alliance of Research Libraries is a nonprofit consortium of twelve libraries in Colorado and Wyoming. Gold Rush was created to serve some common needs of Colorado Alliance libraries, and it continues to evolve with these libraries' input. Plans for Gold Rush, originally called the "Database of Databases," began in 1999 with a concept paper and the formation of a focus group. The Database of Databases would be a central repository of Web-based resources held by Colorado Alliance libraries. This database would allow library patrons to identify both databases and full-text journals subscribed to by Alliance libraries, as well as the full-text publications embedded within aggregated databases. It would improve access to electronic content via a linking mechanism. It would help library staff identify database redundancy, compare contract terms and conditions, and facilitate consortium purchases. Perhaps most importantly, the Database of Databases would provide member libraries with an affordable electronic resource management tool and URL linker in a difficult budget time.[13] In early 2001, the Colorado Alliance announced the Database of Databases' new name, Gold Rush, and invited a focus group to evaluate the beta version of the product. Gold Rush was launched on July 15, 2001, and due to widespread interest, has evolved into a highly-affordable commercial product available to any library.

The Colorado Alliance is conscious of the importance of standards in electronic resource management systems. The Gold Rush project team has been monitoring the work of the DLF ERMI, and has incorporated many of the ERMI's functional requirements into Gold Rush.

The Gold Rush suite includes Web-based public and staff interfaces, Gold Rush Reports, and an OpenURL linker called Gold Rush Linker. The Gold Rush suite is hosted on Colorado Alliance servers. Gold Rush is licensed on an annual basis, and can be licensed for a single library or a group of libraries in a consortium. There are three levels of license available–Gold Rush Reports, Gold Rush Basic (Gold Rush Reports, and the Web-based public and staff interfaces), and Gold Rush Complete, which includes everything in the Gold Rush Basic package, and the Gold Rush Linker.

The Colorado Alliance maintains an inventory of content providers, the associated databases and e-journal packages, and the associated title lists, URLs and coverage information. Libraries that use Gold Rush are encouraged to suggest additional resources to be added to the inventory. As of March, 2004, the inventory contained more than 50,000 unique journal titles from more than 700 content providers. The Colorado Alliance updates the existing data and adds new resources whenever possible, but due to limited staff resources, that information is not as current or comprehensive as other commercial vendors' information. Libraries implementing Gold Rush begin by setting their electronic journal and database holdings. Typically, this is done by compiling two spreadsheets: one listing journal titles, ISSNs, and URLs harvested from the OPAC, and one listing databases and associated vendors. Libraries may also set their print journal holdings if desired; these holdings can be linked to the record in the local OPAC by ISSN. Gold Rush then integrates the libraries' holdings with its inventory, creating the ability to generate title lists that include journal titles in aggregated databases that may not have been cataloged.

The Gold Rush Staff Interface, called the Staff Toolbox, is divided into five parts: Reports, Holdings, Subscriptions, Cataloging, and Settings. The Gold Rush Reports module features a series of pre-defined reports on Gold Rush resources and system activity. The Holdings module provides tools to establish and manage database holdings and related URLs. The Subscriptions module includes more than eighty fields for storing and tracking detailed information on each of a library's electronic resources, including license terms, vendor information, purchase details and links to resources, administrative modules, usage statistics, and scanned copies of licenses.

The Cataloging module allows library staff to add descriptors and alternate titles to increase access to electronic resources. Finally, the Settings module allows local Gold Rush administrators to establish and manage Gold Rush accounts. Gold Rush administrators have the ability to establish accounts for individuals or groups and specify privileges for each account. A list of "permission details" for each area of the staff toolbox is displayed when a new account is created; boxes corresponding to each tool can be checked to grant privileges to the account.

Gold Rush provides some key tools to facilitate the tracking of license data in the Subscriptions area. License terms such as downloading, copying, printing, ILL, course packs, and electronic reserves can be recorded with a standard yes/no flag that facilitates searching and report creation. Other license information, such as negotiation details and links to electronic copies online are also tracked in the subscriptions area (see Figure 1).

FIGURE 1. Gold Rush Staff Toolbox Subscription Module

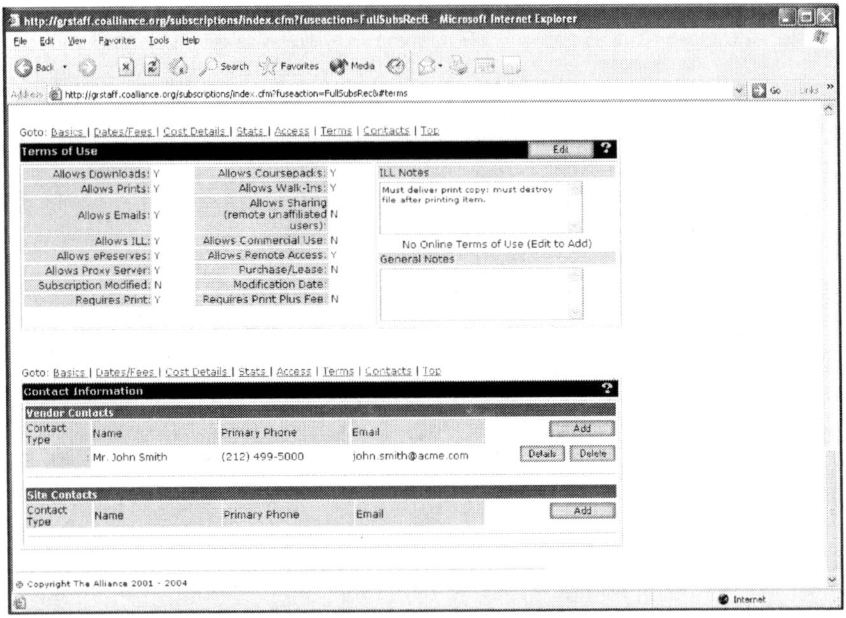

Reprinted with permission.

The "Search Subscriptions" basic search tool searches vendor or product information, while the advanced search feature enables staff to perform Boolean searches against many of the fields listed in the Subscriptions area. There is also an alert tool that generates e-mails to specified recipients to notify them 30, 60, 90, or 120 days in advance, based on specified subscription or trial ending dates.

The patron interface offers several tools to facilitate the discovery of electronic resources. Patrons can search and browse A-Z and subject lists of journal titles. However, the subject terms currently being utilized in the subject search and browse are Library of Congress Subject Headings, which are highly specific and numerous. This subject browse does not facilitate browsing as well as a brief list of broad subject terms. Patrons can also search by keyword and database title. All searches can be limited to free-of-charge resources (including open access titles) and full-text journals. The Colorado Alliance plans to add article level searching in the future, and is working on a revised public interface that can be customized with colors and fonts more closely resembling libraries' OPACs and Web sites (see Figure 2).

FIGURE 2. Gold Rush Patron Interface

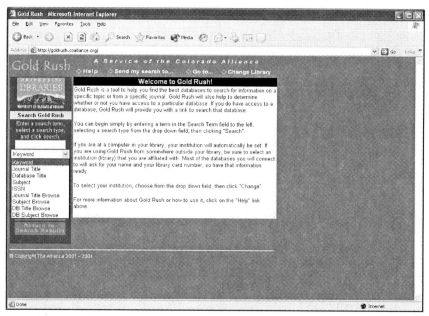

Reprinted with permission.

The patron interface also provides lists of journals and databases available at Colorado Alliance libraries. Patrons may be affiliated with more than one Alliance library, so this feature is intended to allow patrons to compare holdings at various Alliance libraries. Staff can use this feature to plan shared purchases with other Colorado Alliance libraries.

Gold Rush Reports features a report that allows libraries to compare content coverage (both citations and full text) between two similar databases. This report returns journal titles ISSN(s) and coverage information. In the future, the Colorado Alliance plans to add reports that compare multiple databases, and compare one library's electronic resource holdings against those of another Alliance library. Other reports include a Unique Titles Report, which lists the number of titles unique to a single database, compared against title coverage in other databases; Journals by Subject and Databases by Descriptor reports, which can be used to create database and journal subject listings; All Database Providers and All Journal Providers, which list all of the providers in the

Gold Rush database for a given database or journal title; and Library Settings reports, which include a Site Activity Report, a Current Users Report, and a Current Public Customization Settings Report. All reports can be downloaded and saved in a variety of common file types, including Microsoft Excel.

GR Linker is an OpenURL compliant link resolver. The link resolver provides links to full text, primarily at the journal title level. The Alliance is currently working with vendors to provide increased article-level linking. GR Linker also supports article-level linking by working with CrossRef to obtain Digital Object Identifiers (DOI) when they are not included in the citation information. There are further options available when no electronic full text can be found. If a library has set its print journal holdings, patrons can follow print links to check the print holdings; clicking on a print link executes an ISSN search in the local catalog. GR Linker can also send citation information to interlibrary loan systems such as OCLC ILLiad and WebZap, developed at Colorado State University Libraries.

Electronic Resource Management (ERM)

In late 2001, Innovative Interfaces customers began communicating with Innovative regarding challenges they were experiencing in managing electronic resources. These libraries needed a database to store license details, legal details and vendor information. They needed to be able to produce reports and track cost information. The University of Washington was at the point where they had to commit to developing an in-house database, or work with a vendor to develop a module that would be integrated into their library system. Soon after an initial meeting with the University of Washington, Innovative entered a development partnership with the University of Washington and four other institutions.[14] The five institutions had a great deal of input into the development of the module. They described the variety of electronic resources available and the relationships between publishers and aggregators. They described their workflow, the importance of storing specific data elements, and the types of reports they needed. Innovative Interfaces has also been working closely with the DLF ERMI, and has incorporated the group's functional requirements in the development of ERM.

By the fall of 2003, twelve institutions had participated in an early beta test of the Electronic Resource Management (ERM) module, including two that had an ILS from another vendor and were using ERM as a stand-alone module. A general release of ERM was scheduled for mid-2004 as part of Innovative's Millennium Silver software release. The following functionality descriptions are based on information provided by Innovative in early 2004.[15]

ERM has separate public and staff interfaces. The staff interface features a series of fields for entering data, including license details, subscription and holdings information, contract notes and vendor contacts, prices and payment information, access details and URLs, IP addresses, resource links, and administrative details–login information and usage statistics links (see Figure 3). ERM also provides variable fields that can be assigned according to a library's individual needs. The field labels are utilized in creating reports with the Millennium create lists tool. Administrators can restrict viewing and editing of license and resource data to the appropriate levels of staff using field-level permissions.

ERM provides a notification tool that sends e-mails to selected recipients any number of days before an event occurs. Events can be created, each with trigger dates.

FIGURE 3. ERM Resource Record Detail

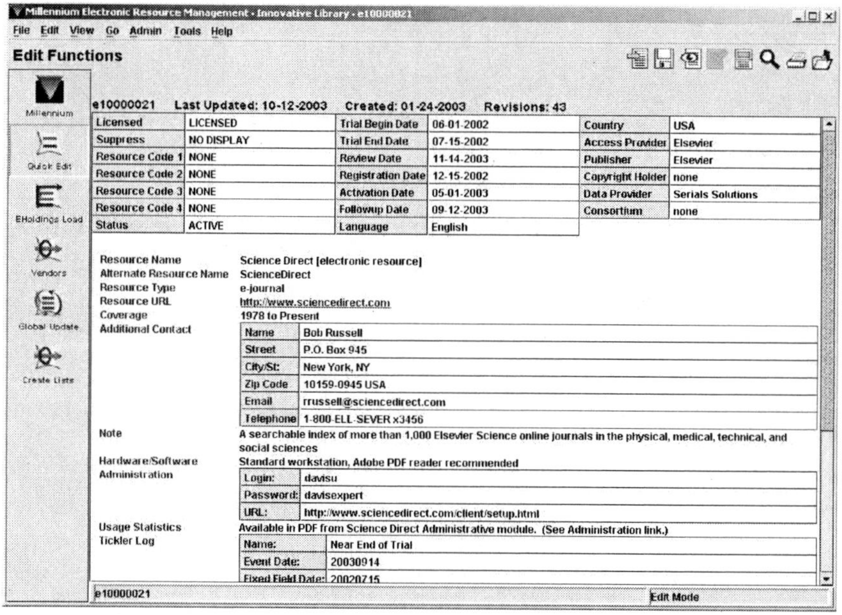

Reprinted with permission.

ERM is used to create "resource records" that are linked to one or more related bibliographic records (see Figure 4), and information attributed to each resource record is also attributed to the related bibliographic record(s). For example, if a system downtime note is placed in a resource record, that note automatically populates all of the bibliographic records attached to that resource (i.e., titles in a bundled subscription or publisher package).

The public interface integrates information from the resource record and from related records in other modules, such as serials, acquisitions, and cataloging (see Figure 5). Staff can control the extent of electronic resource information displayed to the public. Electronic resource information that would typically be displayed to the public includes license terms, system downtime information, and holdings information.

ERM also provides A-Z and subject lists for searching and browsing databases (see Figure 6). License conditions and access information for each resource are displayed to patrons as they navigate to the databases. Again, each library determines the extent of electronic resource infor-

FIGURE 4. ERM Resource Record

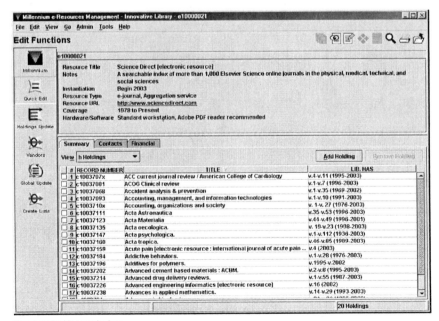

Reprinted with permission.

FIGURE 5. ERM Resource Record, Patron View

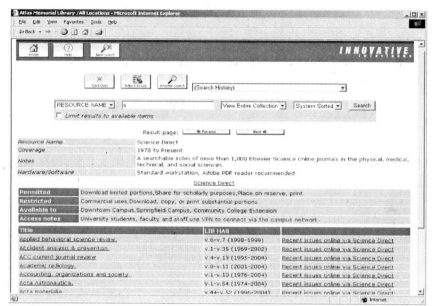

Reprinted with permission.

·mation that is displayed to patrons. Currently, the list displays broad subject areas developed by Innovative, but Innovative plans to allow libraries to customize these subject terms in the future.

DISCUSSION

Gold Rush and ERM both offer tools to assist in license management, such as tracking and displaying license details, permissions, access and authorization parameters, and linking to scanned copies of licenses. Gold Rush differs from ERM in that it offers the ability to search and browse electronic resources held by other Alliance libraries, the ability to perform database comparisons (and forthcoming, comparisons between two or more Alliance libraries' electronic resource holdings), and it offers an OpenURL compliant link resolver. It is also within an affordable price range for most libraries seeking a stand-alone product for license management support.

Some libraries have limited their implementation of Gold Rush primarily to the GR OpenURL linker, and continue to track license infor-

FIGURE 6. ERM A to Z and Subject Lists

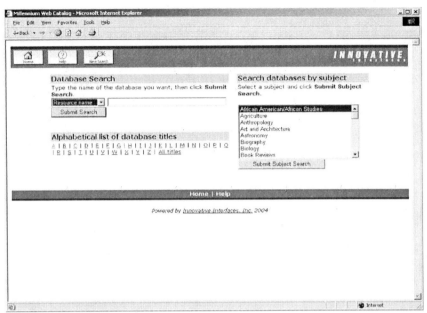

Reprinted with permission.

mation outside of Gold Rush.[16] One institution manually inserts a link to Gold Rush in the 856 MARC field of bibliographic records. This link takes the user to the Gold Rush interface which connects to full-text and indexing sources for that title. This feature allows the library to centralize access to electronic content in OPAC records.[17] Libraries that have integrated this linker report that the utility is relatively successful.

Gold Rush does, however, have some limitations. Although the Alliance maintains an inventory of publishers, vendors, and associated databases and journals, this list is not comprehensive, and is not updated as frequently as it is in other software products. If libraries discover omissions when setting their database holdings, they must request that the Alliance add these resources before they can be included in the library's Gold Rush database holdings. Although journal holdings can be batch-loaded, populating database holdings and electronic resource metadata is a manual process that requires a large initial time investment and ongoing management responsibilities.

Because of the cooperative nature of the Gold Rush project, libraries that are implementing the software have taken an active role in influencing its future development, which is valuable to all, yet represents another investment of time. In addition, although the Alliance has tried to make the public and staff interfaces easy to navigate, they are still new interfaces and users must spend time learning to navigate them. As a stand-alone product that does not utilize data already in an ILS, implementation must include a significant amount of training and internal promotion to encourage adoption by all library departments.

For libraries that use Innovative, ERM has several advantages when integrated into an existing Innovative Millennium system. The most obvious is that information related to electronic resources is managed in the ERM module, but is integrated into the other Millennium modules. Conversely, information that already exists in other modules, such as data from bibliographic and order records, does not have to be entered again, requiring less of an initial time commitment. Also, library staff who are already familiar with the Millennium interface and the create lists function require less training to use this new module, and they can easily incorporate electronic resources information into their current tasks and reports. Library-wide access to (and adoption of) the ERM module enables departments to work cooperatively to enter and maintain electronic resources information. ERM is also able to leverage the global update tool (essentially a find and replace tool) as well as the create lists tool, both accessible from other Millennium modules and familiar to some departments in the library.

ERM does not provide e-journal management information, such as full-text title lists, publisher information, coverage information, and URLs. It is expected that this information either exists in the ILS or will be obtained from an external e-journal management service. As an ILS module, the implementation of ERM is an intensive endeavor requiring library-wide planning, testing, customization, training, and ongoing maintenance. In a time of widespread budget reductions, ERM also represents a significant financial investment.

CONCLUSION

This article highlights the state of electronic resource management software available at the time of this writing. Clearly these products are still in development, and undoubtedly other vendors will be introducing similar e-resource software. The two e-resource management modules investigated were developed to support the tracking of license information, along with other features. To varying degrees, both products meet many of the desired requirements needed in a dynamic, Web-based electronic resource management system. However, they were developed from two different perspectives, one with a consortium focus, and the other as an individual library ILS module.

It is also important to keep in mind the complex issues facing library professionals engaged in selecting, negotiating, and providing access to e-resources. In order to determine appropriate software solutions, there are a number of factors related to an institution's local environment that need to be considered. This will affect how a product can be implemented and how it will perform. These factors may include policies and procedures related to the cataloging of electronic content, state funding regulations, the existence of institutional portals, the availability of technology support, the costs for new hardware, and other constraints. Will the initial and ongoing effort invested justify the acquisition and implementation of a software product? Will the benefits outweigh the monetary costs and commitment of staff needed to implement a product?

Unfortunately, there is no single software solution that addresses all of these challenges.[18] Managing license compliance is just one piece of the larger e-resource puzzle for libraries. Libraries may also need additional pieces of the puzzle, such as e-journal management tools, OpenURL linking, and federated metadata searching. In the end, the answers may have more to do with budgets and local needs than with finding the most comprehensive, integrated, and cost-effective solution.

NOTES

1. Ellen Finnie Duranceau and Cindy Hepfer, "Staffing for Electronic Resource Management: The Results of a Survey," *Serials Review* 28, no.4 (2002): 316-20. See also, Timothy D. Jewell, *The ARL "Investment in Electronic Resources" Study: Final Report to the Council on Library and Information Resources*, December 24, 1998, www.arl.org/stats/specproj/jewell.html.

2. Timothy D. Jewell, *Selection and Presentation of Commercially Available Electronic Resources: Issues and Practices*. Washington D.C.: Digital Library Federation Council on Library and Information Resources, 2001.

3. Ibid., 51-55.

4. Ibid., 25.

5. Terry W. Brandsma, Elizabeth R. Berhhardt, and Dana M. Sally, "Journal Finder, a Second Look: Implications for Serials Access in Today's Library," *Serials Review*, 29, no. 4, (2003): 287-294.

6. Michelle Sitko, Narda Tafuri, Gregory Szezyrbak, and Taemin Park, "E-journal Management Systems: Trends, Trials, and Trade-offs," *Serials Review*, 28, no. 3

(2002): 176-194. See also: Ellen Finnie Duranceau, "E-Journal Package-Content Tracking Service," *Serials Review*, 28, (2002): 49-52. See also: Jill Emery, "A Comparative Review of Three Electronic Journal Management Systems: Journal Web Cite, Serials Solutions and TDNet," *Charleston Advisor*, (October 2001): 16-19.

7. Mark Czyk and Nathan D.M. Robertson, "HERMES: The Hopkins Electronic Resource Management System, *Information Technology and Libraries*, 22, no. 1 (2003): 12-17. See also: Marie R. Kennedy, Michele J. Crump, and Douglas Kiker, "Paper to PDF: Making License Agreements Accessible through the OPAC," *Library Resources and Technical Services*, 48, no. 1 (2004): 20-25.

8. Ellen Finnie Duranceau, "License Tracking," *Serials Review*, 26, no. 3 (2000): 69-73.

9. Ibid., 70.

10. Robert Alan and Lai-Ying Hsiung, "Web-Based Tracking Systems for Electronic Resources Management," *The Serials Librarian*, 44, no.3 (2003): 293-297.

11. Robert Alan, "Electronic Resource Management: An In-house Approach," Presented at the Charleston Conference, October 2003.

12. Ibid.

13. Steve Oberg, "Gold Rush: An Electronic Journal Management and Linking Project," *Serials Review*, 29, No. 3 (2003): 230-232.

14. Ted Fons, Innovative Interfaces Product Manager, in discussion with authors, October 2003 and January 2004.

15. Ibid.

16. Meg Brown-Sica and Cynthia Hashert, "Gold Rush Linker: Making Better Use of Our Electronic Resources," *Colorado Libraries*, 29, No. 1 (Spring 2003): 25-28.

17. Elizabeth S. Meagher and Christopher C. Brown, "Gold Rush: Integrated Access to Aggregated Journal Text through the OPAC," *Library Resources & Technical Services*, 48, No. 1 (January 2004): 69-76.

18. See also: Marshall Breeding, "The Many Facets of Managing Electronic Resources," *Information Today*, 24, No.1 (January 2004) http://www.infotoday.com/cilmag/jan04/breeding.shtml.

Licenses, the Law, and Libraries

Anna May Wyatt

SUMMARY. As libraries move into the digital age, they will be forced to rely upon licensing agreements to obtain electronic information. These licenses are often drafted by the vendor with terms favoring the vendor. Librarians need to be aware of the current status of the law so that they may better negotiate licenses which protect the library's rights of interlibrary loan, fair use, and archival rights. Some licenses, such as shrinkwrap and clickwrap licenses, may not be negotiable. Librarians need to send materials back or refuse to use services which have shrinkwrap licenses which do not meet the needs of their patrons. *[Article copies available for a fee from The Haworth Document Delivery Service: 1-800-HAWORTH. E-mail address: <docdelivery@haworthpress.com> Website: <http://www.HaworthPress.com> © 2005 by The Haworth Press, Inc. All rights reserved.]*

KEYWORDS. UCITA, licenses, contracts, library services, electronic access, databases

INTRODUCTION

Licensing is a hot topic in today's library. As libraries move further and further into the digital age, an increasing number of library services

Anna May Wyatt is Assistant Professor/Cataloger of Science and Technology, University of Oklahoma.

The author would like to thank Eric Wyatt for his thoughtful reviews.

[Haworth co-indexing entry note]: "Licenses, the Law, and Libraries." Wyatt, Anna May. Co-published simultaneously in *Journal of Library Administration* (The Haworth Information Press, an imprint of The Haworth Press, Inc.) Vol. 42, No. 3/4, 2005, pp. 163-176; and: *Licensing in Libraries: Practical and Ethical Aspects* (ed: Karen Rupp-Serrano) The Haworth Information Press, an imprint of The Haworth Press, Inc., 2005, pp. 163-176. Single or multiple copies of this article are available for a fee from The Haworth Document Delivery Service [1-800-HAWORTH, 9:00 a.m. - 5:00 p.m. (EST). E-mail address: docdelivery@haworthpress.com].

are controlled by licenses. Every service the library provides which depends upon software, database, or electronic access is governed by a library license. A license is merely a contract between the library and a vendor. Normally, these contracts are written by the vendor, with contract terms favoring the vendor. Some contracts may be negotiated; others, like the shrinkwrap licenses accompanying books with CD-ROMs, are not negotiable. Although the law is not settled, recent cases which have been decided in this area are moving toward making the library liable for breaches to a shrinkwrap license just as it would be liable for breaches to a negotiated license. This article will examine the current status of the law concerning database, shrinkwrap, and clickwrap licenses and the effect these laws have on library services.

As the concern over licensing has grown among librarians, numerous articles have been written concerning various aspects of licensing. Many have written about the serials crisis and how library database and site licenses are controlling the journals to which the library will provide access.[1] Some have written about negotiating the license agreement,[2] while others have written about understanding the various clauses in the licensing agreement.[3] There is even an article written from the publisher's perspective concerning how the publisher makes decisions to treat different items, such as e-books and other online products, under different licensing agreements with different contractual terms.[4] However, this article will focus on the changes in the law which affect library licenses and the effect these licenses have on library services and library rights under the Copyright Act.

DATABASES

Licensing became an issue for libraries with the growth of databases. Databases have been defined by Webster's dictionary as "a comprehensive collection of related data organized for quick access, generally by computer."[5] Almost all databases contain facts. However, copyright does not protect facts. According to the Copyright Act of 1976, "copyright protection subsists . . . in original works of authorship. . . . "[6] This has been interpreted by the courts to mean that in order for an author's work to qualify as original, the work must be an independent creation and it must be creative.[7] In *Feist v. Rural Telephone Service Company*,[8] Feist copied a large portion of Rural's telephone directory without obtaining Rural's permission. The Supreme Court stated that facts could not be copyrighted and Rural's directory, being in alphabetical format, did not exhibit sufficient creativity to be protected under the copyright law.[9] Moreover, the court stated that "only the arrangement of the database would be protected."[10] Thus, many databases fall under the *Feist* ruling and the data, compiled at much expense to the database owner, cannot be protected from being copied in substantial amounts.

Database owners began to look to the software industry for guidance in protecting their labor and products. When software first became prevalent in the marketplace, many vendors thought that the copyright laws did not apply to software.[11] However, the Copyright Act was revised in 1980 to include protection of software.[12] By this date, the software industry had already moved in the direction of licenses to protect their products.[13] Database owners began utilizing licensing agreements to restrict the access and usage rights of users to their information as well. Thus, database owners turned to contracts to protect their products.

DATABASE AND COLLECTIONS OF INFORMATION MISAPPROPRIATION ACT

In addition to contracts, database owners have also lobbied both state and federal legislatures for laws in addition to copyright to protect their investments. The Database and Collections of Information Misappropriation Act (H.R. 3261) and Uniform Computer Information Transaction Act (UCITA) are two proposed laws which would offer additional protections to database owners. The Database and Collections of Information Misappropriation Act is the latest version of a bill which was first introduced in 1996[14] to strengthen database protection laws. The act defines database as "a collection of a large number of discrete items of information produced for the purpose of bringing such discrete items of information together in one place or through one source so that persons may access them."[15] A person will be held liable under this act for making a substantial amount of a database available in commerce without authorization when the database was collected and maintained "through substantial expenditure of financial resources or time"[16] "in a time sensitive manner"[17] which "inflicts injury on the database"[18] and the ability of others to free-ride on the efforts of the database owner "would so reduce the incentive to produce the product or service that its existence or quality would be substantially threatened."[19] An exception is granted to "nonprofit educational, scientific, and research institutions"[20] and their agents who make available databases for "nonprofit educational, scientific, and research purposes . . . *if the court determines that the making available in commerce of the information in the data-base is reasonable under the circumstances.*"[21] Government databases were excluded from protection under this act.[22]

If this law passes, libraries, whose service orientation is toward serving as many users as possible, could potentially be sued for making databases available in commerce. The courts would determine whether the library's actions were "reasonable under the circumstances." Although libraries should not have to worry about being sued by databases with which they maintain licenses, there are collections of discrete items, which could fit under the definition of databases, located at various Web sites which could be accessed using the libraries Internet servers. In interpreting the Database and Collections of Information Misappropriation Act, courts might turn to the European Database Directive, the model for this act. In Europe, courts have given database owners excessive protection which has included Web sites as databases.[23]

Moreover, the passage of this bill would allow protection of all the information in a database, even facts. As stated previously, facts cannot be copyrighted and therefore, may be copied, shared, and used without citation of a source by the public without infringing copyright. If this bill should pass, it will be interesting to see whether the law would be struck down as unconstitutional for providing protection to facts. The bill passed the House Judiciary Committee's Subcommittee on Courts, the Internet and Intellectual Property in October, 2003, over objections that it would provide "copyright-like protections on facts within databases."[24]

UCITA

The second proposed law, UCITA, is a uniform state law which would regulate transactions and contracts in digital media. Although UCITA has been passed in Virginia and Maryland, it has received so much opposition that the National Conference of Commissioners on Uniform State Laws (NCCUSL), the drafters of UCITA, issued a press release stating that they would no longer spend their resources promoting the act.[25] UCITA is still a concern because it is still possible for proponents of UCITA to introduce this legislation in other states and because courts have cited UCITA in their opinions, thus giving legal precedent to some of the legal principles stated in UCITA. UCITA has many legal principles which adversely affect library services.

First, UCITA provides numerous protections to database owners and vendors. A database vendor may change the content of the information in a database without materially breaching the contract.[26] The vendor will only be held to be in breach if he removes an item which is expressly stated in the contract. The vendor may also take the system offline intermittently without breaching the contract.[27] If the vendor wants to make changes to the contract, he may do so by posting a notice in an accessible location, such as a Web site or any place that a library might have electronic access.[28] Even if the library never actually receives notice of the change, the very posting fulfills the vendor's duty of notice. Moreover, the library can be held responsible for glitches in the database if they do not inspect the database when they have an opportunity to inspect.[29] Thus, the library needs to review database licenses carefully to ensure continuous and quality service from the vendor. The library must include in the contract each journal title that the library wants to receive to prevent the vendor from dropping a journal title from its database. The library should negotiate maintenance of the database and specify when and under what conditions the database may be taken offline. The library should also expressly state the method that the vendor will be required to use to provide notice of contract term changes to the library and if it is by Web site, ensure that someone is given the responsibility of monitoring the Web site on a weekly basis.

UCITA AND THE COPYRIGHT ACT

UCITA also affects the library's rights under the Copyright Act. The rights granted the library under the first sale doctrine, which allows libraries to lend their copy of an item, fair use, which allows libraries to make copies of journal articles for interlibrary loan as well as allowing patrons the right to make copies of journal articles and chapters in books for educational purposes, and the library's archival rights may all be nullified by a vendor's contract or by accepting materials which are accompanied by shrinkwrap and clickwrap contracts. Under the first sale doctrine, an owner of a copyrighted work may sell or dispose of the work without obtaining permission from the copyright holder.[30] Thus, when the library purchases a book, the first sale doctrine allows the library to lend the copy to a patron, withdraw the copy when the library deems it no longer useful in the collection, and sell the book at a book sale or throw it in the trash if the condition of the book warrants. However, if the library has a license to use materials, such as computer software or a database, the library does not acquire ownership; thus, the first sale doctrine does not apply. The library instead is a licensee and may only use the copy of the item in accordance with the license terms.[31] This means that if the license states the item cannot be loaned or leased, the library cannot lend it even though the Copyright Act allows libraries to lend items, including computer programs.[32]

Under UCITA, the vendor may restrict the right to make copies of any item in the database, thus preventing the library from exercising its fair use rights. Under the Copyright Act, "the fair use of a copyrighted work, including such use by reproduction in copies or phonorecords or by any other means specified by that section, for purposes such as criticism, comment, news reporting, teaching (including multiple copies for classroom use), scholarship, or research, is not an infringement of copyright."[33] The statute sets out a four prong test to determine when an action qualifies for fair use: (1) the reason for the use; (2) nature of the work; (3) the amount used in relation to the whole; and (4) the effect of the use on the market.[34] Since most of the copying done in and by libraries is for teaching, research, and scholarship, libraries and their patrons normally fit within the parameters of fair use, provided the patrons do not copy an entire book. However, database vendors may include in their licenses read-only rights for library patrons. This would be perfectly legal and waive the patron's fair use rights. The vendor may also state whether journal articles may be shared with other libraries through interlibrary loan. Many vendors feel uncomfortable allowing libraries to interlibrary loan digital materials.[35] Therefore, librarians need to ensure that their contracts with vendors allow articles in a database and other electronic information to be copied by patrons and made available through interlibrary loan.

Librarians should also ensure that they have the right to make archival copies written into their vendor contracts. Under the Digital Millennium Copyright Act of 1998 (DMCA),[36] the Copyright Act of 1976 was amended to allow a library the right to make up to three copies, including digital copies, of an item for preservation purposes if the item is deteriorating or exists in an obsolete format and another copy of the item cannot be obtained at a fair price.[37] However, under UCITA, the right to make copies, even for archival purposes, is subject to the terms in the contract. Many vendors prohibit copying works for archival purposes.[38] Moreover, with the move from print to digital serials, libraries may be faced with a situation where they no longer own back issues of a journal in print format and they are no longer able to access back issues electronically due to nonrenewal of a contract or perhaps the vendor's decision not to archive older materials due to lack of profitability.[39] The library should negotiate archiving rights to ensure continued access to current journal holdings in the future.

SHRINKWRAP AND CLICKWRAP CONTRACTS

Even though UCITA only controls contracts in Virginia and Maryland and any contract in which the parties choose the laws of Virginia or Maryland in the choice of law clause, many courts have issued rulings which mirror the legal principles set out in UCITA. First, shrinkwrap and clickwrap contracts,[40] which in the beginning were considered unenforceable adhesion contracts, are now fully enforced by the courts. The court in *ProCD v. Zeidenberg*[41] stated that "shrinkwrap licenses are enforceable unless their terms are objectionable on grounds applicable to contracts in general."[42] Although the lower court had stated that the contract in *ProCD* was unenforceable under federal copyright law,[43] the circuit court held that "a simple two-party contract is not 'equivalent to any of the exclusive rights within the general scope of copyright' and therefore may be enforced."[44] This case began a trend of cases which held that shrinkwrap and clickwrap contracts would be upheld, even if the terms of the contract violated copyright law. In *Hill v. Gateway*,[45] the court held that the Hills had assented to a shrinkwrap license by failing to return the merchandise after thirty days as required by the shrinkwrap license enclosed with their computer.[46] Thus, the Hills were bound to the terms in the shrinkwrap license by the court reaching the same result which a court would have reached under UCITA.

Courts have also looked to *ProCD* in determining whether clickwrap licenses should be found enforceable. Relying on *ProCD*, the court in *I. Lan Systems v. Netscout Service Level Corp.*[47] enforced the clickwrap license agreement stating that I. Lan Systems accepted the contract when they clicked the "I agree" icon.[48] However, courts distinguish between clickwrap agreements which require the user to click assent to the contract and those agreements, sometimes called webwrap agreements, which require a user to click on a link which takes them to the license agreement, but does not require the user to click an icon or box stating that the user agrees to the terms of the contract. In *Specht v. Netscape*,[49] Specht and several other plaintiffs had downloaded free plug-ins from Netscape without noticing any license terms. The license terms would have been found had the users scrolled to the next screen and clicked on a button asking the user to "please review and agree. . . . "[50] The court stated that "a consumer's clicking on a download button does not communicate assent to contractual terms if the offer did not make clear to the consumer that clicking on the download button would signify assent to those terms."[51] Moreover, the court discussed UCITA stating "the model code UCITA . . . generally recognizes the importance of conspicuous notice and unambiguous manifestation of assent in online sales and licensing of computer information.[52] Thus, the court did not enforce the contract because they found the users did not have notice of the contract and did not assent to the contract terms. However, the court did use UCITA for insight and the same ruling would have been issued had UCITA been the law in that state.

Moreover, courts have enforced shrinkwrap licenses which limit the liability for damages of the software provider. In *Mortenson Co. v. Timberline Software Corp.*,[53] Mortenson, a construction contractor, purchased software from Timberline which Timberline installed on Mortenson's computers. Although the software came with a shrinkwrap license on the diskettes and manuals, Mortenson claimed he had not seen the contract because a representative from Timberline installed the software for him. Mortenson, relying on the software, placed a bid which was $1.95 million too low due to a bug in the software of which Timberline was aware. Timberline stated that they were not liable for more than the price of the software because of their limitation of remedies and liability clause in the contract.[54] The court, relying on *ProCD* and *Hill*, stated that even if Mortenson had not seen the contract, "use of the software constituted its assent to the agreement, including the license terms."[55] Moreover, the court found that the limitation of remedies and liability clause was not unconscionable.[56] The court stated that Timberline, or other parties trying to enforce a limited liability clause, could prevail by showing the clause was a "reasonable usage of trade."[57] Thus, current case law is implementing many of the legal principles stated in UCITA.

Under UCITA, an information provider may disclaim all warranties by stating language such as "except for express warranties stated in this contract, if any, this [information] [computer program] is being provided with all faults, and the entire risk as to satisfactory quality, performance, accuracy, and effort is with the user."[58] The Reporter's Notes also state that "an information provider is not responsible for defects that were either (1) known by or disclosed to the other party, or (2) could have been discovered on reasonable inspection if the opportunity to inspect was available."[59] Thus, an information provider may provide the library with software and/or databases which have bugs and glitches, disclaim any liability for damages or for fixing the system in a shrink-wrap license, and have no liability under current case law. It is hoped that not all circuit courts will follow this precedent, but state and federal courts from California to New York have all decided cases using the same legal analysis which is set forth in UCITA.[60]

Therefore, courts have enforced shrinkwrap and clickwrap agreements which gave consumers notice of a contract and the ability to opt out of the contract by returning the merchandise. Although all the cases so far have dealt with contracts between merchants and consumers or copyright owners and distributors, it is conceivable that libraries would also be bound by shrinkwrap and clickwrap agreements. For example, libraries will be bound by the agreements which accompany software programs such as word processing programs, Internet browsers, and other programs placed on computer workstations. It is also conceivable that libraries could be held bound to shrinkwrap agreements which come with CD-ROMs accompanying books if the library does not return the materials within the time frame allotted in the contract. However, no cases have been litigated on this issue. In addition, it is not known whether the library would be bound by a contract entered into by one of its employees who does not have the authority to enter such contracts. For example, staff members or student employees might agree to clickwrap agreements on the Internet to obtain plug-ins, access online news services or newspapers. Some of these services are free for a limited time and then require payment. The library should have a written policy stating what librarians and library employees are allowed to download and what types of Internet services may be accessed without obtaining permission from the appropriate library official.

LICENSING GUIDELINES

With the increase in the number of licenses which libraries are required to review and sign in order to maintain current library services, librarians have begun to work together to draft guidelines for negotiating licenses which will protect library services.[61] Some concerns voiced in the various guidelines include defining the user, access to materials, the content of the materials, ensuring copyright rights are protected, and archiving of material. Library licenses must include a definition of user which will encompass all patrons. Library users should include walk-in patrons as well as students, faculty, and staff in an academic library. If the library offers distance education classes, the license should allow these students access to the materials as well. Libraries should spell out in the license how material will be accessed, whether by IP addresses or log-ins, as well as when library materials may be accessed. Some vendors, in an attempt to ensure that the library maintained its print collection in addition to the electronic version, have withheld the most recent digital versions of journals[62] and thus denied access to materials the library expected to be able to use. Libraries must negotiate with vendors to ensure that if they withhold the most recent articles in the database, the vendor will be in breach of the contract.

Since fair use and archival rights granted under the Copyright Act may be waived by contract, the library must make sure these rights are included in the final version of the contract. Patrons expect to be able to download or print an electronic version of an article in the same manner that they would photocopy a print journal article. These rights should be ensured along with the right to interlibrary loan a copy of a journal article according to CONTU guidelines. Moreover, the library should ensure that someone, whether it be the library or the vendor, is archiving all electronic material so that it will not be lost in the future. If the library is depending upon the vendor to archive materials, the library needs to negotiate the right to access this material in perpetuity.

CONCLUSION

As libraries move further into the digital age, they will be forced to rely upon licenses to obtain electronic information. Vendors of electronic information, fearing that their products may easily be pirated, have chosen to license, not sell, electronic information to their consumers. These licenses are typically drafted by the vendor with favorable terms for the vendor. Libraries need to take an active role in negotiating these licenses to ensure that the library can continue to provide the patron with quality services such as interlibrary loan, electronic journal access with copying and printing privileges, Internet access, use of word processing and spreadsheet programs, usage of materials on CD-ROMs, and database access. Libraries need to be aware of their current rights under the Copyright Act and ensure that these rights are not waived by any licensing agreement into which the library enters. Libraries also need to negotiate for archival rights to ensure future access to all current electronic information.

In addition, libraries need to be aware that many licenses which they cannot negotiate, such as shrinkwrap and clickwrap agreements, are still legally binding contracts to which the library will be bound if they accept materials or services which have these license agreements attached to them. Librarians must decide in a timely manner whether they will accept the terms of these agreements, send back materials, or refuse Web-based services having contractual terms which do not meet patrons needs. If these materials are regularly rejected, perhaps the vendors will be more willing to write contractual terms which are library-friendly or actually negotiate licensing agreements with libraries in the future.

Unfortunately for libraries, software companies and electronic information providers have powerful lobbies which have been instrumental in drafting legislation at both the federal and state levels which is favorable to the vendors. UCITA and the Database and Collections of Information Misappropriation Act are two such proposed laws currently under consideration. Although the library community lobbied successfully against the passage of UCITA in many states, the legal principles underlying UCITA are now becoming law through the decisions in numerous court cases across the country. These legal principles are favorable for the vendors, not for libraries. Librarians need to consider the current status of the law to ensure that they protect library services in the final version of the licensing agreement.

Finally, librarians need to continue to band together to discuss licensing issues. The current licensing guidelines drafted by several groups of librarians are invaluable tools to librarians in libraries of all sizes to sort through the maze of contractual terms, definitions, and obligations found in most licensing agreements. Librarians do not need to be lawyers to enter contracts, just informed.

NOTES

1. Kenneth Frazier, "The Librarians' Dilemma: Contemplating the Costs of the 'Big Deal,'" *D-Lib Magazine* 7, no. 3 (March, 2001), [Online]. Available: http://www.dlib.org/dlib/march01/frazier/03frazier.html [2003, October 26]; Jean-Claude Guédon, "Beyond Core Journals and Licenses: The Paths to Reform Scientific Publishing," *ARL* 218 (October, 2001), [Online]. Available: http://www.arl.org/newsltr/218/guedon.html [2003, October 26]; Walt Crawford, "Beware What You Wish For: Online Journal Quandaries," *American Libraries* 33, no. 10 (November, 2002): 65.

2. Sandhya D. Srivastava, "Licensing Electronic Resources," *The Serials Librarian* 42, no. 1/2 (2002): 7-12; Duncan E. Alford, "Negotiating and Analyzing Electronic License Agreements," *Law Library Journal* 94, no. 4 (Fall, 2002): 621-644.

3. Kathryn Metzinger Miller, "Behind Every Great Virtual Library Stand Many Great Licenses," *Library Journal Net Connect Suppl.* (Winter, 2003): 20-22.

ble.”

6. Copyright Act of 1976, U.S. Code, vol. 17, §102 (2000).

7. Dov S. Greenbaum, “Commentary: The Database Debate: In Support of an Inequitable Solution,” *Albany Law Journal of Science & Technology* 13 (2003): 454.

8. 499 U.S. 340 (1991).

9. Ibid., 345.

10. Greenbaum, “Database Debate,” 455. See: *Feist*, 499 U.S. 360.

11. Kwong, Deanna L., “Annual Review of Law and Technology: V. Business Law: A. Copyright-Contract Intersection: The Copyright-Contract Intersection: SoftMan Products Co. v. Adobe Systems, Inc. & Bowers v. Baystate Technologies, Inc.,” *Berkeley Technology Law Journal* 18 (2003): 353.

12. Michael J. Madison, “Article: Legal-ware: Contract and Copyright in the Digital Age,” *Fordham Law Review* 67 (December, 1998): 1039.

13. Kwong, “Copyright-Contract Intersection,” 353.

14. Greenbaum, “Database Debate,” 468-469.

15. *H.R. 3261. Database and Collections of Information Misappropriation Act (Introduced in House)*, §2(5)(A). (2003), [Online]. Available: http://thomas.loc.gov/cgi-bin/query/F?c108:2:./temp/~c10828W9AU:e744 [2003, October 13].

16. Ibid., §3(a).

17. Ibid.

18. Ibid.

19. Ibid.

20. Ibid., §4(b).

21. Ibid.

22. Ibid., §5(a)(1)(A).

23. Greenbaum, “Database Debate,” 465.

24. Grant Gross, “Subcommittee Approves Database Protection Bill,” *InfoWorld* (October 16, 2003), [Online]. Available: http://www.infoworld.com/article/03/10/16/HNsubbill_1.html [2003, October 21].

25. American Library Association. (2003). “NCCUSL Announces Decision about UCITA,” *ALAWON* 12, no. 73 (August 5, 2003), [Online]. Available: http://www.ala.org/washoff [2003, August 5].

26. American Law Institute and National Conference of Commissioners on Uniform State Laws. (1998). §2B-615, in *Uniform Commercial Code Article 2B: Software Contracts and Licenses of Information* (August 1, 1998 draft), [Online]. Available: http://www.law.uh.edu/ucc2b/080198/080198.html [2003, October 27].

27. Ibid.

28. Ibid., §2B-303 Reporter's Notes.

29. Ibid., §2B-406 Reporter's Notes.

30. Copyright Act, §109(a).

31. Elizabeth J. McClure, “Note: Uniform Commercial Code Article 2B & the State Contract Law-Federal Intellectual Property Law Interface: Can State Statutes Even Begin to Address Copyright Preemption of Shrink-wrap Licenses?” *Journal of Intellectual Property Law* 6 (Fall, 1998): 140.

32. Copyright Act, §109(b)(2)(A).

33. Ibid., §107.

34. Ibid.

35. Alford, "Negotiating and Analyzing Electronic License Agreements," 625; Laura N. Gasaway, "Article: Values Conflict in the Digital Environment: Librarians Versus Copyright Holders," *Columbia-VLA Journal of Law & the Arts* 24 (Fall, 2000): 148.

36. *U.S. Statutes at Large.* 1998. Vol. 112, p. 2860. *The Digital Millennium Copyright Act of 1998.*

37. Copyright Act, §108(c). The statute states, "The right of reproduction under this section applies to three copies or phonorecords of a published work duplicated solely for the purpose of replacement of a copy or phonorecord that is damaged, deteriorating, lost, or stolen, or if the existing format in which the work is stored has become obsolete, if- (1) the library or archives has, after a reasonable effort, determined that an unused replacement cannot be obtained at a fair price; and (2) any such copy or phonorecord that is reproduced in digital format is not made available to the public in that format outside the premises of the library or archives in lawful possession of such copy. For purposes of this subsection, a format shall be considered obsolete if the machine or device necessary to render perceptible a work stored in that format is no longer manufactured or is no longer reasonably available in the commercial marketplace.

38. Jennifer Femminella, "Note: Online Terms and Conditions Agreements: Bound by the Web," *St. John's Journal of Legal Commentary* 17 (Winter, 2003): 118.

39. Ibid.

40. Shrinkwrap contracts are agreements, for software, CD-ROMs, and even for books with computer disks or CD-ROMs inside, which appear on the packaging, usually covered with cellophane, which state that by opening the packaging the purchaser has agreed to all the terms of the enclosed license. Clickwrap contracts are contracts, for software, databases, and other electronic information, which require the user to click an "I agree" icon or click an unchecked box, before use of the software or electronic information. If the user clicks on the icon, they are then bound to the terms of the contract. See: Garry L. Founds, "Note: Shrinkwrap and Clickwrap Agreements: 2B or not 2B?" *Federal Communications Law Journal* 52, no. 1 (December 1999): 100; Ryan J. Casamiquela, "V. Business Law: A. Electronic Commerce: Contractual Assent and Enforceability in Cyberspace," *Berkeley Technology Law Journal* 17 (2002): 476.

41. 86 F3d 1447 (7th Cir 1996).

42. Ibid.

43. Ibid., 1453.

44. Ibid., 1455.

45. 105 F3d 1147 (7th Cir 1997).

46. Ibid., 1150.

47. 183 F. Supp2d 328 (D. Mass. 2002).

48. Ibid., 338. The court also stated that "if ProCD was correct to enforce a shrinkwrap license agreement, where any assent is implicit, then it must also be correct to enforce a clickwrap license agreement, where the assent is explicit."

49. 306 F3d 17 (2d Cir 2002).

50. Ibid., 23.

51. Ibid., 29.

52. Ibid., 34. The court also stated that "UCITA does not govern the parties' transactions in the present case, but we nevertheless find that UCITA's provisions offer insight into the evolving online 'circumstances' that defendants argue placed plaintiffs on inquiry notice of the existence of the SmartDownload license terms."

53. 140 Wash.2d 568, 998 P2d 305 (2000).

54. Ibid., 575. The clause stated: "LIMITATION OF REMEDIES AND LIA-BILITY. NEITHER TIMBERLINE NOR ANYONE ELSE WHO HAS BEEN INVOLVED IN THE CREATION, PRODUCTION OR DELIVERY OF THE PROGRAMS OR USER MANUALS SHALL BE LIABLE TO YOU FOR ANY DAMAGES OF ANY TYPE, INCLUDING BUT NOT LIMITED TO, ANY LOST PROFITS, LOST SAVINGS, LOSS OF ANTICIPATED BENEFITS, OR OTHER INCIDENTAL, OR CONSEQUENTIAL DAMAGES ARISING OUT OF THE USE OR INABILITY TO USE SUCH PROGRAMS, WHETHER ARISING OUT OF CONTRACT, NEGLIGENCE, STRICT TORT, OR UNDER ANY WARRANTY, OR OTHERWISE, EVEN IF TIMBERLINE HAS BEEN ADVISED OF THE POSSIBILITY OF SUCH DAMAGES OR FOR ANY OTHER CLAIM BY ANY OTHER PARTY. TIMBERLINE'S LIABILITY FOR DAMAGES IN NO EVENT SHALL EXCEED THE LICENSE FEE PAID FOR THE RIGHT TO USE THE PROGRAMS.

55. Ibid., 584.

56. Ibid., 588-589.

57. Ibid.

58. American Law Institute and National Conference of Commissioners on Uniform State Laws, *Article 2B*, §2B-406(b)(4).

59. Ibid., Reporter's Notes.

60. See *Specht*, 306 F3d 32-34.

61. See: Patricia Brennan, Karen Hersey, Georgia Harper. (2000). *Licensing Electronic Resources: Strategic and Practical Considerations for Signing Electronic Information Delivery Agreements* (March 13, 1997), [Online]. Available: http://www.arl.org/scomm/licensing/licbooklet.html [2003, November 1]; American Association of Law Libraries . . . [et al.]. (1997). *Principles for Licensing Electronic Resources* (October 6, 1997), [Online]. Available: http://www.arl.org/scomm/licensing/principles.html [2003, November 1]; CIC Collection Development Officers and CIC Electronic Resources Officers. (1998). *Preferred Practices For CIC Licensing of Electronic Journals* (July 1, 1998), [Online]. Available: http://ntx2.cso.uiuc.edu/cic/cli/cdo_preferred_practices.html [2000, May 15]; Task Force on the CIC Electronic Collection. (2000). *Assumptions & Guiding Principles for Near-Term Initiatives* (February 11, 2000), [Online]. Available: http://ntx2.cso.uiuc.edu/cic/cli/licguide.html [2000, May 15]; CIC Electronic Resource Officers. (2000). *Standardized Agreement Language* (March 9, 2000), [Online]. Available: http://ntx2.cso.uiuc.edu/cic/cli/contracts/standardized_agreement_language.htm [2000, May 15].

62. Alford, "Negotiating and Analyzing Electronic License Agreements," 629-630.

Licensing:
An Historical Perspective

David C. Fowler

SUMMARY. The history of licensing for the electronic resources that are utilized by academic libraries, though short, has been extremely complex. This history has moved from the humble beginnings of simple single-user or single-workstation CD-ROM licenses to the complicated consortial licenses of today that cover hundreds of journals, potentially for several campuses. This paper examines how licenses moved away from the early days and reviews how the mechanics of, and expectations for, these licenses have evolved over time, both from the perspective of libraries and of vendors. *[Article copies available for a fee from The Haworth Document Delivery Service: 1-800-HAWORTH. E-mail address: <docdelivery@haworthpress.com> Website: <http://www.HaworthPress.com> © 2005 by The Haworth Press, Inc. All rights reserved.]*

KEYWORDS. Licenses, history, electronic resources, licensing terms, licensing conditions, negotiations

David C. Fowler is Assistant Professor and Electronic Resources Coordinator for Acquisitions, Technical Services Division, Parks Library, Iowa State University, Ames, IA. His professional experience began when he became the Serials Services Librarian at Texas A&M University, Corpus Christi. Mr. Fowler has previously published an article in *Collection Management*, and is presently working on a series of articles on time and costs studies in a library acquisitions department.

[Haworth co-indexing entry note]: "Licensing: An Historical Perspective." Fowler, David C. Co-published simultaneously in *Journal of Library Administration* (The Haworth Information Press, an imprint of The Haworth Press, Inc.) Vol. 42, No. 3/4, 2005, pp. 177-197; and: *Licensing in Libraries: Practical and Ethical Aspects* (ed: Karen Rupp-Serrano) The Haworth Information Press, an imprint of The Haworth Press, Inc., 2005, pp. 177-197. Single or multiple copies of this article are available for a fee from The Haworth Document Delivery Service [1-800-HAWORTH, 9:00 a.m. - 5:00 p.m. (EST). E-mail address: docdelivery@haworthpress.com].

http://www.haworthpress.com/web/JLA
© 2005 by The Haworth Press, Inc. All rights reserved.
Digital Object Identifier: 10.1300/J111v42n03_12

INTRODUCTION

The history of licensing for electronic resources utilized by academic libraries, though short, has been a complex and, many would argue, a long and torturous process. It has moved from the humble beginnings of simple single-user or single-workstation CD-ROM licenses to the complicated and lengthy consortial licenses of today that cover hundreds of journals, potentially for several campuses. This paper will examine how licenses moved away from those early days, and view how the mechanics of, and expectations for, these licenses have evolved over time, both from the perspective of libraries and of vendors.

WHAT IS LICENSING?

So, what is a license, and what is licensing? A license is a physical or virtual document between two or more parties that allows an intellectual resource owned by one party (the licensor), to be used by another or multiple other parties (the licensees) for a fixed duration of time, usually for a one-year or more subscription period. In other words, a license is the permission given by a competent authority to engage in an activity that would otherwise be unlawful, without the presence of the license. Licensing then, is the act performed by the licensor (the vendor), giving that permission to the licensee (the customer, usually a library).

Before any in-depth examination of the history of license development is begun, it would be helpful to briefly review the types of licenses in use, as well as the various components that are common to the majority of licenses.

TYPES OF LICENSES

End-User Agreement

End-user agreements tend to be the most common type of license, and they will specify how a piece of software (presumably a database) could be utilized by a licensee. An end-user agreement may specify that a given piece of software may only be installed on a particular machine in a library, or it could alternatively specify that it could be installed on multiple workstations in the library as long as a maximum number of users (one, two, or more) have not been exceeded. "Shrink-wrap" licenses, which are licenses that come into force when a piece of software is opened, are usually grouped within this category.

Site License Agreement

These licenses tend to be more complicated and lengthy, but are the kind preferred by universities, colleges, and other large organizations with libraries, as they allow for campus-wide, system-wide, or consortium-wide access to an electronic resource, usually via IP-range access, so that log-ins will be completely transparent to the end-user(s). Site licenses may be fairly standard for all institutions, or they may be very particular and individualized, requiring much negotiation between the vendor and licensee. When complete, these licenses will generally set a negotiated price (frequently based on the size of an institution or consortium) in return for specific services from the vendor, chief among them, campus-wide access to their product, but which also may include such "extras" as usage statistics, hook-to-holdings features, table of contents notifications, use of the product for course packs, and so on.

There may also be a number of restrictions specified that the user must abide by, including copyright, interlibrary loan, installation and usage restrictions, and others. All of these items are usually negotiable, at least to some degree, with most vendors.

Next, what are the common components of e-licenses?

1. Introduction

Where the parties involved are listed, as well as their legal addresses, and how they will be referred to in the remainder of the document.

2. Key Definitions

This section provides specific descriptions of vital terminology that follows throughout the document, such as: agent, authorized users, course packs, fees, licensed materials, servers, and subscription periods, so that ideally, there will be no confusion on what any of these terms signify later on.

3. The Agreement

This section introduces the main body of the license, and sets up the remainder of the agreement by addressing the grant of the license, subscription period, termination of the license, and other items.

4. Usage Rights

This section defines what the end-user may expect to do with the product in question; e.g., accessing the licensed materials, (including searching, retrieving, and displaying), printing out copies of articles, saving articles to disc, and e-mailing articles to other authorized users.

5. Interlibrary Loan/Electronic Reserves

This section or sections specifies if copies are permitted to be provided to other libraries, by post, fax, or electronic transmission, to be used by patrons of those libraries. It would also specify if the licensed materials could be used as part of course packs and electronic reserve. Usually, there will be a specification that such materials be deleted upon the completion of a class that utilizes them.

6. Prohibited Uses

This important section details to the licensee the things that they may *not* do with the licensed materials, including removal of author names or copyright notices, systematic printing or downloading of the licensed materials, or mounting or distributing of the licensed materials. This section may also specify when the publisher's permission must be obtained in order to perform certain restricted activities, such as utilizing licensed documents for commercial use, publishing or distributing the materials and altering, abridging, adapting, or modifying the licensed materials in any way.

7. Publisher's Responsibilities

This section details what the licensee may expect from the licensor, including: making the licensed materials available in a specified format, notifying the licensee of any changes in the product, the reliability of access to the licensed materials, as well as the reservation of rights in terms of withdrawing certain materials to which rights have been lost, that have been deemed objectionable, or that copyright has been infringed upon. This section may also define the publisher's intentions in terms of archiving materials.

8. Terms and Termination

This section details the circumstances in which the license can be terminated by either party, including defaulting on financial obligations, committing material breaches of the license and so on. It also specifies disposition of any fees paid, should termination occur.

9. General Provisions

This section usually indicates that the agreement will supercede any prior contracts established, that alterations to the license after the fact are only valid if recorded in writing and signed by both parties, as well as a number of other miscellaneous provisions. This section will also usually contain the clause indicating the court of jurisdiction if any disputes arise over the license.

10. Signatures

Where the authorized signatories of both licensor and licensee are affixed, making it a valid legal document.

CHANGES OVER TIME

In the beginning, one of the most frequent and pervasive problems encountered with licensing was that every publisher re-invented the wheel with every license they generated, not only in the sense of negotiating every license from scratch, but also particularly in the larger sense, with each vendor failing to benefit from the experience of others, or allowing themselves to rely on the institutional expertise of libraries. One reason for this could be perception: libraries were somewhat regarded as opponents, rather than partners in those days.

Licenses in general in the earlier days were fairly spotty in terms of quality and usefulness. Two early vendors that provided good-quality licenses were JSTOR (established in August 1995 by the Andrew W. Mellon Foundation) and Project Muse (also launched in 1995 by the Johns Hopkins University Press). They produced licenses that were very library-friendly, and were receptive to feedback from the library community. At the time, however, they were the exceptions rather than the rules.

It appears that many publishers conducted their businesses in the early days of online publishing in reaction to an innate fear of losing profits and market share if they allowed online licenses that were too "permissive." Their fear was that allowing such unfettered online access would drive people away from their proven and reliable money making print journals. The vendors thus continued to be focused on print profits, unwilling to risk a rapid shift to the new online or even to the middle-of-the-road "print + online" paradigm. This resulted in much difficulty for libraries that were attempting to negotiate reasonable licenses that recognized libraries' needs and concerns, as well as those of its end-users, and also in being able to recognize the sea-change that was now occurring in how intellectual information was being communicated to the academic community.

In the last ten years, as the publishing (and license) industry has evolved, the situation has largely improved for all parties. But what accounts for this? A learning curve was conquered, for one; there was also the eventual development of a growing acceptance by publishers that their lifeblood would not be sucked out by librarians in the frightening new electronic environment. Yet, another reason was a dawning realization by both sides that time really does equal money, and that the endless hours spent arguing over minute details in ever-changing licenses was in fact, not time well spent. This became an extremely important factor in the overall picture of evolving licenses.

Smart and nimble publishers have realized that standardization of license terms and conditions saves everyone work, including themselves. Perceptive publishers have also paid attention to the dialogue that has occurred between their peers and the library community over the last ten years, and have benefited from the hard-fought license work of others. In other words, they have realized that the re-invention of the wheel with each and every license negotiation was a futile practice, and they have since constructed their licensing terms and procedures upon those things that had already been battled over, worked out, and refined by other parties.

Alas, not all publishers have gotten on board with this philosophy. Many, due to reasons of competitive paranoia, still will not look to their peers for useful advice and experience, and when that happens, both sides suffer. These vendors are the ones who end up poorer for their experience (or lack thereof). They are less likely to have user-friendly licenses, or to have positive experience with negotiating licenses. It can only be hoped that the number of these vendors will continue to dwindle.

Next, we turn to some of the battles that have been fought to shape the more uniform licenses of today.

INTERLIBRARY LOAN RIGHTS

This has been one of the primary battlegrounds in the licensing war. Publishers would often initially take a position that only print interlibrary loan (ILL) was acceptable, primarily because they feared the loss of control over their copyrighted material if electronic materials were electronically transmitted between libraries. One such restrictive license reads:

> Systematic or programmatic downloading, service bureau redistribution services, printing for fee-for-service purposes and/or the systematic making of print or electronic copies for transmission to non-subscribers or non-subscribing institutions (such as in "interlibrary loan") are prohibited.

Some vendors have even attempted to extend some electronic licenses to cover print materials. Nixon has noted, " . . . where licenses attempt to tie the sales of a print version of a resource to license of an electronic version, the license may also require libraries to restrict patron access to the print materials. As this practice becomes more prevalent, libraries will be able to fill few, if any remote patron or ILL requests for material."[1] Clearly, librarians are unable to stand by and let basic ILL rights continue to erode like this.

Thus, libraries have taken the position that they were responsible stewards of these copyrighted materials, and were only conducting interlibrary loan transactions with authorized ILL partners, using only materials that the library owned (or had rights to), and which they had a legal right to conduct ILL transactions with, and were doing so according to accepted library practice. To the libraries, the medium of the material was irrelevant. What mattered was ownership. To this end, a more reasonable license would read:

> The Licensee may supply to an Authorized User of another library within the same country as the Licensee either by post or fax transmission, for the purpose of research or private study and not for Commercial Use, a single paper copy of an electronic original of an individual document being part of the Licensed Materials. For the avoidance of doubt, electronic transmissions are nor permitted without the expressed prior written consent of the Publisher.

As time progressed, publishers eventually adjusted their own ILL paradigm, and most began allowing some electronic transmission (fax or Ariel) of a paper printout of an electronic resource that they had licensed. Although not quite a full measure, this compromise was acceptable to most library operations, and this continues to be the standard order of business for many electronic products and for the libraries that use them. Some vendors do now allow direct electronic transmission of their licensed products, providing that standard interlibrary loan policies are followed, and it is hoped that the trend toward this will continue, especially as academic libraries increasingly drop print copies out of their journal collections for economic reasons.

While most vendors have been cooperative, in particular (and perhaps surprisingly) the more commercial publishers, a number of influential and major physics societies have maintained strict "no-electronic ILL" clauses in their contracts. Some large academic institutions had been holdouts on signing this type of contract for quite some time. In fact, these universities had often maintained policies that any ILL restrictions would be deal-killers during negotiations. Due to the importance accorded to some of the publications of such learned societies by influential faculty members (including many serving on editorial boards), some universities may decide to "make a deal with the devil," and make exceptions to their licensing policies for these particular publishers. These however, continue to be exceptions to the general rule, and most universities will continue to fight these restrictive clauses whenever they do appear. Fortunately, most commercial publishers and learned societies have become more enlightened, and only a few holdouts remain in this area. An important, and somewhat labor-intensive, side effect of this type of inconsistency to note is that university interlibrary loan departments may now be forced to maintain and consult two different lists of electronic journals for every ILL transaction: one for those items that can be loaned electronically, and another for those that cannot. It is hoped that the last remaining holdouts will alter their anachronistic stance, and that this sort of needless inconvenience will not last much longer.

E-RESERVES AND COURSEPACKS

These are provisions that are somewhat related to the interlibrary loan rights situation, and which involve an institution's right to download and use properly licensed materials in an organized and systematic way for classes. As most licenses prohibit any such systematic downloading or copying of their materials under normal circumstances, publishers originally objected to requests for the adoption of a relevant license provision from client institutions; in some cases, they would allow such downloading, but would either charge exorbitant royalties or require that the institution seek permission for each and every course, which would often prove to be a large logistical problem for a busy ILL staff. A provision in such a license reads:

> Subscribers and users may not disseminate content outside the geographically contiguous campus by any means . . . and use of contents and articles in coursepacks are expressly prohibited.

Without such permissions being specifically spelled out in a license, libraries can be forced to make individual applications for each article requested for a coursepack, which can be a huge administrative burden. Ferullo has noted "Permission to use materials varies from one publisher to another. Some are more amenable to the use, particularly if the library owns a copy of the work, while others will charge royalties for each use. There can certainly be an occasion where a publisher denies permission, but generally an exorbitant royalty fee is just as effective in discouraging use. As much lead time as possible is recommended when trying to obtain permission. Many publishers will respond in as little as a week whereas others might take months to process the request."[2]

Today this is rarely a concern, as publishers seem to have come to the conclusion that they are not losing sales by allowing licensed materials to either be placed temporarily on a school's server for the purposes of access by a particular, limited population such as a class (e-reserve), or by the systematic downloading of several sets of a particular article for a specific and legitimate academic purpose (course packs), as long as appropriate royalties per copyright law are paid. A typical modern license would thus read:

> Licensee may include copies (hardcopy or down-loaded) of items from the online form of Publications (1) in anthologies (coursepacks) in print or digital form for sale and/or distribution to the Authorized Users for their use in connection with classroom instruction and/or (2) in reserves (print or digital) set up by Licensee's libraries for access by Authorized Users in connection with specific courses offered by Licensee. Copies of items in digital form which are included in online coursepacks or reserves will be deleted by Licensee after the end of the semester in which the related course concludes.

AUTHORIZED USERS

Another point that had often been contentious in licenses was the question of who was, and who was not, an authorized user of a licensed database. Librarians at public institutions have held to the long-established principle that any walk-in user of the library was authorized to use any resource, electronic or otherwise, within the library. Some vendors however, wished to restrict authorized users in academic libraries only to faculty and students (sometimes to particular subsets of faculty and students), and perhaps also to other university staff. A reasonable definition of authorized users would be:

> Authorized Users means persons who are authorized to use Licensee's library facilities who (a) are affiliated with Licensee as students, faculty or employees of Licensee (as hereafter defined) or (b) are physically present in the Library.

This proved to be a battle that was fairly easily won by libraries. Part of the reason for this is that publicly funded libraries have the force of state legislatures and courts behind them, and these have legally defined whom a public institution must serve; thus, this proved to be an unfruitful fight for publishers. Now, authorized users are generally defined to comprise faculty, staff, full- and part-time students, and walk-in users. Alumni and some other special classes of the university community do not generally and automatically receive access to university e-resources unless they are registered users of the library system (a concession to publishers). Another questioned issue is that some university campuses will have corporations renting space in university-owned research parks, and from time to time, they have also sought access to licensed resources. In this case, unless such a company is populated by university faculty members, both libraries and licensors have generally been in agreement that merely having an office on university property does not automatically translate into being a member of the university community, and such requests have had to be denied.

However, what about campus units that do not necessarily neatly fit into a licensor's view of what a "physical" campus is? A restrictive license would read:

> (Vendor) grants you a nonexclusive, nontransferable, limited right to use the software for personal or internal business use by you on

the permitted number of Licensed Computers at a single, physical location designated by you (the "Licensed Location").

One that deals less with a physical location, and more with the type of users allowed would read:

> Authorized Users may be persons remote from the Subscriber's physical location whose access is administered from the Subscriber's site or campus.

Generally, university dormitories and housing units have not had any trouble in being considered on-campus authorized users, but a number of schools have had experiences with justifying to publishers that two particular types of non-traditional campus units are integral parts of the university community, and thus, worthy of being authorized access to all e-resources subscribed to by the parent university and library.

Land-grant universities possess a duty, as part of their legislated mission, to provide academic and support services statewide, via their university extensions, located at remote sites throughout a state. These extension offices will possess some facilities allowing electronic access to the central library facilities. A few, though fortunately not a large number of vendors, have questioned libraries on the legitimacy of pro-·viding access to these offices. The licensors have proven to be persuadable on this issue when they have been educated about a land-grant university's mission, and that this was, subsequently, a legally non-negotiable item for such schools.

In a similar vein, many public and private universities maintain physically separate research or classroom facilities that are not administered separately, and thus, should not bear the definition of being a "separate" campus. A number of publishers have attempted to define such facilities as not being an administrative part of the parent campus, and subsequently have made attempts at requiring them to purchase a separate license, or go without access. Universities in such situations have had to provide documentation and legal materials that these units are integral parts of the main campus, and that they were only separate by reasons of geography, not by reasons of administration. A license provision that would specifically address this would be:

> This document also confirms that two off-site laboratories will be included in the contract.

Another issue that some universities have faced has been with federal government units located on the university campus. This has proven to be a somewhat more thorny issue for universities with several vendors, especially with a leading chemical abstracts publisher, Chemical Abstracts Service (CAS). In an example that the author is familiar with, CAS contended that a Department of Energy (DOE) unit located on a university campus was purely a federal government owned and operated entity, and thus had no right to utilize its abstracting service without a separate (and expensive commercial) license of its own. The publisher then essentially placed the burden of proof upon the university to justify why this access was not a material breach of contract.

During an investigative campus visit from this publisher, the university in question was able to demonstrate a number of factors that led this particular publisher to realize that the university and laboratory were correct in their assertations. There were several reasons for this change of heart. One factor was proximity: The DOE facility in question was located centrally on the campus in question and was, in fact, directly across the street from the university library itself. Another issue was economic: The lab was able to prove that its research was not directed toward profitability and was academic in nature. A third issue was staff: The university was able to show that all of the laboratory's research and support staff were on the payroll of the university, rather than the DOE, including many who were research faculty. Thus, they were unquestionably integral parts of the campus community. Another issue was size. The university was able to demonstrate that the laboratory was a very small DOE facility, tightly bound to its partner university by history and geography, unlike large and independent DOE labs such as Los Alamos, Brookhaven, or Lawrence Livermore. The final, and perhaps most important issue, was legal: This university had a signed services contract with the DOE facility that guaranteed the lab would receive complete access to any electronic resource fielded by the library. The library's only other alternative would be to eliminate a questioned resource from its inventory. In the end, the publisher decided that this would not be an outcome in their favor, and relented.

While the outcome was positive for this particular university, other universities have had to deal with campus units that may have received funding and/or staff from other sources, and have had to spend significant amounts of time and money defending their licensing relationships with such organizations. Thus, over time, universities have realized that it is necessary to ensure that they negotiate broad-enough definitions of "authorized users" to cover all the people that the university library is legally and morally obligated to serve. After all, a university campus has become less a physical location today than a virtual place, one that many people, in many physical locations, can access.

SITE LICENSES AND PROXY SERVERS

In the early days of electronic licensing, libraries essentially signed a license and paid for access to a single CD-ROM workstation for a particular resource to be mounted on. The next stage was for CD-ROMs to become networked over multiple workstations, and licenses then began to reflect this change, allowing access to multiple seats within the library (e.g., 2-3 simultaneous users, 3-5 simultaneous users, etc.). When the World Wide Web had developed enough for publishers to start providing resources previously available only on CD-ROM, a similar pay-by-the-seat model was also initially followed. This model has since been largely, but not yet completely, discarded.

The definition of what a modern library was and what it could evolve into began to change, however. No longer was it to be bound by physical walls, and defined as a merely physical place. The Web now enabled resources to be provided or denied to any authorized computer via recognition or non-recognition of its unique IP (Internet Protocol) address. Today, in late 2003, most major publishers have switched to IP address recognition, which allows access to an electronic product to any computer in a campus network. The implementation of new campus Wi-Fi networks is also now beginning to allow wireless Internet access (including to licensed resources) to laptop computers within the boundaries of the campus as well, inside and out.

At many universities, licenses that continue to offer access to an e-resource only on a per-seat basis are routinely rejected for practical and policy reasons. These institutions cannot and will not maintain repositories of usernames and passwords for their electronic resources. In some cases, libraries have elected to script usernames and passwords into URLs, but this is a very labor-intensive process from an information technology department standpoint. Fortunately, there have been only a very few major holdouts. In particular, one very notable e-journal exception, the *New England Journal of Medicine*, finally elected to switch to a site license model in mid-2003.

Licensors also had an initial bad reaction to the introduction of proxy servers into the mix. Murray has noted four reasons that libraries install proxy servers: " . . . to enable access to resources by patrons outside a library's network, to filter Web requests or responses on public stations, to conserve bandwidth and improve response time, and to gather statistics on Web usage."[3] Proxy servers thus enable authorized users to access e-resources from off-campus locations. When an authorized user attempts to access such a resource, they are prompted by a dialog box to enter an authentication code, such as a library card number. Unauthorized users, without such a number, would automatically be turned away. In the early days, however, licensors did not view this process logically and apparently feared that this was yet another attempt to wrest control over unauthorized users from them. They reacted by instituting "no proxy" clauses into their licenses, which then caused numerous disputes with their client libraries.

This, fortunately, proved to be another example of rationality winning the day, and most vendors now allow and even encourage proxy server arrangements for their products, as they have come to realize they only enhance controls over unauthorized users. A permissible and relevant license provision would read:

> This document confirms that the license allows for remote access. The phrases "an address within the range identified . . . " and "Authorized Users may be persons remote from the Subscriber's physical location whose access is administered from the Subscriber's site or campus . . . " are interpreted by both parties as allowing the licensee's use of a proxy server from the Main campus to offer remote home/office/travel use.

CONFIDENTIALITY

Another frequent sticking point over the years has been a licensor insistence on maintaining total confidentiality of the terms of a signed license agreement. While this is a not-uncommon provision within the realm of contract law, public universities and other institutions are unable to sign any contracts that require total secrecy, as their public status, requires (1) legislative oversight, (2) that the public, upon request, be able to review public records, and (3) compliance with state law, which in some instances will include "sunshine" provisions in the state code, mandating transparency in all transactions conducted by governmental units, including any contracts that have been entered into. A troublesome license provision could read:

> Customer agrees that it shall not use or disclose information relating to (1) the terms of this Agreement, (2) the content of reports delivered hereunder, or (3) pricing terms or arrangements under this Agreement.

Most vendors have complied with the requirements in this area, and allowed such clauses to be modified or stricken. They also proved to be quick learners; the author has not encountered any instances where the striking of this license provision was objected to by a licensor. Another way of neutralizing the problems with state law would be to amend it thusly:

> To the extent allowed by and consistent with State Law, Customer agrees that it shall not use or disclose information relating to (1) the terms of this Agreement, (2) the content of reports delivered hereunder, or (3) pricing terms or arrangements under this Agreement.

JURISDICTION

This remains one of the most adjusted clauses in license agreements, but fortunately, the vast majority of vendors are amenable to altering it. In earlier days, a few were adamant about retaining legal jurisdiction over the license agreement in their "home court," be it the Southern District of New York, or the Kingdom of the Netherlands;

> This Agreement shall be governed by and construed in accordance with the laws of the State of New York, without regard to its choice of law or conflict of law provisions.

Alford notes that the passage of the Uniform Computer Information Transactions Act (UCITA) in Virginia and Maryland (as well as its pending consideration in others states) also requires librarians to carefully consider the governing law in any contract, as UCITA terms are generally not favorable to libraries.[4] Because of this, and due to the fact that many public universities cannot sign any contracts that move legal jurisdiction out of state, licensors now, with very few exceptions, either allow jurisdiction to be transferred to the state of the licensee, or will strike the clause entirely, thus remaining mute on the issue.

INDEMNIFICATION

Indemnification clauses have been inserted in order to hold harmless both parties of the agreement against any claims by third parties that were the result of their performance under the license agreement. Alford indicates that " . . . under state law, public institutions are not authorized to indemnify a third party for anything. In a publicly funded institution, the librarian should determine what authority, if any, the library has to indemnify a third party and for what types of claims."[5] Librarians then should know what their obligations are in this area, and be prepared to say "no" if necessary. An acceptable license for libraries will specify that both parties to the agreement should agree to be financially responsible for their respective breaches of the warranties in the license agreement.[6]

Some publishers have attempted in the past to shift the majority of the financial burden of the indemnification clause to the licensee. A one-sided indemnification clause might read:

> Licensee agrees to hold (vendor) and all their employees, staffs, and agents harmless from any claim, suit, or proceeding arising out of the subject matter of this Agreement, including indemnification of (vendor) for reasonable expenses incurred in defending such claims.

Libraries have routinely objected to such provisions, and over time many licensees have agreed to routinely strike such clauses, much as they do with objections to jurisdiction clauses. In the event of keeping the clause, these would be much more favorable terms:

> Each party shall indemnify and hold the other harmless for any losses, claims, damages, awards, penalties, or injuries incurred by any third party, including reasonable attorney's fees, which arise from any alleged breach of such indemnifying party's representations and warranties made under this Agreement, provided that the indemnifying party is promptly notified of any such claims.

ANNUAL MAINTENANCE FEES

Annual maintenance fees are a cost paid separately from any capital outlay for a particular product or from content fees. In effect, these are fees to pay for use of a platform itself, not for the information actually contained on the platform. Rationally, there is probably no substantial reason to separate these fees from regular content fees; rather, these appear to be an attempt by the publisher to make users take note of a specific platform that they are promoting via the extra fees. There has been speculation that publisher intent is that institution of these maintenance fees will make the platform stand out and look "important." As long as such fees are reasonable, it is unlikely that libraries will mount any major objections to them, and will regard them as part of the cost of doing business.

A MODEL LICENSE?

Many library professionals have labored for a model license that protects both library rights and interests, and that gives reasonable deference to publisher rights as well, all while maintaining as much simplicity as possible. While admirable model licenses have been developed, their implementation has not been universally, or even widely adopted.

One of the most widely regarded model licenses is the CLIR/DLF Model License, sponsored by the Council on Library and Information Resources and the Digital Library Federation. Yale University's Liblicense Web site states that this license " . . . represents the contributions of numerous college and university librarians, lawyers, and other university officials responsible for licensing, as well as significant input from representatives of the academic publishing community."[7] As such, it represents an excellent cross-section of library professionals' opinions, and it can be hoped, will become the basis for fair and balanced electronic license agreements in the years to come. The model license can be viewed in its entirety at: http://www.library.yale.edu/~llicense/standlicagree.html.

CONSORTIA

Consortial arrangements have provided a more economical way, in today's world of academic publishing hyperinflation, for institutions to provide access to expensive electronic resources to their patrons. Consortia tend to be made up of schools within a state system, or within a regional grouping. Other models are also possible.

Licensing arrangements for consortia become more complex, unsurprisingly, because of the increased number of parties involved. The multiple licensees may have entered the consortial arrangement for the common goals of financial benefit, or for better access, but each participating institution will bring its own agenda and its own priorities to the table, and these positions must be harmonized into a common consensus for a consortium to successfully negotiate with the vendor.

WHERE WE ARE NOW

Where do licensing arrangements stand in late 2003? Overall, for many licenses, life has become quite a bit simpler for all involved. Vendors have learned a lot more about library concerns, and have adapted to these, incorporating many of these provisions into their licenses. As well, vendors have become more comfortable with the post-print, all-electronic academic publishing world, and are for the most part no longer taking prophylactic measures in licenses to protect their print sales. Interlibrary loan of electronic materials, which was once a battle to obtain the rights to do, is now less often a major concern when negotiating an agreement.

WHAT IS ON THE HORIZON?

What does the future of licensing hold? Standardization is an important goal. Bosch states that several elements need to be considered in this area:

1. Development, acceptance, and use of common templates/boilerplates. Accomplishing this would make the process much easier and reduce costs for all.
2. The development and acceptance of common principles. This would dramatically reduce the amount of time finding common ground.

3. A common vocabulary. Simply put, if everyone speaks the same language, misunderstandings are avoided and licenses are simpler.
4. Blanket licenses by company for a range of products as opposed to individual products. Licenses that cover a group of common products, or products by a common vendor are much more efficient than having a single license for each item.
5. Third party brokering of licensed products. This involves working with a vendor to purchase a number of titles under a unified license.[8]

USAGE STATISTICS

Another area that is being rapidly exploited is the requirement by libraries that publishers provide some kind of regular usage statistics for their products. Many publishers initially resisted this, probably fearing that statistics might lead to the elimination of some of their weaker-performing journals. For publishers, it is also a significant initial expense, as Luther has noted: "Providing usage data is a new role for publishers and aggregators–one that requires not only much learning but also a financial investment. While it appears that the data would be as useful to publishers as to librarians, publishers must first develop the capability to serve their own purposes and then provide additional analyses and support to present the data so that librarians can use them."[9] Many publishers now seem to be offering monthly or quarterly statistical packages of varying thoroughness, thus allowing libraries to track what their most cost-effective journals are. It is now becoming a common expectation for all moderately sized publishers to include a statistics package and statistics provision in their licenses.

BACKFILES

Now that many publishers have current journal issues online, a major focus has become the retrospective conversion of older backfiles for journals that have already been online for some time. This sort of thing has been the bread and butter of organizations such as JSTOR and Project Muse for years, but many other publishers are just now following suit. Licenses for products that are now offering the option of such backfiles have begun to include archival clauses that reflect costs, terms, and conditions for such files.

Retrospective conversion of older journals into PDF or HTML files for online access is a very labor-intensive process. Most licensees recognize this and also understand that new costs are involved. Thus, they will generally be prepared to pay for the backfiles, if they are desired. The standard model has been for a one-time access fee to be paid for such backfiles. An emerging issue of contention is what will happen if licensees balk when certain vendors begin instituting annual fees for backfiles, in addition to the annual fees for current content.

TRADING TITLES

Another issue that needs to be addressed, and which would come under the heading of publisher responsibilities, is how to respond to the increasing trend of e-journal titles being bought and sold between vendors. In particular, what are the publisher's responsibilities in a license insofar as notifying licensees of the impending loss of an e-journal title from an aggregate package, and its possible transfer to another package, or perhaps to some other arrangement? Further, if such a title is lost from a package with a fixed price that has already been paid for, will the publisher need to be responsible for some sort of financial compensation to a customer? Libraries will need to determine what their rights and expectations are in this area, and how to press for modifications to licensing language to protect their interests.

GENERALIZATIONS AND CONCLUSION

Licensors have largely emerged in good shape from the past model where each new vendor who entered the electronic marketplace started constructing and negotiating licenses from scratch. A decade of experience with electronic licenses has created a set of shared experiences between libraries and publishers, the emergence of model licenses, and the standardization of many elements within licenses. While there are still some vendors who seemingly insist on making negotiations an excruciating experience, most publishers now realize that librarians are better to have as partners than adversaries, and have worked to create much more palatable electronic licenses with which all parties can be happy. Such licenses serve the interests of vendor, librarians and end-users equally well.

NOTES

1. Nixon, Donna. 2003. Copyright and Interlibrary Loan Rights. *Journal of Interlibrary Loan, Document Delivery & Information Supply,* v. 13, no. 3, p. 70.
2. Ferullo, Donna L. 2002. The Challenge of E-Reserves. *School Library Journal,* July 15, 2002, pp. 33-35.
3. Murray, Peter E. 2001. Library Web Proxy Use Survey Results. *Information Technology and Libraries,* v. 20, no. 4, pp. 172-178.
4. Alford, Duncan E. 2002. Negotiating and Analyzing Electronic License Agreements. *Law Library Journal,* v. 94, no. 4, p. 13.
5. Ibid., p. 11.
6. Licensing Digital Information: Warranties; Indemnities; Limitations on Warranties, viewed at http://www.library.yale.edu/~llicense/warrgen.shtml on Nov. 3, 2003.
7. Licensing Digital Information: CLIR/DLF Model License, viewed at http://www.library.yale.edu/~llicense/modlic.shtml on Nov 3, 2003.
8. Bosch, Stephen. 1998. Licensing Information: Where Can We Go from here? *Library Acquisitions: Practice & Theory,* v. 22, no. 1, p. 46.
9. Luther, Judy. 2001. White paper on electronic journal usage statistics. *The Serials Librarian,* v. 41, no. 2, p. 120.

REFERENCES

Alford, Duncan E. 2002. Negotiating and Analyzing Electronic License Agreements. *Law Library Journal,* v. 94, no. 4.

Association of Research Libraries. 1998. License Review and Negotiation: Building a Team-Based Institutional Process. Washington: Association of Research Libraries.

Bosch, Stephen. 1998. Licensing Information: Where Can We Go From Here? *Library Acquisitions: Practice and Theory,* v. 22, no. 1, pp. 45-47.

Brach, Carol A. 2001. Electronic Collections–Evolution and Strategies: Past, Present and Future. *Science & Technology Libraries,* v. 21, nos. 1/2, pp. 17-27.

Chadwell, Faye A. 2001. A License to Kill For . . . *Managing Electronic Serials: Essays Based on the ALCTS Electronic Serials Institutes 1997-1999.* Chicago: American Library Association, pp. 109-128.

Davis, Trisha L. 1997. License Agreements in Lieu of Copyright: Are We Signing Away Our Rights? *Library Acquisitions: Practice and Theory,* v. 21, no. 1, pp. 19-28.

Ferullo, Donna L. 2002. The Challenge of E-Reserves. *School Library Journal,* July 15, 2002, pp. 33-35.

Luther, Judy. 2001. White paper on electronic journal usage statistics. *The Serials Librarian,* v. 41, no. 2.

Murray, Peter E. 2001. Library Web Proxy Use Survey Results. *Information Technology and Libraries,* v. 20, no. 4, pp. 172-178.

Nixon, Donna. 2003. Copyright and Interlibrary Loan Rights. *Journal of Interlibrary Loan, Document Delivery & Information Supply,* v. 13, no. 3.

Yale University Library. 2003. Liblicense: Licensing Digital Information, A Resource for Librarians, available at: http://www.library.yale.edu/~llicense/index.shtml.

Index

Numbers followed by f indicate figures.

BOOK ORDER FORM!

Order a copy of this book with this form or online at:
http://www.haworthpress.com/store/product.asp?sku=5566

Licensing in Libraries
Practical and Ethical Aspects

_____ in softbound at $29.95 ISBN-13: 978-0-7890-2879-2. / ISBN-10: 0-7890-2879-4.

_____ in hardbound at $49.95 ISBN-13: 978-0-7890-2878-5. / ISBN-10: 0-7890-2878-6.

COST OF BOOKS _____

POSTAGE & HANDLING _____
US: $4.00 for first book & $1.50
for each additional book
Outside US: $5.00 for first book
& $2.00 for each additional book.

SUBTOTAL _____

In Canada: add 7% GST. _____

STATE TAX _____
CA, IL, IN, MN, NJ, NY, OH, PA & SD residents
please add appropriate local sales tax.

FINAL TOTAL _____
If paying in Canadian funds, convert
using the current exchange rate,
UNESCO coupons welcome.

❑BILL ME LATER:
Bill-me option is good on US/Canada/
Mexico orders only; not good to jobbers,
wholesalers, or subscription agencies.

❑Signature _____

❑Payment Enclosed: $ _____

❑ PLEASE CHARGE TO MY CREDIT CARD:
❑Visa ❑MasterCard ❑AmEx ❑Discover
❑Diner's Club ❑Eurocard ❑JCB

Account # _____

Exp Date _____

Signature _____
(Prices in US dollars and subject to change without notice.)

PLEASE PRINT ALL INFORMATION OR ATTACH YOUR BUSINESS CARD

Name

Address

City   State/Province   Zip/Postal Code

Country

Tel   Fax

E-Mail

May we use your e-mail address for confirmations and other types of information? ❑Yes ❑No We appreciate receiving
your e-mail address. Haworth would like to e-mail special discount offers to you, as a preferred customer.
We will never share, rent, or exchange your e-mail address. We regard such actions as an invasion of your privacy.

Order from your **local bookstore** or directly from
The Haworth Press, Inc. 10 Alice Street, Binghamton, New York 13904-1580 • USA
Call our toll-free number (1-800-429-6784) / Outside US/Canada: (607) 722-5857
Fax: 1-800-895-0582 / Outside US/Canada: (607) 771-0012
E-mail your order to us: orders@haworthpress.com

For orders outside US and Canada, you may wish to order through your local
sales representative, distributor, or bookseller.
For information, see http://haworthpress.com/distributors

(Discounts are available for individual orders in US and Canada only, not booksellers/distributors.)

Please photocopy this form for your personal use.
www.HaworthPress.com

BOF05